To Bombeau
with love from all of us
Merry Christmas
Nancy and Crawf
and Frank and Bost

I'LL TAKE TEXAS

☆

I'LL TAKE

Texas

BY MARY LASSWELL

in collaboration with Bob Pool

with illustrations by Jo Alys Downs

HOUGHTON MIFFLIN COMPANY   BOSTON

The Riverside Press Cambridge

BOOKS BY MARY LASSWELL

Suds in Your Eye

High Time

Mrs. Rasmussen's Book of One-Arm Cookery

Bread for the Living

One on the House

Wait for the Wagon

Tooner Schooner

I'll Take Texas

☆

This book is lovingly dedicated
to
two southern gentlewomen
Annie Barnhart Giles, of Austin, Texas
and
Saint Rita of Cascia, patron saint of
the Impossible

☆

CONTENTS

1. YOU *CAN* GO HOME AGAIN

How would Texas feel to a prodigal going home after nearly thirty years of absence? Twenty-seven years had taken her halfway round the world in space, across the Atlantic and Pacific Oceans, and into a world of experience far removed from the state where her ancestors had engraved the names of Lubbock and Grayson on the land and in the history books.

"All things come home at eventide," and my voyage of discovery and rediscovery was long overdue. Another milestone was looming up, my fiftieth birthday.

Even shut up in the capsule quarters of a roomette aboard a pitching Katy train as it crossed the Red River headed for Dallas in the murky dawn of Armistice Day, 1953, I did not need any signs to tell me I was in Texas: I could feel it. There was no need to turn on the light and consult the schedule, no need

to raise the window blind. The familiar atmosphere, un-
changed and changeless, had already seeped in through the
hermetically sealed windows — bringing Texas to me.

Texas is an aura made of dry dust, Johnson grass, mesquite,
and cactus. It is an essence compounded of hot wind over pine
and post oak, with the tangy spray of the Gulf thrown in. It is
leather, and horse sweat, and Bull Durham. It is heady gusts
of clean air coming off the Caprock.

A Texan can, by taking thought, conjure up this magic essence without any of those ingredients at hand, perhaps while
standing in Westminster Abbey, or walking up the steps of
the Taj Mahal.

As I dressed I wondered how many Americans spent the
largest portion of their lives away from their native regions.
Life in the great cities of America had shown me how few of
their citizens are native. The adaptability of a still-young people like Americans makes most of us tend to take on the color-
ing of the region we inhabit. The local accent ceases to be
alien, and we soon forget our own. Generally, we have not the
passionate nationalism of the older races, say, of Frenchmen
living in Spain, or Germans living in Italy. Neither do we cling
to the sense of "home" as the Briton does, with fierce resistance
to being assimilated by any other locality or country.

The philosophy of "You can't go home again" makes us think
we have outgrown the old ways "back home" beyond hope of a
comfortable readjustment.

Can it be, I thought as I slid the door of the roomette open,
that many Americans are harboring, in a mildly shamefaced
way, an unacknowledged longing for their home "country"
even though they still live in the United States? Isn't America,
after all, one great big union? Or is it?

Must we go far away to find out what it is that marks us in-
delibly for what we are? Long absence and varied experience
over the years had sharpened my perceptions. The disturbing

reports of the press, fond of exploiting the flamboyant and the sensational in Texas and Texans, had created in my mind some serious doubts and not a little trepidation. I was almost afraid of what I should find there. Along with the rest of my baggage I had a bundle of half-truths, misconceptions, and misrepresentations. Taken altogether, they added up to a decided ambivalence, an uncomfortable state of being of two minds about Texas: loving the old and noble that I had known, and questioning the new and ignoble that I had read and heard about.

On high days and holy days, the Lone Star flew from the tall flagstaff at Old Fort Farm, my home in Newport, Rhode Island. When my Alma Mater, the University of Texas, beat the Texas Aggies at football on Thanksgiving Day, I salaamed my forehead to the floor, facing in the wrong direction, it turned out later. And I believed firmly that there was no trouble in the world that could not be settled instanter by the Texas Rangers.

In spite of this lip service, I was not what could be called a Practicing Texan. In fact, I was rather pleased when people said: "I'd never take you for a Texan. You don't say 'I'm from Tax-iss!' the minute you open your mouth." In the light of these facts, why was I thrilled when a Boston newspaper referred to "tiny, highpowered, Texan Mary"?

It came home to me that each of us carries within him an imperishable core of regional memory: the Down-East Yankee has his lobster pots and the sound of slatting canvas. The Kansan the creak of the tall corn as it stretches upward in the hot night. The New Englander, lilacs and stone fences. The Southerner remembers in terms of mockingbirds and magnolias. The Westerner distills his memory out of painted sands and desert sunsets. Each man must decide for himself how much is reality, how much illusion.

You are going to feel like an orphan boy at a picnic, I thought as I walked between the car couplings on the way to the diner for coffee, coming back without getting in touch with any of your friends. I knew who was to blame for that. Over the years I had written more books than letters.

As the train whizzed by the railway platform at Terrell, I saw ranks of brown and white bales of cotton, that precarious crop that had paid for a considerable part of my education. Although this was a part of Texas I had never seen, the familiar sight of the cotton bales was too much for me. As the tears rolled down my struggling face I realized that I was plain, "country" homesick.

I thought I had come back to Texas for professional reasons. The itinerary from my publishers listed autographing appearances in Dallas, Lubbock, and Amarillo. I had just come from Boston, New York, and St. Louis. Why didn't I go to Omaha, Los Angeles, or Denver? I know now that these professional reasons were merely rationalization, a sort of subconscious subterfuge to get back home. Unrecognized nostalgia, all the more painful for having gone underground, was working in me in many ways, and this particular choice of itinerary was one of them.

When I got out of the cab in front of the hotel, I thought I heard someone calling my name. I turned my head to see that it was only a truckload of lonesome, bawling, white-faced calves. But it was music to me: as Texan a welcome as anyone could wish.

Later that day at a luncheon celebrating an important railroad book, I sat between two literary figures well known to America, Lon Tinkle and E. de Golyer. Dr. Herbert Gambrell, author and distinguished Professor of History at Southern Methodist University, gave me the kind of introduction every author dreams of and seldom gets, certainly not when the master of ceremonies does not know in advance that the writer is to be present. He quoted verbatim from one of my books! He spoke with feeling of my Texas lineage, and then came the moment of chagrin when I had to stand up and acknowledge publicly that I, a fourth-generation Texan, had never been to Lubbock, a city and county named for my great-grandfather, nor to Amarillo, nor even to Dallas for that matter. It might have helped to know that Lubbock County was created thirteen years after my great-grandfather's death — and that he had never seen the city of Lubbock either. But I did not possess that knowledge at the time!

As I talked with literate, well-informed men and women that day, creative workers in many fields, I began to be painfully aware of how little I knew about Texas, its land and its people. Before the sun went down I had resolved to remedy *that*, scientifically and systematically.

I wondered why so many other Texans don't know Texas. They are no strangers to Foyot's in Paris, and have lunched by the blue Aegean Sea, but few of them know the majesty of the Big Bend or the mystery of the Big Thicket. My own lack of knowledge of the state, surprising in one with deep roots and extensive family connections, was due to an overprotective family. My Scottish mother brought me to the University of Texas at Austin from the Mexican border country so that I should "know someone from every town in Texas." I made friends quickly enough, but was never allowed to visit these classmates in other parts of the state. Prior to 1953, I could truthfully say that I knew Texas from A to Z . . . from Austin to Zapata, a distance of about four hundred miles!

In 1952, when many Americans living near strategic military and industrial areas were feeling anxious owing to the prospect of nuclear bombings, I too began to cast about for a good place to hide. My knowledge of Texas geography was so accurate and extensive that I told my editor I was going to the Big Ben Davis Mountains.

"Where are they?" she asked, intrigued. We got out the map and found no such mountains marked on it. I might have been poring over that map yet if a book tour had not taken me back to Texas.

Less than a day after my arrival in Dallas, I learned, with a red face, that I had combined into one composite creation the Big Bend region of the Rio Grande and the Davis Mountains of West Texas, with an overtone from a deep-sounding bell on a clock spire in London. Probably the rest of my life I shall continue to get solicitous inquiries from straight-faced friends, asking if I would not care to hear them sing:

> In the Big Ben Davis Mountains, where the people never wash their socks,
> And the alcohol comes trickling from the crevices in the rocks . . .

One compassionate soul told me there was such a thing as a Ben Davis apple, but it takes more than apples to comfort me.

My own ignorance began to produce in me a great sympathy for the "tenderfoot" writers who had come to Texas, spent a few days in Dallas and Houston, collected a handful of "Big Rich" anecdotes, gone back home and written about Texas from the outside in. They were armed only with superficial experience, at best. This might make good reading for the uninformed, but I had just made up my mind to retire permanently from the uninformed segment of the population.

To redeem myself in my own eyes, I had to see and know the real Texas from the inside out. I had to learn as much as was feasible about all the principal sections of Texas. I wanted to delve beneath the surface of its colorful history, to acquire firsthand knowledge of its folklore and folkways, to go into settlements, towns, and ranches, and meet the people on their own dunghills. I wanted to observe them at work, play, and worship. I planned to ride Texas' borders, cross its rivers, and circle some of its vast lake shores. I wanted to climb those mountains and examine them close-up, to assure myself they were real. I planned to ride over the glistening beaches that stretch along most of the 370 miles of Gulf Coast, and I would penetrate deep into the heart of the eastern pine forests of the state. All this and more I was to do. For I was determined to find out "Is it true what they say about Texas?"

Maturity had shown me how prejudicial and prevalent the minotaur complex is. Like Minos, the judge in Hell, we pass judgment, sentence the prisoner, and then order him to plead — all without having heard the evidence! I wanted, more than anything else, to remove all prejudice from my outlook.

Texas was a gigantic topic, one people discussed avidly, with special emphasis on its future. No man, and certainly no woman, has seen all of Texas. But I would not give up until every dollar was spent and every bullet fired. My ambition was to be able to discuss the vast subject, not from a quick perusal of periodicals, but from valid, firsthand study. If I spoke, I wanted to know what I was talking about.

I dropped the hocus-pocus of objectivity before I started. A Texan trying to be objective about Texas is like one of those Impossible Interviews that appeared in *Vanity Fair* years ago, say, between the Distillers' Corporation of America and the WCTU, or between a promoter of bullfights and the SPCA. When all was said and done, the "facts" would be my side of the story!

Although I had no intention of writing a book about Texas when I began my project in 1953, I obeyed the instinctual drive of my nature and found that once more I was letting life make my selections for me. That prime necessity of feeling myself intensely alive, of learning — and therefore growing — must be fulfilled at any cost. When I felt the familiar heart's climate, and saw the treasures of writing material spread out before me, I knew of a certainty that I should emulate the tall stranger, far away from home, who stood by the graveside at the funeral of the friendless man and said: "If nobody's gonna say anything about the deceased, I reckon I'll say a few words about Texas."

Being me, I knew I would have to communicate, to share what I thought was most impressive and most worth sharing. I would avoid making a dry, grim survey. No dreary Baedeker for me, if I could help it.

Out of all the experiences and adventures that I knew lay before me, why shouldn't fact be fun, especially in Texas? Such a project would involve, I felt sure, work harder and more baffling than any I had ever known, knotty problems, some sacrifice, and many stormy situations. But tackle it I must, for the result would be a sadly needed postgraduate education, if nothing else. Even in that, my most lonesome November, I knew the emotions that were pushing me around were doing so for some productive purpose, for some creative cause. I must fulfill that longing so common to men everywhere, and go back to the old house where our growth marks are still on the wall, to see old friends, and to hear familiar voices, to walk into a store after a generation of absence and hear the proprietor say: "You been outa town."

Some sixth sensitivity told me the time was NOW. Texas has been known to barbecue the fatted calf for a returning prodigal, and I had a feeling that she was going to put on a real show, pull out all the stops, and let 'er rip.

"Texas has a way o' turnin' out for a feller sometimes," Jimmy Meek said to me. Like other oil men, Mr. Meek is not always successful, not always on the crest of the golden wave, but being Texan he always believes that "things will be better next year."

"A few years ago," he said, "I hit a dry hole an' was broke. I had me a good big *mains*ion over in Houston, but I was havin' trouble payin' the paperboy! Long about that time, here came a wire from some friends o' mine in New York sayin' they were on their way to Texas. I had got acquainted with 'em when I was in the money, an' knew what they would be expectin' from Texas."

I could sympathize with Jimmy Meek there.

"Well," he said, "it's funny how Texas is there when you need her! She puts the big pot in the little one. Here come these folks in the spring o' the year, expectin' just about everything. Happened one o' my friends had gone off on a round-the-world-cruise an' left a brand-new Cadillac with me to put out to pasture for him. I just loaded my New York 'company' into the Cadillac an' took off for Deep East Texas. Another friend o' mine over there in the heavy money was throwin' a three-day shindig: barbecue, ball, an' fox hunt. 'Course we were all invited, an' the New Yorkers just lapped it up! Nature kinda turned it on for us, too . . . bluebonnets splattered all over creation! Never saw so many or so pretty in my life. That three-day spree didn't cost me a cent but the gasoline.

"Then they wanted to see the Alamo, so we took a runnin'-fit an' went to San Antonio. Lady Luck was doggin' my heels. I had a winnin' streak that wouldn't quit!

"When we got to San Antonio, we hadn't no more than walked into the lobby of the Saint Anthony Hotel than this visitin' feller's wife let out a squeal: 'Oh! *That's* what I think of as being a Texan!' She wasn't too far wrong. She was lookin' at six foot six o' man in old-time Texas garb, boots, brush jacket, and hat: the works. I grinned myself, because she was lookin' at the real thing! It seemed most too good to be true, but anyway I said: 'Do you want to meet him? That's Bill Sterling, Cap'n o' the Texas Rangers.'

"She almost fainted, an' accused me o' makin' it up for her benefit. 'Show her your guns, Bill,' I told him to convince her he was real. Ol' Bill acted kinda timid, but he pulled back his jacket an' showed her the guns. That convinced her."

I hoped devoutly that for the sake of the story, Mr. Meek's "company" would fly back to New York at once, for I could not see how he could top that one.

"Then," he said, "we lit a shuck for Dallas. I called a friend, manager o' one o' the best hotels in town, an' told him about the fix I was in. 'Come ahead on, boy,' he said. 'Got the Presidential Suite saved for you, complimentary. Good public relations.' Things just do fall that way for you sometimes.

"We were livin' it up big, an' they were sayin' how high, wide, an' handsome Texas oil men treat their guests. Everybody was havin' one hell of a good time! After dinner (on the hotel, you understand), I decided they'd oughta hear a quartet o' singin' Negro waiters down in Houston that I liked so well. Man, could they sing! My 'company' was flyin' back to New York next mornin', so I phoned the waiters in Houston, told 'em to rent 'em some tuxedos, an' to take a taxi from Houston to Dallas. They got high an' behind an' came on over quicker'n a minnow could swim a dipper."

I looked Mr. Meek right in the eye, but he never flinched. "You never brought those waiters two hundred and fifty-five miles from Houston to Dallas in a taxi," I reproached the sometime-Texas-Maharajah, "besides, who paid the taxi bill?"

"Woman, when you want your singin' waiters, you want 'em! Who paid the taxi fare? Hell, the waiters did!"

That Armistice Day of 1953, when "it all started," began tearfully but ended rewardingly for me, bringing not peace, but adventure. I smiled inwardly as I thought how wisely my epitaph had been chosen for me years ago: MANY A HEADACHE, BUT NEVER A DULL MOMENT.

As I was leaving the scene of this momentous luncheon, I began to wonder how I could accomplish the task I had set myself, a goal that was all but unfeasible for a woman who had never changed a tire by herself, especially in a land where service stations are sometimes a hundred miles apart.

Bill Johnson, the regional editor of *Time* Magazine whose wife Liz Ann, owner of MacMurray's Book Shop, had brought me to Dallas, stopped me at the door and introduced the man he was talking to.

"You've been back in Texas half a day, Mary," Johnson said. "In that length of time you're bound to have heard of Pool's Perimeter of Texas trip!"

My publishers lost no time in securing the collaboration of Bob Pool, a man who had given a lifetime to formal and informal research on Texas, who was thoroughly familiar with every nook and cranny of the state. He was to be my guide and mentor as I sought a new dimension of knowledge, not just height, depth, and breadth, but a heart of wisdom.

Here I was, almost by accident, embarked on a Texas-size odyssey, in quest of a homeland I had never really known, setting my compass by a star I had never seen, but one I knew had to be here.

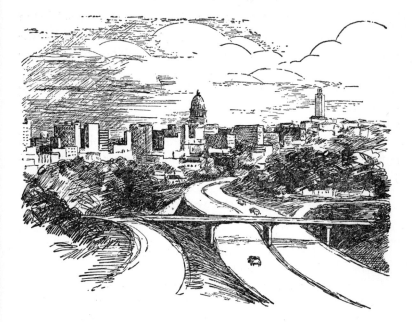

2. THE BIG MIDDLE

WHERE BETTER than Austin, the big middle of that enormous
abstract quality that is Texas, could I set up a base of operations? In the shadow of the Capitol, where the archives house
treasures from the past, near the vast resources of the library
facilities of the University of Texas, I would be on solid ground.
Here I could take up the threads of the past in a section of the
state that I knew well. From there I would work out to the unknown and try to make the prodigious scene before me specific
and concrete. Here at the very crossroads of Texas, I would
be in the direct path of events.

From the hub I can ray out over the state, when the mountains won't come to Mahomet, I reasoned. There would be
stimulus and excitement in the capital city. Friends old and
new were bound to turn up at least once a year. People driv-

ing through from the West Coast or from the East would stop for a visit. Politics would bring some, and the thirst for knowledge would bring others to the University. The annual meetings of the learned societies, such as the Texas Folklore Society and the Texas State Historical Association, would lure the scholarly creative people from their studies over the wide reaches of the state.

Austin is the heart of Texas, geographically, politically, and culturally, I thought. Townsend Miller's narrative poem, "A Letter from Texas," has this description of the capital:

> There lies the central city, the westering wall beyond
> Rising out of the plain under the blue plateau
> Naked by morning to the incredible sun
> Shielded and shadowed in the long afternoon —
> Austin, the central city, and she is crowned with sun
> And twice-crowned westward with the violet hills.
> John, the thick white roses swarming over the wall
> The moon in the white courts, the quivering mornings!
> John, the girls and the young men walking in the streets
> Tall, splendid, easy as wind over the prairie
> Wind in their blue eyes and in the afternoon
> They shake the day off in the cold shadowy pools,
> By night on the great starlit river, the Colorado,
> Their hands open and their hearts. This is the central city
> And they walk in it and their hearts high.

Evocative and accurate, the lines convey the stately beauty of Austin, water-rich, solid, and steeped in tradition. This is a Texan city, not a cut-rate Chicago nor a reprint Rochester. No smelly industry mars the natural beauty that attracts so many retired persons to her hospitable hills and lake shores.

The advantages, for me, were many. Within ten minutes' drive I could be in the fragrant hills looking down on Austin's links in the chain of six Highland Lakes within a sixty-mile stretch, man-made lakes that had appeared as if by magic during my absence. I could look at the sapphire sky reflected in their waters, and watch, with the approach of night, the myriad twinkling lights that bejewel the bosom of the city that wears the Violet Crown. This was the beginning of Texas' "Hill Country," at the Balcones Fault, that great escarpment that separates the Edwards Plateau in the west from the Coastal Plains.

Inside of fifteen minutes, in my car, I could go back more than a hundred years in time by talking to a cedar cutter who wanted to get deputized so he "could kill his brother legally." "My granddaddy fit in the Sandy Anna War," he told me.

I could visit with my "stove-up cowboy," Uncle Will, survivor of thirty-two lung hemorrhages, "all alone, out in the pasture, Miss Mary . . . me lyin' on the ground rippin' an' stavin'! In my lungs I got forty plastic balls rattlin' round right now, but that was after I'd been to Paris, France, an' fought in World War I. That vinn roudge an' vinn blank done it! 'Co'se the shrapnel never helped none."

Uncle Will never got out of the fourth grade, he said, because a little girl with blond curls always looked up at him so pretty, scarcely daring to breathe, each day as he read with feeling from the Fourth Reader the account of a grizzly bear killing a valiant dog: "I spit that part out loud and savage." What man could graduate from that!

"You gonna write *me* in a book, Miss Mary?" A long, significant pause, and then: "Well, I reckon I've not said a word that could hurt ary soul livin' or dead." And because this is Texas where anything can happen and does, back in town Miss Fannie Ratchford with her erudite arrangement of *Gondal's Queen*, a novel in verse by Emily Brontë, was exciting the scholarly on both sides of the Atlantic.

A few blocks away, Eloise Roach, a public school teacher, was coming into her own with her inspired translation of Jiménez's *Platero and I*, winning belated recognition for her perceptive understanding twenty years after her translation had been turned down by publisher after publisher. She had felt Jiménez's greatness before the seal of approval, the Nobel Prize, was conferred on him.

In four hours of driving I could be in Houston looking down on the Ship Channel from the top of the San Jacinto Monument. In five hours I could be at a meeting of the Texas Institute of Letters in Dallas, or deep in the Piney Woods at the Prison Rodeo. In the same length of time I could be listening to the pounding surf at Galveston, the Oleander City. Or I could be wading in the warm Gulf of Mexico, breathing air that is as soft as a whiff of chloroform and just as relaxing to taut nerves. I might pry oysters from their beds, if I could get up sufficient energy to pull my rake, but the soft air off Copano Bay at Rockport, near Goose Island and Austwell, the Aransas National Wildlife Refuge, is not conducive to physical effort. It would be enough just to contemplate the enchanting mottes of inside-out live-oak trees, their limbs blown together by the prevailing winds into solid roofs, arbors of twigs and branches all facing the same direction. The clumps look like long-haired women, their backs to the wind, hair blown forward and up from the nape of the neck, to stream out in front of their faces.

These inducements, and many more, pointed to Austin as the logical place to set up shop.

It's always moonlight in Austin! Will the moons still be there? I wondered. The tower lights, 165 feet high, were built six years before the turn of the century. Their mercury vapor lamps give off a lovely blue glow. Each tower of the twenty-seven illuminates more than four square blocks, and they are on from twilight till dawn. I had the "moons" all counted, as bird watchers keep track of the vanishing whooping cranes. By my count, there should have been thirty-two, but I was told that the missing five were used as parts to repair the remaining "moons." There are small elevators in the center of each tower for repair work, and they are all inspected regularly. To me, they are a very real part of Austin. Built to light the hilly, wooded areas of the town, Austin traded her narrow-gauge railway for the towers in lieu of cash. They are costly to operate, but worth every penny of the expense. Their charm and beauty, plus the fact that Austin is now the only city in the world with tower lights, makes perpetual moonlight cheap at any price.

I was almost afraid to turn the page of my memory when I came back to Austin in November of 1954, but old friends had changed not at all. All the rest had changed almost beyond recognition.

After twenty-seven years' absence, I picked up the telephone scarcely daring to hope for the voice of the friend who had been my housemother as a student, but since the "moons" were still active, I was encouraged to call and find out.

"Mary Lubbock, you get yourself out here right this minute!" The voice was the same one that had called to me down the block when I had forgotten my books as a freshman.

Four blocks from the campus of the University of Texas, under the wide eaves of the white house with the hundred-year-old red cedars, I began to take in the heady blend of the strange and the familiar. The curious sensation of observing the "now" through the eyes of the "then" resulted in a kind of double exposure. I began to understand that all Texas is an eternal synthesis of past and present, superimposed one upon the other. It produces a feeling of being in two places at once. Skyscrapers for pigeonhole parking in one block, and a few blocks away an ancient wooden store with a false front high above it bears the crudely lettered words Raw Furs Bought. The frontier past and the urban present of Texas are separated by a very short span of time.

A modern air conditioner hummed in my bedroom in the house that stood on cedar blocks. They are still in perfect condition, almost as hard as granite, although they were cut while Indians were still a menace to the builder.

Out of my south window I could see the dome of the Capitol,

high above the building made of red Texas granite, shaped like
a Greek cross in Doric architecture. That sturdy structure was
completed in 1888 at the cost of 3,000,000 acres of Texas land,
valued at that time at one dollar per acre. Sixteen oxen hauled
the 18,000-pound cornerstone from the quarries near Marble
Falls to Burnet, and on to Austin by a special railroad built to
handle the granite for the Capitol building. The "Goddess of
Liberty" stands sixteen feet tall on top of the dome, and holds
aloft the Lone Star of Texas with her left hand, while her right
hand holds a sword pointing down. At night a rosy glow comes
from the dome, reminding me of the warm red earth of Texas'
fruit lands.

From my east window I could see the University Tower,
new and a little strange to me, an ornament whose charm has
been much debated. Its height caused Frank Dobie to say: "If
they'd lay the damn thing down on its side and run a gallery
around it, it would look a lot more Texan." On victorious nights
the tower is lighted with brilliant orange, the University color
that stands out in startling contrast to the deep navy blue sky.

All day the chimes from the giant carillon in the tower followed me with their prayer, one sentence added for each quarter hour:

> Lord, through this hour
> Be Thou my guide,
> For in Thy power
> I do confide.

On certain days there are concerts by the carilloneur, weird
combinations of Thomas Moore and George Gershwin. No
kind of one-fingered musical performance has much appeal for
me, but there was one chime concert I regret having missed.
The day Stalin died, a student played the chimes loud and fast,
beginning with "I'll Be Glad When You're Dead, You Rascal
You!" Then he swung into "Massa's in the Cold, Cold Ground,"
and ended up with "Old Black Joe."

Waking up to music was no new experience in the old white house. Every Sunday morning for four years I had waked to the sound of two unvarying selections on the phonograph of the housemother: "Whispering Hope" sung by a soprano and a contralto in closest harmony, followed by the strutting trombones of "The Saint Louis Blues." Did a more typical Texas combination ever exist? A sugary religious song and Brother Handy's earthy classic, the great granddaddy of the blues! The Victrola doesn't look so stylish as it did, and the spring is a little weaker, but it still plays. And the two records are still intact.

I am glad things haven't changed in this neighborhood, I thought as I prepared breakfast, but I should have withheld that opinion for a minute or two.

The breeze carried in the voice of a young Rabbinical student from the apartment next door, yammering at the Moslem classmate who shared his apartment and would like to keep a kosher house, also. According to the budding Rabbi, the Moslem was "too stingy to pay for good kosher meat," which was brought over for him from San Antonio and lodged for safekeeping under lock and key in the ritually pure refrigerator of the Hillel Foundation a few blocks away.

"You go to a dance," the future holy man shouted, "you want to wear a plain suit, but because everybody else wears a tuxedo, you go out and rent one too! Nothing but dogma! You like to sleep on the floor, you're used to it. But in the U.S. everybody sleeps in a bed, so you sleep in one too! That's dogma."

I was beginning to get a grasp of "dogma" for the first time when a young Iranian petroleum engineer who lived in the apartment next to the Jewish boy began to play the slow movement from Lalo's *Symphonie Espagnole* on a violin. He played extremely well, with a rich throbbing tone. I was struck by the Morse code quality of music, a universal means of communication.

"An Iranian, whom I think of as Persian, probably Paris-trained, playing Lalo in Austin, Texas," I said to myself. The vital Hebraic melody was broken off suddenly when a bunch of GI's arrived at the apartment of an army nurse next door to the Iranian. The boys brought cartons of beer to the nurse, who was going to school on her GI Bill of Rights. Good old Bill, I thought. Uncle Sam ought to change his name to Bill, he foots so many of them. The nurse's record player blasted out with "Party Doll," and that put the violin in the case with a kind of despairing shriek from the bow.

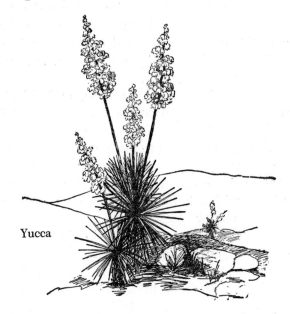

Yucca

A pair of young Turkish newlyweds passed in front of my window and waved. They were affable because the previous day I had heard them trying out their creaky new English on the butcher at the chain store trying to ascertain whether or not the hamburger had pork in it. I assured them that it did not and we chatted a moment. They were pleased with the amount and variety of food in Texas markets but deplored the lack of seasonings. I was able to show them jars of saffron, sesame seed, and garlic on the shelves of the same shop.

"It is not quite the same." I smiled to myself as I thought of my student days when the most exotic foodstuff available in the neighborhood was soggy barbecued gray brisket at the Helpy Selfy and a greasy hamburger on the Drag, the row of shops opposite the campus. There had not been even one first-class Mexican restaurant in Austin then, although Walker's cannery for Mexican foods was going strong. Now Americanized Mexican food is a major industry in Austin, both in grocery stores and in restaurants.

A Chinese with a thick Mississippi mouth-full-of-mush accent runs an excellent Cantonese restaurant and drives a violet Cadillac. "What lil ol' thang you want me to fix you-all tonight? Fix you some real nice foo yung, little lady!" The first time I heard him speak as a guest on a television cookery program I was certain that the heat had got me, and that I had finally flipped my lid.

And this sample of the globe's people I have seen with scarcely the bother of leaving my apartment, I thought as I looked at the changed life of Twenty-second Street and the people who had wrought the change. We used to be vastly amused by the fact that some of the students came from Pflugerville, a scant nine miles away.

A Ceylonese student passed by, very lovely with beautiful teeth and hair. Her sari-like dresses would make a designer gnash his teeth in envy. How did one drape fabric in such graceful folds?

"Yes, I will come to tea, and I will show you how we arrange the material," the girl said and glided off on her white wedgies to work on her Master's thesis. Her subject is History of Education, and she is writing the thesis in French. Her exotic appearance attracted very little attention, which astonished me when I remembered that the only unusual mode of dress seen on Twenty-second Street in "the old days" was a pair of Boy Scout shoes, tightly laced around the ankles of a lady poet. The same poet, shortly after my return, sent her daughter a box full of Texas earth to put in her shoes when she was married so she would "be married on Texas soil" even though the ceremony took place in another state.

My chat with the Ceylonese girl ended on a pleasant note, but as I turned to go into the house my thoughts were stampeded by a nuisance that is the plague of most of America today: a youth from Muleshoe, Texas, with a burr-cut and open sport shirt, shot by in a red Buick convertible screeching his tires in the fashionable way to the tune of about five dollars' worth of peeled rubber. I tried to remember what we used to do that was equally annoying, but all I could dredge up was ukulele playing. These lads and their tire screeching would have been welcome recruits for Torquemada and the Inquisition.

Here at the heart of the state, I realized that Austin had become "occupied country." Outlanders of every description had invaded the place and infiltrated the familiar scenes. Foreign faces, unknown tongues, outlandish dress and costume were everywhere on the streets and the now unrecognizable campus. Saris and sarongs. Turbans and togas. Blue jeans and boots. And most startling of all, very pregnant girls were much in evidence about the campus, lugging stacks of books uncomplainingly. It was hard for me to reconcile the present with the past, to conceive of the enormous number of married students I should find enrolled in the University, when during my student days marriages were carefully kept secret, and if discovered meant certain expulsion for both students. Now the University owned many special housing units for married students, they formed clubs and associations, had meetings to solve baby-sitter problems, and even elected a wife of the year: Mrs. Co-Wed.

I was surprised at the decline in the number of "Queens." There had been "Queens" of practically everything on the campus, but now most of them had been changed to "Miss." My all-time favorite is "Miss Service Station of Austin," who went right to the top as "Miss Portable Appliance of Texas," with a two-week, all-expense paid vacation in Hollywood!

There was no way to figure out what brought them — maybe the climate, or Texas' legendary advantages — but there were students here from nearly every state in the Union. A Texas accent was now almost a rarity on the campus. The tower might well have been likened to the Tower of Babel. During one lunch hour at the Commons I heard seven different languages spoken — and that was counting only those I could identify. During the twenties, I remember only one Chinese co-ed, who was stared at everywhere she went. A man from Belgrade, then Serbia, was a popular engineering student. With his roommate, a Belgian, these students made up our United Nations of that day. I am not including Latin Americans because there were always quite a few of them. A treasurer of the Republic of Mexico worked his way through the University of Texas and married an Austin girl.

I was struck by the desire of many of the foreign students to be assimilated into the American way of life. A Japanese chemistry-fellow had finished his course of studies and was returning to Japan. His friends in the lab noticed that he got through school on two nylon sport shirts. When he was leaving they took up a collection and bought him "a pair of Ivy League pants, and an Ivy League shirt, the kind with the little button in back of the collar, you know. There was even enough money to buy him a belt! He wanted that outfit more than anything!" The fact that the *sine qua non* of the Ivy League, a coat, was missing marred his bliss not at all.

The influence of the automobile is felt strongly at the University and the parking problem is serious. I heard that 18,000 students owned 24,000 cars. To anyone trying to park his car in front of his house in the University neighborhood, the remark is less facetious than it seems.

Around the beginning of the Christmas holidays, I saw signs on the bulletin board of the Student Union soliciting passengers for a car pool "going to Connecticut for the holidays." There was even a member of a service fraternity on duty to check in applicants.

Strange unclassified religious sects had made their appearance on the campus over the years. The status and influence of these groups is not clearly defined. What was known as the "bull session" is now conducted in some quarters on a quasi-religious, "do-it-yourself analysis" basis that may produce some serious repercussions. Certainly the proceedings give the various Deans' offices grave concern.

To my surprise, I heard football games in the stadium opened with prayer, to the infinite distress of the intelligent segment of the faculty who were opposed to asking God's blessing on the mayhem they were about to witness. When some of the local divines got the bit in their teeth (in this case, the microphone), they ran away with the prayer and turned it into a fair-sized sermon to their captive audience.

A few local medical men, slipping a fast one over on the "No Advertising" edict of the American Medical Association, had themselves paged over the public address system several times during the game, to show the crowd in the stadium how greatly they were in demand. But the University outsmarted them. A system was devised whereby each physician was called by the last three numbers of his narcotics license. The calls fell off substantially.

I followed with great interest the firing of a football coach at the University, saw photographs of him being hanged in effigy, and was told that his children were taunted so badly that they had to be taken out of public school . . . all because his team had lost.

"This in Texas? A land that has been the last resort and hope of losers over the centuries?"

I could only wonder how many people would ever have heard of the Alamo if the Texans had won.

But along with un-Mexican Mexican food like puffy tacos, athletics had become Big Business and part of a Public Relations Plan. The "silent persuasion" was strong here, and I wondered what crazy swing the pendulum would take in the next thirty years.

As I studied these startling additions to Texas' university life, I tried to be a Disinterested Observer. I was no longer enrolled in the University, and I had no children to attend it. One fact stood out above everything else: the University was alive.

What counted with me was the change, the yeasty upsurge of independent thought and action on the part of the students, a decided departure from the dogmatic, ironclad years I had known.

The school was demanding — and getting — the right to make its own mistakes. For years it had asked for bread and been given a stone . . . by the keepers of the cash, the Available Fund. Money for impressive buildings had been forthcoming, but little for faculty and great visiting teachers. Now I saw evidence on every side that the Powers That Be were well on the way to distinguishing brains from bricks. The University of Texas is entering its Golden Age.

Recreational and cultural opportunities had increased with the passing of the years. At Batts Hall of the University, Dame Edith Sitwell, rummaging in her reticule, sniffing elegantly and dabbing at the end of her red-tipped nose with a lacy handkerchief held in a sculptured hand that just could support the weight of her jewels, gave a reading from her own works. Then, most unforgettably, she read Lady Macbeth's sleepwalking scene. Pleased with her reception, Dame Edith said affably, almost confidentially, that she was descended from Lady Macbeth, and as anyone could attest who had ever visited her, almost as bad a hostess, although she had not yet stooped to murder. When pressed to read more, her good taste would not permit her to follow Shakespeare with any serious verse. She read from her own *Façade* to the joy of the students and faculty. After reading "Scotch Rhapsody," dealing with a drouthy Sabbath, she said she had read it in Edinburgh the previous summer and that the Scots seemed unreasonably delighted with the poem. She did not know when she read it, she told the audience, that in Edinburgh one could not buy a drink on Sunday. When she read "Green Geese," I noticed four boys sitting in front of me and a little to my left reciting silently and gleefully the words of the poem with Dame Edith.

Edith Sitwell in the Cow Country! And there was talk of T. S. Eliot appearing before long. Those in charge, it was said, could bring these celebrated figures to the University for three days as visiting lecturers, after screening them thoroughly, and having made sure that they did not boggle at the Loyalty Oath. "But," a witty man said, "if they stay longer than three days, they have to have their chests X-rayed." Times had certainly changed "in Texas, down by the Rio Grande."

From the campus, I wandered down to the First Methodist Church across from the Capitol, where I had been a paid soloist as a student. It stood solid as ever, but the charming red brick house across the street where I met Paul Whiteman and his band when they played at a party there had been razed to make a parking lot. "Ma" Ferguson, Governor of Texas, had been there that night with her daughter Ouida, guests of the gay, golden girl for whom I played piano accompaniments. It was during Prohibition, but that was no "cold-water doin's."

A few doors away I saw the antique shop of the gifted lady who used to waltz into the shop to serve her patrons to the music of "The Blue Danube Waltz," played on a tinkling music box.

I went back up to All Saints' Chapel, my own church, where I used to sing "for free" on my Sunday nights off. It was changed considerably, but is still probably the only church in the world

where General Robert E. Lee, in Confederate gray, stands enshrined in stained glass along with the rest of the saints.

The pews had been moved back, apparently to make room
for the multitude, but they were jammed so close together that
even a person with my short wheel base had difficulty in kneel-
ing. I do not think Bishop George Herbert Kinsolving, who
built the chapel for students in order "to reach the best minds
in the state," approves of such squeezing as he lies there in his
crypt under the altar. Bishop Kinsolving was a Texas-size man
of the cloth, of generous proportions spiritually and physically.
The Indians would have called him a heap-big sleeve man.
His amethyst ring was the size of a hard-boiled egg. He was the
biggest man I ever saw in my life, and as he sat there three decades ago in his Episcopal robes I was convinced that God Almighty had a thick, droopy pepper and salt mustache, too.
When "Big Bishop" laid his hand on a head in confirmation, the
candidate stayed confirmed — and never grew an inch.

"Where do the students go to dance?" I asked. "I see no signs
of the old Saturday night Gym Struggle we looked forward to
so eagerly." I was told that students go dancing in night clubs,
drinking beer or toting their own bottles.

I wanted to know if they still held the Junior-Senior Prom.
Blank looks and "never heard of it," was all the response I got.

Back in what I am beginning to think of as the Tacky Twenties, it was the custom at the University of Texas for the girls of
the Junior Class to honor the women of the Senior Class with a
ball — the Junior-Senior Prom. Each junior girl drew a name
from a box, and the senior girl whose name she drew was her
"date" for the ball. Short or tall, that's how it was. The junior
had to borrow men's clothing of a reasonable fit, preferably a
dinner jacket, from some boy, buy a corsage for her "date," get
a taxi, call for the unlucky woman, and escort her to the dance.
It was also obligatory to see that the senior's dance card was
filled, and to make sure that enough "stags" cut-in to assure the
lady of a respectable "rush."

As I described this traditional event to some younger people, I began to understand the incredulous looks they gave me. I was begining to wonder if I had not dreamed it up after a surfeit of novels by Guido da Verona. But I certainly remembered my own junior year, when I borrowed a dinner jacket and a pair of white flannel pants from Harry Levy of Galveston, the smallest boy I could find on the campus who owned evening attire. I can still see the housemother, my own mother, and three other mothers of daughters who lived in the same house, standing over Harry in the reception hall as he fixed the bat-wing collar for me, and tied the black bow tie to his satisfaction. Sta-Comb, I think, was what he slathered on my head to make my hair lie flat. But there was nothing he could do about the thimblelike derrière in the tight white pants. No "date" was ever escorted by a funnier-looking, more "feisty" beau.

"Here it is!" One of my classmates, now the keeper of cash and documents on the campus, produced a copy of the 1925 *Cactus*, the school yearbook. There, undeniably, in black and white were photographs of the revelers. "Of course we had the Junior-Senior Prom!" She was almost indignant! "I remember trying to borrow a silver flask to make my outfit complete."

I remembered the laughter the description of the Prom always elicited in the various corners of the world where I had mentioned it. Looking at it as students would now, in the full light of the psychological implications, I have to agree with the classmate who wanted to borrow the flask: "And it was all so innocent!"

As I wandered up and down the hilly streets of Austin looking for landmarks, I was filled with admiration for the canny pioneers who selected this site for the capital of Texas. Here was water, rushing from Barton Springs, crystal clean and icy cold. Wood and stone were readily available for building a city that even in 1839 marked out on the map a plot for the Hospital, then called in most sections an Alms House, where Breckenridge, the City Hospital, still stands.

But these natural endowments alone are not sufficient to give character to a town, I thought. Human experience is what it takes to do that. I passed by Colonel E. M. House's solid red stone residence, still in good condition. He certainly had experience of life in Austin — and elsewhere. Counselor and confidant of President Woodrow Wilson, Colonel House helped elect and served as adviser to several Texas governors, James S. Hogg, Charles A. Culberson, Joseph D. Sayers, and S. W. T. Lanham, a fact that is little known outside Texas. The fields Colonel House operated in at the United States Capitol may have been wider, but the situations he controlled there were no tougher than those he handled in Texas. Self-effacing and unobtrusive in his manipulations, he seems to have been a man who was satisfied to be the neck which turns the head, rather than the head itself.

Here O. Henry "got into trouble at the bank," and was sent to the penitentiary. Although they named a Junior High School for him in Austin, there are two schools of thought about the famous writer of short stories. Every few years, somebody writes a book about him . . . even years, he seems to be proved innocent; odd years, guilty. In 1957, a group interested in its preservation moved O. Henry's Honeymoon Cottage away from a rundown neighborhood to a piece of land on Lamar Boulevard, near an attractive residential section. The cottage was said to be of doubtful authenticity, but there was no doubt about one thing: the residents of the neighborhood did not want it near their property! It "caught fire" twice and finally burned to the ground. Now the occupants of these push-button paradises can watch Thomas Mitchell in peace, as he portrays O. Henry in the network television dramatization of the stories, many of which O. Henry wrote in Austin.

A man not popular in Austin, even in 1840, was Alphonse de Saligny, chargé d'affaires of His Majesty, Louis Philippe, King of France, to the Republic of Texas. He built a charming house which has been known from the beginning as the French Embassy, said to be "the only Embassy ever built by a foreign power on Texas soil." I have even heard it said that it was the only Embassy owned by a foreign power on American soil.

I was astonished to learn from *The Handbook of Texas*, the Holy Bible of any Texas researcher, that Anson Jones bought the land the so-called Embassy stands on in September 1840 for five hundred dollars, and sold it to de Saligny for one thousand dollars. The chargé d'affaires paid for it with his own money, and started building the charming dwelling with the latticed porch. Before construction was finished, de Saligny sold the house and land to Bishop Odin of San Antonio, agreeing to finish the building and arranging in the transfer to occupy the house until April of 1842. Apparently de Saligny used the place as an Embassy, but it appears to have been his own personal property. I feel sure this information comes as a surprise to numerous Texans, many of them better informed than I was.

It is unfortunate that, owing to the shifting of neighborhoods and industrial changes, the "Embassy" sits on Tin Can Heap, a sordid setting for so painstaking a labor of love as the restoration of the house and grounds by the Daughters of the Republic of Texas. De Saligny was not famous for paying his bills and made a number of enemies during his tenure. The pigs of his landlord got loose in de Saligny's garden, and almost provoked an international incident. The Republic of Texas, always hard up for money, was negotiating for a loan from France. The Franco-Texienne relations were flourishing until the pigs started "depredating" in the chargé d'affaires' garden. De Saligny managed to get the loan squashed, doubtless by a word in the ear of his brother-in-law, the French Minister of Finance. Probably he did Texas a favor in the long run!

Roaming in the State Cemetery I came upon an antipathetic reminder of Reconstruction Days. E. J. Davis, the tyrant of Texas, carpetbag ruler after the Civil War, was governor of Texas when Confederate citizens were disenfranchised by his order. He was said to be the pawn of Sheridan and Grant, although Texas historians insist that he was a man of personal probity. There is a pretentious monument to Davis, but it was not placed there by the State of Texas. His brother paid for it.

The sight of the stone brought to mind an Austin woman who wrote an all-but-forgotten book called *The Refugees, a Sequel to Uncle Tom's Cabin,* "by a devoted daughter of the South, Annie Jefferson Holland." It is quite certain that the refugees, or the survivors of the Reconstruction, did not need a monument to remind them of E. J. Davis. There was little chance of their forgetting him!

In the book, written in 1889, Annie Holland claims that "since Mrs. Stowe crucified him [Uncle Tom], I have a right to resurrect him for the benefit of The Refugees." I wonder if Annie Jefferson Holland knew that *Gleason's Pictorial Drawing-Room Companion,* of Boston, in the Saturday, July 2, 1853, number printed the following comment eight years "before the shooting started." "The Boston Museum has been outraging decency by reviving a vulgar negro extravaganza — *Uncle Tom's Cabin.*"

Mrs. Holland's touching little volume is written in a style so bad as to be almost good. The heroine has to sew the white satin dresses, the wedding gowns of the invading Yankee women in order to buy food, but "she did not have to accept the invitation to the wedding." The story involves the sending of Uncle Tom to the Texas State Legislature to spite the carpet-bagger overlords and defeat a scalawag candidate. It is a witty record of the feelings of many Texans during the now almost forgotten Reconstruction Days.

The flyleaf of my copy of this collector's item bears the signature of a gay, much married Austin lady of whom it was said: "She's had some FINE husbands!" The last of this gallant band is credited with making the startling statement that he was papering his house with black wallpaper so that when he murdered his wife, the blood wouldn't show.

I looked with very different emotions at another tomb in the cemetery. As I admired the recumbent statue of Albert Sidney Johnston, lying in its weatherproof glass case inside a small chapel of ornamental iron with a Lone Star in each gable, I wondered what the Confederate General, lying there on a battlefield stretcher, covered with an army blanket—all terribly real even in white marble — thought of the talented and unconventional woman who had carved into his statue so much dignity and sorrow. Dignity and sorrow, but no defeat. How did anyone breathe emotion into white marble? By living, I decided, and remembered the scandal in reverse that had Austin and other parts of Texas by the ears for so long a time.

Not far from Twenty-second Street stands Formosa, as solid and impervious to ruin as its chatelaine, the Westphalian sculptor, Elisabet Ney. "The sculptress of kings," she has been called. It seems there is no getting away from the condescension of the "ess" that is the lot of sculptors and authors. "First sculptress of Europe, friend of Alexander von Humboldt and Schopenhauer, Ludwig of Bavaria, and a host of others," Miss Ney came to Hempstead, Texas, in 1873 with the great love of her life, Dr. Edmund Montgomery. She was wearing a Grecian robe embroidered with gold at sleeves and hem, the waist bound with a golden chain, and her throat circled with a diamond necklace given her by the King of Prussia. One arm was adorned with a bracelet, the gift of Queen Victoria, and on the other was a circlet of diamonds and emeralds bestowed by George V of Hanover. She arrived in this garb while Indians were still a threat and a great many of the settlers were wearing homespun.

After purchasing the great plantation Liendo, the house built by Leonard Groce's slaves, still in perfect condition, beautifully proportioned in its classic simplicity, Miss Ney rode over her lands in the Grecian costume on top of which she had strapped two six-shooters and a dirk. Her life was wretchedly unhappy

and full of misfortune at the plantation. Her youngest child
died and she cremated the body in the fireplace, and placed the
ashes in a leather pouch. She rejected her surviving son and
dressed him in silks and satins, making a little Lord Fauntleroy
out of him, perhaps to thwart the fates.

In the early 1900's she came to Austin, built her odd house,
and made statues of famous Texans. Here she wore Turkish
bloomers and turbans, also a long linen duster. She used to
take her hammock with her when she went to spend the night
with friends. At Formosa she served her favorite dish, clabber.
She rode in the first electric automobile in Austin, owned by a
man named Shipe. He was driving Miss Ney in the electric one
day when the car misbehaved. The engine was under the front
seat and heated up to such a degree that the motorists were
forced to get out and sit on the cool but chigger-infested grass.
The chiggers must have held high carnival in the voluminous
folds of Miss Ney's Turkish trousers.

All this time, Dr. Montgomery, a quiet scholarly Scot, sat in
his study and wrote. From all accounts a brilliant but conventional man, it must have pained him over the years to maintain
the role upon which Miss Ney insisted.

Elisabet told her son that she and Dr. Montgomery were not
married, and that she had picked him up in rags in the street of
a fisherman's village because she was sorry for him.

I have been told by people who were children at the time
their parents sat for Miss Ney that they were allowed to ride to
the sittings in the carriage, but not to go inside the studio on account of "Miss Ney's irregular arrangements." During my girlhood I served frequently as a hostess at Formosa, which had
then been turned into a museum, and I talked to many people
who remembered her well. Most of them say that she maintained her spinster status assiduously.

When Dr. Montgomery "visited" her, he brought his tent
and pitched it on the lawn. They always slept in separate

rooms, and even when Miss Ney was seventy, her maid slept in front of her door as guard. With two children as accessories after the fact, it always seemed to me like locking the stable door after the horse was gone.

In actual fact Elisabet Ney was soundly married, but hating the ordinary and the bourgeois, she maintained to the end of her life that she was not. It was only after Miss Ney's death in 1907 that Dr. Montgomery explained to the public that the woman he had lived with so long was actually his wife.

I wonder how many people seeing Elisabet Ney's statue of Lady Macbeth in the Capitol at Washington know the story of the woman who chiseled it? Had Texas played a part in the formation of her eccentric personality?

All around me were fascinating stories and interesting people. The way Texans thought and felt seemed to be changing daily. I talked to anybody who would "stand hitched," for only so could I find out what they were thinking and becoming.

Texans, bless God, are a vociferous lot and there is nothing they would rather do than talk. I found others of my breed who had come home after long absence. I noticed that nearly all of them took a more intelligent interest in things Texan than they had done previously.

I began to wonder if we should not be required by law to go away for a period of years in order to be able to appreciate the heritage of our homeland.

One of these returned Texans is Laura Krey, a scholarly writer whose *And Tell of Time* I had read with great pleasure and an odd feeling of identification back in 1942. We met to be photographed for our initiation into the woman's journalism fraternity, Theta Sigma Phi.

"I know your people go away back in Texas," she said.

"Santa Anna was held prisoner on my great-grandfather Grayson's boat, the *Yellowstone*, after the battle of San Jacinto. My great-grandfather Tom Lubbock founded the Texas Eighth

Cavalry of Civil War fame, with Frank Terry. He named it the
Terry Rangers, in honor of his friend and cousin by marriage.
Francis Richard Lubbock, comptroller of the Republic, was my
great-granduncle."

Her eyes twinkled under arched brow: "Terry was *my* great-
grandfather! Colonel Tom Lubbock married Obedience Smith,
who was my Great-grandaunt Bedie. That makes us cousins,
twice removed."

Neither of us would have been any great success as Trappist
monks, even if our sex had not barred us from that order vowed
to eternal silence. When the excitement of discovering blood
kinship simmered down, Laura Krey told me she had been away
from Texas forty years. She, too, felt a strong desire to know
more about the fabled land our forebears had helped wrest from
the wilderness. I knew from her writing that the old days and
the old ways would be strong in her. We sat in the Kreys' pleasant book-filled study and talked of the tremendous changes we
had observed in Austin, the only part of Texas that we shared.
We soon found out that aside from this common meeting
ground, our lives might just as well have been spent in two different worlds of space and time.

"Here we are, blood kin, reared in Texas by old-time Texans,"
she said, "you on the Mexican Border, and I on an antebellum
plantation on the Brazos. The difference in the settings and in
the customs we have known wouldn't be nearly so great if we'd
come from different countries in Europe."

"I spoke Spanish as soon as I spoke English," I said, "and had
never known a colored person to talk to until I was fourteen. On
the border, I don't suppose I had seen more than half a dozen
Negroes. When I was a freshman, I asked a colored woman in
Woolworth's one Saturday afternoon if she would let me hold
her baby."

"In my part of Texas no one spoke a word of Spanish," she
said. "Yet I know that our common ancestors always got along
beautifully with the Spanish colonial governors — they were

the same kind of people, rugged and elegant. That combination is what has escaped some of the historians. The hard-bitten fearlessness of the Old Texican, never hesitating to make his own law or to take the existing one into his own hands, was often combined with elegance of mind and a cultured spirit. His essential dignity made him at home with the Spaniards. Benjamin Fort Smith would have been completely at home in Spain." He was our common ancestor who owned an Indian reservation on the Angelina River, long before Sam Houston brought the Alabama-Coushatta to their reservation. He spoke sixteen Indian dialects. "We always enjoyed the society of the Spanish families when we visited in San Antonio during my girlhood," Mrs. Krey said.

"The only Spanish left in most of those families is the name," I said. "During my lifetime, I have known only three or four families of unmixed Spanish blood in Texas. Most Anglos use the word 'Spanish' in referring to Mexicans they like and admire; they think it's more complimentary than 'Mexican.' But the highest type of Mexican is fiercely proud of his nationality. There's a song of the people which begins: '*Yo soy Mexicano!*' 'I am Mexican, and it is my pride to be called so.'"

"The only Mexicans we had were field hands and day laborers in the Brazos plantation country. We didn't associate with them," she said.

"Even a sandal-footed bird catcher has a certain distinctive character. How could he not have dignity, descended from the Indian and the Spaniard? I think you would have liked your laborers if you'd known them."

Mrs. Krey shook her head: "In the tight circle of the planters, we didn't associate with foreigners of any kind. It surprises me now, looking back, for there must have been several high-born German families there. But it was a closed society. We mingled only with our own kind of people."

I knew that Richmond, Columbus, and West Columbia were still Old South, unreconstructed.

"And yet you married a charming German-born professor of medieval history," I said.

"Recently," Mrs. Krey said, "I drove into the plantation of a relative without letting him know I was coming. I had to hurry and identify myself when the owner came out to see what a car with a Minnesota license was doing on his land. When he heard my voice, he was all affability and charm. 'Get down! Get down and come in! All of you!' "

Having driven better than fifty thousand miles, including some of the less "reconstructed" sections, in Texas in a car with a Rhode Island license, I could appreciate her speed in singing out in answer to the unspoken "Who goes there?"

"And you say that during your life in Brownsville Mexican families were accepted socially?" Mrs. Krey persisted.

"They were not only accepted, they were the social arbiters. If there was any condescension, it was on the part of the Mexicans. Anglos are prone to forget that these Texans measured off their land grants from the kings of Spain in *varas*, some of them from as early as the year 1675. Certainly some of those who patented their lands between the Nueces River and the Rio Grande can show records to that effect."

"What is that measure, the *vara?*" she asked. "It appears again and again in land grants and other documents."

"The *vara*, originally, was simply a straight twig or switch. It came to serve as a lance, and then as a badge of office carried by mayors, judges, and other officials. The judge's *vara* began to assume a position of official importance in the eyes of the people, and eventually was used as a measuring stick. Finally it became an official unit of measurement, about thirty-three and a third inches. I have heard Mexican seamstresses ask how many *varas* of material I had for a dress, but that was before *varas* and *metros* were corrupted into *yardas*."

Mrs. Krey smiled: "Wait till some of my relatives in Virginia hear how long these families have been in Texas!"

"Even Texans forget that the Mexican and Spanish-American

had more than a hundred years headstart over any English-speaking family. They were here before the Pilgrim Fathers landed at Plymouth Rock. They're the true breed of indigenous Americans, made up of the mingled blood of Conqueror and Conquered."

It seemed incredible to us that all this, these separate worlds, and divergent points of view, different planes of existence could all be Texas. Earth, spirit, and blood: all Texas, and all different.

"I wonder if any writer could possibly convey this tremendous diversity," Laura Krey asked.

"I ask myself that question daily," I replied, "but something Dorothy Sayers said in *The Mind of the Maker* encourages me to keep trying. She was speaking of writing, but I think what she said applies equally to so composite and complex a creation as the evolution of a people. 'The vital power of an imaginative piece of work demands a diversity within its unity, and the stronger the diversity, the more massive the unity.' The blending of the Spaniard and the Indian into the Mexican is, in a sense, 'an imaginative piece of work.' In *Iberoamérica* Dr. Américo Castro says that Cortes deliberately put his ships out of commission. So the Spaniard had only one alternative: to conquer or to die."

"There isn't much chance for decadence in such a new world," she said, and I agreed enthusiastically.

"I believe that the strength of Texans, and most Americans, springs from the diversity of their racial mixture; here there's an underlay of color from the cultural heritage of Texas' existence under six flags. French, Spanish, Mexican, Republic of Texas, United States, and the Confederacy — each has made its influence felt. Not to mention the German, Irish, Scottish, Alsatian, Czechoslovakian, Polish, and Scandinavian influences in Texas. All that holds these heritages together is Texas history. It puts them all under a common denominator. If they don't know the history, they are not really Texans. Even my illiterate friend whose 'granddaddy fit in the Sandy Anna War' knows history . . . and at first hand. It is the awareness of Texas' history that brings about the final assimilation. Without it, the hoops that hold the staves of the barrel together are missing. I'm astonished to find that there are some Texans whose roots go deep into the state, who know next to nothing of her history, even when their own ancestors had a part in making that history. What encourages me is the passionate zeal newcomers show in wanting to find out all they can about Texas, past and present. I've heard them say sheepishly, after a few months' residence, 'We *were* damyankees!' "

"Yes, it is either that, or an instant and lasting antipathy to it," Mrs. Krey said. "Some of them can't bear the way of life and Texas is a naughty word to them."

"Did you ever hear the story about the prisoners the Texans brought home after the Civil War?" I asked. "They were captured in some Gulf Coast engagement, and kept in a rude stockade, guarded by rough embittered soldiers. The Texans had scarcely any food for themselves and naturally the Yankee prisoners weren't exactly gaining weight. A brash reporter wanted to interview them, and did so over the protest of the guards. The weather was sticky and sultry, and on top of everything the poor Yankees were being eaten alive by mosquitoes, but the reporter went in among them with the stock question that Texans have asked outside visitors over the years — and still do: '. . . and how do you like Texas?' The reporter recorded their answer simply: 'They expressed themselves as being well pleased with Texas!' "

I kept thinking of the different paths our families had taken and of the different points of view these had led to. Yet I knew that the Spanish influence was inextricably interwoven in the fabric even of plantation life. The very names of the rivers proved that: the Brazos de Dios that had watered the Terry sugar plantations was Spanish for Arms of God. All the major rivers of Texas have Spanish names and the place-names tell the story, too. There is no hamlet so small that one cannot buy a bowl of chile or find at least one hot tamale man.

"In seven hours' driving," I said, "I can take you to streets in Brownsville where strangers passing you by will still reach out and touch you, if they admire you, to keep you from getting the evil eye. I can take you to weddings where the *arras* are still a part of the marriage ceremony."

"*Arras?* What is that?"

"The *arras* symbolize the gift of marriage, what corresponds to our phrase, 'with all my worldly goods I thee endow.' The Mexicans use little golden coffers about an inch long, with curved lids like tiny pirate treasure chests. The ring bearer carries the ring on a white satin cushion; another child carries the little gold coffer. The wealthy place small gold coins in the chests . . . and the poor, never to be outdone, take dimes to the jeweler and get them washed with gold leaf. Thirteen coins make up the dowry: one gold and twelve silver. The gold coin stands for Christ, and the others for the twelve Apostles. 'With this dowry I thee wed' — it is very beautiful and moving."

"How I should love to know your world," Laura Krey said. "I am beginning to see Texas through a new pair of glasses."

I was seeing a new Texas myself — and longed to stand once more under the deep, colorful shadow of Spain.

3. THE SHADOW OF SPAIN

IN TEXAS the shadow of Spain is a long one. I wanted to go back where that shade falls thickly and deeply, to the Old World atmosphere of Brownsville where the old Spanish ways had colored my behavior, my speech, and my philosophy of life.

That shadow will travel the length of the River Road, the nine hundred miles from Brownsville to El Paso, I thought as I began to replenish the coffers of my memory. I'll never be out of sight of the architecture I love, nor far from the sound of the language in which I have always been so completely at home. Along part of the way, there will be some of those friends left who go far back into my childhood, who shared the events that made so deep an impression on me. From them I will get corroboration of my memories.

I wondered about the part memory plays in writing. Since

writing and printing were the first adjuncts to memory, they are
bound to walk hand in hand. The ineradicable quality of the
formative years of my life struck me. What happens from the
age of five to fifteen is what stays to color the feeling and thinking of the individual forever. The kind of life, and the land it is
lived in, seem to mark the person for its own.

I tried to put into tangible form the characteristics that Mexican Border life developed in people, what it was that made
them different. I decided that they could be characterized as
being cosmopolitan, charitable, and close-mouthed. Nothing
much could ever shock them, and the surest way to start trouble would be to offend a person's dignity. I recalled that Border people had a great fondness for outdoor festivals, and an
enormous love of children. Love in its truest sense, with respect for their budding identities. The Latin influence always
seemed to bring the young up to adult equality. There was no
talking down, rib tickling, and "Whose little girl are you?"

In a calculated risk, I dared to measure my memories against
the present. The disappointment could be overwhelming if
none of the sights and sounds remained as I recalled them,
but I decided to take the chance.

Over the widely separated spaces of the earth that I had
covered, out of all the sights and sounds, the experiences that
make up a life, above all, most vividly these things remain:

A windmill whirring in the breeze, and the sweetest of comforting sounds, the splash of the water tank running over.

Feathery green mesquite, honey-laden catkins and ferny
leaves that quiver in the little hour before the dawn when the
sleeper reaches unconsciously for cover.

Satin blooms of prickly pear against gray-green; colors as
resonant and translucent as old stained glass.

The rustle of heart-shaped leaves of the cottonwood tree,
exactly like the patter of rain.

The smell of rain when it finally falls on powdery earth, and tiny toad frogs springing from the dust by magic. The deep disappointment when the shower stops, and the sound of dry flies rasping out a buzzing metallic drone commences once more. Heat shimmering up in waves from hard-packed adobe and bleached cement sidewalks. Lakes and resacas sending out a muddy, primordial smell as the water in them gets lower and lower. Cattails growing at the edge with green slime washed against their stems. Tadpoles and minnows dipped up in an old straw hat, and the sickly-sweet smell of water lilies.

The round pasteboard tag from a sack of Bull Durham hanging out of the pocket of a khaki shirt, a brown, lean left hand rolling a cigarette while the right hand scratches a match along the rough trouser leg. The Mexican woman's corn-shuck cigarette of strong black tobacco, the smell of the charcoal in the clay furnace as she heats the sadirons. The tiny hiss as she spits on one to test its heat. The tamale man, trading a dozen hot ones for three red roses for his girl.

The wild geese, honking in the night and the blue norther next morning. The scrape of a granite spoon on a cast iron skillet and the snarl of the coffee grinder.

Waking in the night. "They sent word Miss Laura Mc-Kinney died." You heard the horses champing oats in their feed-bags and knew your mother was going to help the rest of the womenfolk wash and lay out their dead, dressing the maiden in the fine white underlinen that she had made for her hope chest.

The thudding sound of hoofs and the cloud of dust as the vaqueros cracked long leather whips like pistol shots at the herd. The high clear whistle, like the song of a whippoorwill, that the cowboys used to keep the cattle on the trail. The lonesome bawling of the stragglers, a sound that never quite left your heart. Birds and chickens picking ticks off the backs of cattle when they lay down to rest.

Coyotes yapping in the moonlight, gouging out holes in the finest watermelons in the patch. A plowman whipping his team of mules and cursing endlessly in a high monotone of bitter, quintessential words. The dry bed of the Resaca de la Palma, full of cracks and crevices so large a child could be lost in them by daylight. By nightfall, scurrying feet, lantern light and the cry: "The flood is coming." The tiny trumpets of the tree toads were never wrong. The raging wall of water roaring over the river bed and haystacks floating away. Chicken coops and pitiful livestock. A man in a rowboat trying to open the top drawer of a dresser in his house.

The constant Texas wind that had sent too many plainswomen into a flight from reality, staring straight before them with faded blue eyes. The sand and the grit, sifting, sifting, sifting through closed windows and doors. In the beds and in the food, into empty bottles tightly stoppered. The blessed relief when it stopped.

Your first twenty-two rifle, and the day you shot the hawk trying to carry off a fine game hen. The look in his eyes when he tried to rise and found he was crippled. The tightness in your chest when you had to back off and put him out of his pain.

March, and your first kite. Lying flat on your back in the middle of a prairie covered with verbenas, opal cups, and bluebells while the kite soared what seemed like miles into the limitless azure sky, tugging like a great fish on the end of a long stout line, your first touch with the infinite.

A little town rodeo. "There ain't a horse that can't be rode. There ain't a rider that's never been throwed."

Shells cutting your toes in the sand, and a Portugese Man-o'-War washing up against your leg, stinging into a blister. The phosphorescent gleam of flounders as you speared them at night, knee-deep in warm salt water of the Gulf of Mexico, a lantern in one hand and a fish gig in the other.

The interior goose flesh that rose when the whisper went round: "The Rangers are coming." The night the Ku Klux Klan was to march, and a little auburn-haired woman before the School Board: "If they march, as principal I'll order every child in the grammar school onto the bandstand in the park to sing 'My country, tis of thee . . . under a sheet. Sweet land of liberty . . . under a sheet.' Shall I go on?"

The time you hid in the brush all day at the edge of the re-saca trying to get a snapshot to send to *St. Nicholas Magazine,* a picture of a raccoon opening and washing a clam, dipping it up and down in the water with his oddly human hands. The Sunday you saw the two bobcat kittens.

The smell of Mexican pecan candy on Soledad Street and your first visit to the Alamo. The silver souvenir compact and the presentation by your grandaunt, the curator: "Remember Davy Crockett, and keep your powder dry!" The feeling of being on sacred ground, more holy than a church, and the knowledge that your own flesh and blood had answered the cry: "Who'll go into San Antonio with Old Ben Milam?"

Violet dusk and a tangle of children and dogs in a rolling wheel on the hard-swept earth, puppy-breath, pungent as pepper in the nostrils, and raspy pink tongues licking your face. Bull bats swooping low in the soft darkness over the squirming, indistinguishable mass of life.

Chile joints and the cool, dim smell of ice-cream parlors, marble-topped tables and wire ice-cream chairs. In the background, white wooden trelliswork covered with artificial flowers and small colored lights; overhead the slow slatting of the big mahogany blades of the ceiling fan. Election Day — the Blues and the Reds, each side wearing its chosen rosettes, hacks full of *músicos*, blasting out "El Veinte y Tres" and "Zacatecas March." The baseball game between the Fats and the Leans.

The smell of orange blossoms and jasmine; the unbearably sweet singing of a mocking bird at three in the morning. Lightning bugs tied in your pigtails, and the stark emotion on the faces at the rare spectacle, a Revival.

The whinnying of a horse in the night, pawing in agony at the door of the sleeping porch, his belly ripped open as he jumped the picket gate to the corral. Your father in his white nightshirt carrying a lantern and a Winchester. The sound of the mercy shot.

The high, whangy voices of Texas with the "haow" and "naow" of Vermont. The velvety voices of Texas, lazily resonant, and those like silver filigree, spun out in lovely tone, no matter how banal the words they may utter. The intense, tight-reined Texas voice with a staccato overlay of Spanish accent.

The long halls of old-time houses, designed to catch the southeast breeze. Old men in undershirts and Scrivens drawers taking their naps on patchwork quilt pallets on the floor, a "pa'm" leaf fan in their hands, stirring the air gently until they fell asleep.

Coffee at daybreak on the sleeping porch, and a man gazing over drouth-stricken acres, looking at nothing but mesquite bushes, withered *granjenos* and *comas*, dusty prickly pear, stunted and dried. No grass on the land but a harsh yellowish stuff like steel wool — and about as nourishing. The air hot and still, flakes of dried manure from the horse-lot quivering up on the heat waves, the windmill motionless. Bleached bones of the man's cattle in plain sight, where the stock came right up to the fence to die, within the smell of the precious water that could not be spared them to drink. Water that was rationed out, a barrel a week to the neighbors — if the well held out. Water that was too scarce for washing dishes — or Texans. The man holding out his coffee cup with a beatific expression under the rolling sweat on his face: "It's a WON-derful country, daughter!"

Held tightly in the golden mesh of memory's net, I rode into Brownsville, that city apart, in late August 1955 at the brief blue hour of the tropic twilight, "pregnant with the old twins, Hope and Fear." At some time or another every returning wanderer has experienced a similiar sensation: wanting to look, yet almost afraid to do so.

Along the highway, lined with towering frondy palms, bordered with small, sly resacas lapping their greedy tongues of water at the grass-edged road, flowers and vines grew luxuriantly. Their colors rivaled old-time calendar art at its worst. The beauty that had once been corralled behind the high walls of patios now ran abroad by the roadside.

After a quarter of a century, would there be one single example of the charming old Brownsville architecture left? Some of the houses I loved were neoclassic, several were French Provincial, and others Spanish. Many were flat roofed, with graceful, well-proportioned columns. Some were soft French brick, with gentle mansards of slate. Most of them were surrounded by lacy fences of wrought iron set into brick or cement walls. Many houses had iron-barred doors to keep out thieves of merchandise — and of honor. All yards once had orange trees in them, seven-sister roses, and oleanders. A few of the pretentious had stiff arborvitaes and an evergreen called monkey puzzle.

Now I saw giant philodendrons, *Monstera deliciosa,* the Swiss cheese plant coddled indoors in the East, here rising to the roof. Fiddle-back palm, climbing fig, many varieties new to the region, flourished as though in the heart of their native jungle. A mixture of regional and exotic, the plants were much like the native people of Brownsville.

What had given Brownsville her unique quality as a town? A curiously indefinable aura has always hung over the city. During the turbulent times of my childhood from 1910 to the Mexican Revolution and period just prior to World War I, there was a faintly nefarious air to the place. The town was a puzzling blend of intrigue and artlessness, frankness and secrecy.

Did the shuttered windows, latticed porches, iron-barred doors, and high brick walls lend themselves to dealings, personal and professional, that if not actually shady, were certainly of a highly inflammable and confidential nature? The perpetual air of secrecy, of notes being carried through the streets by swift, silent messengers, and the long, quiet negotiations by remote control, meetings of epic import between various factions all created an atmosphere of cloak and dagger doings. Did the continual presence of political and social refugees, secret agents of various governments, absconders, and plot-hatchers add to the sinister quality of the town? The continual passing from hand to hand of contraband articles, the disproportionate number of banks and counting houses, the furtive presence of certain doctors, remittance men, and dope peddlers, the midnight rumble of a hack going up Elizabeth Street over the mesquite paving blocks gave a faintly clandestine air to the place. The wood smoke at night, and the high-pitched scream of a man tormented by the vision of a thousand vipers carried home in his stomach from Crixell's saloon combined to create an atmosphere that was medieval and magical. Good or bad, Brownsville was authentic.

Perhaps the pervading music of another language, the Spanish idiom preferred by great and small, whose power and succinctness has colored the speech and thinking of the regional residents forever, leaving ineradicable traces on the accent and vocabulary of natives and newcomers alike: perhaps the language of Cervantes accounts for the separateness and originality of the thinking populace. "Speak to me in Christian!" was the customary retort to a remark addressed to a native in English. The assumption was, and is, that anyone who is capable of speaking Spanish would never, by choice, speak anything else. Could the influence of the French and their language account, in some degree, for the slightly formal manner of the long-time residents? The singsong intonation and the faintly rising inflection of the old-timer is unmistakable in any corner of the world. It is a dead give-away, and no other region in the United States has even a faint approximation of its flavor. In Brownsville, the performance is known as "talking with a lilt." The unfailing notch in the ear of a Brownsville old-timer is the expression "'n' so?" at the end of every declarative statement, turning it into a rhetorical question. It was shortened from "ain't it so?" and undoubtedly grew out of "n'est-ce pas."

Geographically, Brownsville is at the very end of the line. If the sword of Damocles hung over the head of a man, Brownsville was salutary and sympathetic: at several points the Rio Grande could be forded in a single step. During the cotton blockade by the North in the Civil War, international deals were maneuvered from a base in Brownsville, handy to Bagdad and Clarksville, both forgotten now like Nineveh and Tyre.

Spiritually and ethically the town was — and is — broad, and tolerant, with eyelids downcast like those of a high-born lady in an old portrait, not to notice things she shouldn't see. A basic, Latin realism pervaded the city, smoldering under her thick layer of dust like white ashes over a layer of coals. Temperamentally, the residents are self-contained and somewhat wary. A greater town for minding its own business never existed. This ancient wisdom sprung from an inherited culture in two principal languages and ways of life. There were minor influences of other foreign cultures, but they too stressed the sacredness of a man's dwelling, the dignity of the individual, and his inalienable right to privacy and the indulgence of his own peculiarities. *"Cada loco con su tema."* Every crazy man — and woman — had his theme. The three sisters who attended public hangings and who washed their long, wavy hair in the gutter swimming with whiskey from the contraband barrels smashed open by the United States Marshal in front of the Post Office were objects of ridicule, but were in no sense ostracized. The respect of one human being for another was a great and moving thing: the velvety politeness inherited from the Spaniard, the velvetiness increasing in direct ratio to his dislike of the person addressed, added much to the smoothness of life in the daily round. It did not oblige one in any sense to be the friend of all of the world, but it did impart a feeling of courtliness and elegance even to the simple transaction of buying a nickel's worth of coffee cake.

The myserious air common to Border towns was heightened in Brownsville by the occasional presence of colorful birds of passage. Matamoros, less than a stone's throw away, gave refuge to many gaudy personalities who came to town for the space of an evening, and crossed over to Brownsville to a ball or a party. Political refugees, including Porfirio Díaz, often sought the sanctuary of her secret gardens. Cortina, the red-headed Mexican Robin Hood, at one time marauded freely in the town. Tragic figures sometimes passed across the scene. The group of young priests who hobbled pitifully about the walled courtyard of the Church of the Immaculate Conception were said to have been the victims of Pancho Villa, who had them all castrated and thus rendered unfit for further service as priests of God. The incident is remembered by old residents with bitter eyes. Built in 1853, that exquisite church with the vaulted ceiling of celestial blue, the pigment obtained from crushed lapis lazuli, has seen many things, sacred and profane.

These strong, strange forces were at work during my child-hood — influencing the town and, according to their degrees of receptivity, its inhabitants. I wondered what new forces I should find at work. What would it be? Conflict? Conformity? Compromise?

To my joy I saw that the ebony tree, symbol of durability and strength, that evergreen mass of round, emerald leaves and chocolate-brown twigs, had come into its own. No longer were the trees hacked down and burned; they were treasured and nurtured, their beauty adding to the value of the land. Los Ebanos, an impressive, quietly opulent residential section had taken its name from them. One hundred and twenty-five years before, that other Texan Mary, Mary Austin Holley, had deplored the cutting down of giant native trees and their replacement by stiff, skimpy arborvitaes.

Many of these houses belonged to my schoolmates. It was possible in my imagination to pick out the houses of my friends by their looks; substantial, slightly conventional, orderly, and well groomed, with a comfortable air of permanence about them reflecting, as houses so often do, the characters of their owners. These houses were, in a sense, part of the lifework of the men and women who had stayed in Cameron County, had cast their lot in with her and prospered. Many of them had inherited considerable wealth from the early Spanish and Mexican fortunes. Some of them had liquidated the great, rangy old Spanish homes in exchange for the luxury of modern convenience and air conditioning. A few of the old guard had come into oil money. Several aged friends of my mother and father were on easy street at last, having "a lease of their own" given to them by relatives who had more oil money than they knew what to do with. An absence of ostentation and a stubborn insistence on giving prominence to the old nostalgic plants and flowers, not letting them be relegated to the background by the newer, showier specimens of the nurseryman's art, reassured me of what I had always known: that the solid good sense of Old Brownsville, her heritage, was recognized and appreciated by the present generation. Many of my friends share my passionate admiration for the Grand Duke jasmine, close relative of the Hawaiian pikake. It is the Brownsville flower. Grace, beauty, and unsurpassed perfume distinguish it above all flowers for me. It looks like a small cabbage rose carved out of ivory snuggled in lettuce-green leaves.

I must be sure to die sometime between March and November so that someone can place a *jazmín* in my hand. "During those months," the quiet-spoken servant of my friend said, "the bushes are whitened by them every morning."

Yet this dignified lake-studded area had its counterpart in other sections of America, especially in Florida and in California. Many of the Gulf Coast states have the same lush beauty of growth and the identical style of architecture. My mind raced ahead: how would the handsome old houses of the town look to me now? The two-storied cream brick houses with classic white pillars and trim gardens belonging to wealthy Mexicans — we called them the Bride's Cakes as children. How would they impress me now, after a decade of daily awareness of the architectural purity of New England, after long familiarity with the Victorian palaces on the Ocean Drive at Newport? Would they, like so many loved objects seen through the retrospectroscope, be almost unbearably small and shabby? Would they be even worse: brummagem and tawdry? My emotions were sadly mixed as I rode down the no longer familiar streets.

The big white frame house that had been a hospital in 1912 was still there. The chill of waiting for my mother to come out of the anesthetic came back after nearly half a century.

Two blocks down the street I saw the small frame house where she read aloud the entire new book *The Sinking of the Titanic* to the spellbound neighborhood.

The excitement that used to prevail on lawn-party nights came back to me strongly at the sight of a charming two-story landmark in a fine state of preservation. There I had seen my first Japanese lantern, not one, but strings of them strung between the trees, swaying thrillingly and dangerously with lighted candles inside. The smell of grape juice punch and the nostalgic odor of wet gunny sacks over the freezers of homemade ice cream that stood "ripening" behind a vine-covered screen waiting the delirious moment of "dishing up"' came back with startling force. Ben Kowalski, a Polish Jew who was the mayor of Brownsville, and his gentle wife, gracious and lovely, greeting the guests near the iron gate, are dead many years, but I shall remember them always. The sights and sounds, running feet of children scampering discreetly through the guests, careful not to elicit a "look" from Mother, are all part of the mellow memory heightened by the sensation of my hair standing on end when a young lawyer, Lucius Polk, slender and blond, sang a song one line of which has stayed in my mind over the years:

> If I were damned body and soul
> I know whose love would make me whole:
> Mother of Mine.

Could they have known, those gentlefolk, what they were leaving to the young, the impressionable? A well of memory, rich and inexhaustible.

I rode on down Main Street and wondered why few people actually sang any more, instead of listening to so much inferior ready-made performance. Many of the Kowalski family were gifted musicians; the wife of Marcellus Tracy, a newspaper man, was a fine pianist, as was Ruth Holland, a pupil of MacDowell. Dorothea Hoyt and her mother had studied in Europe. Penelope Petersen studied with Leschetizky in Paris and practiced fencing clad in black shorts and a sweat shirt. She was of a build that was then known as "fleshy" and of a temper that even today would be classified as "sudden."

Looking back, the odd assortment of names and nationalities that still mingle at social gatherings in Brownsville seems strange and somehow poetic to me. In a sense the history of Texas is compressed into the patronymics: Brulay, Vieuxtenet, Vivier, Jagou, Putegnat, under the Fleur de Lys.

Celaya, Yznaga, Puig, Fernández, Barrera, Yturria, Forto, San Roman, Cueto, Pacheco, resonant of Mother Spain. Garcías with the classic given names: Macedonio, Ovidio, and Rómulo.

The old Nordic names: Wells, Stillman, Kennedy, Cameron, and Brown. McAllen, Goodrich, Wilman, Barbour, McGarry, Craig, West, Young, Graham, Rentfro, Seabury, Lubbock, McDavitt, Tucker, Clint, and Combe. Creager, Tilghman, and Wallace. Cowan and Grant. Kinder and Rendall. Neale and Tate. Starck and Scanlan. Like a border ballad, these names convey sound and flavor.

There were Slavitcheks and Braunsteins, Edelsteins and Ashcheims, Raphaels and Dwormans: solid custodians of wealth and good living. Cobolini and Calderoni. They made a music that was purely American — and a harmony never to be forgotten.

The harmony extended even to the relations of theoretically opposing groups. Violent Democrats were intimate with rabid Republicans. Protestants looked forward eagerly to the Catholic Bazaar, and large numbers of them attended Catholic schools. One Jewish family attended the Episcopal Church regularly because there was no synagogue.

I stopped before the new Church of the Advent, a monument to the leadership of the Reverend Roland O. Mackintosh and his much loved wife, spiritual father of the Episcopal Church in the Rio Grande Valley, a man loved by every creed and color. He never lost his impish sense of humor, the sly deviltry of a small boy, keen on quips and jokes. The most reverent of men, he kept his flock in a continual uproar of ill-concealed mirth by such sly tricks as announcing in the middle of a blue norther, with the icy wind freezing the hands of the organist, that the hymn would be "From Greenland's Icy Mountains."

The Church of the Sacred Heart, a stout Roman Catholic structure, was built during my childhood just across the corner from our house. Mr. Mackintosh related gleefully a tale that delighted me, since it was characteristically Brownsvillian. At a meeting of the Council of Churches, Mr. Mackintosh was seated between the rector of Sacred Heart and the Baptist preacher.

"You gentlemen are acquainted with each other, are you not?" Mr. Mackintosh said in his Scottish brogue.

"Yes, indeed." The reverend father shook hands with his Baptist confrère.

"I hear, Father," said Mr. Mackintosh, "that the Baptist brother here is soon to be in charge of a fine new church just cater-cornered from Sacred Heart. Now what do you think of that?"

The man in the Roman collar only hesitated a fraction of a second:

"It's splendid, Reverend," he replied. "We shall all live happily in Christian amity and brotherhood."

"Indeed?" Mr. Mackintosh's voice was guileless. "Now, Father, from what direction does the prevailing breeze come in this town?"

"From the southeast, to be sure," the priest said.

"Aha," the Scot's eyes twinkled mischievously behind his thick glasses, "the breeze will carry the incense from your eleven o'clock Mass right in the middle of the Baptist morning service. What will they think of that?"

"They will think it is the finest, most beautiful and inspiring odor they have ever smelt," said the padre.

"So you think!" Mr. Mackintosh chuckled. "Do you know that the Baptists have a great three-inch hose rigged in their Baptistry to put out the fire in your incense pot?"

It is a healthy sign when the assorted faiths of the world are secure enough in their own beliefs to joke good-naturedly about matters of doctrine and dogma.

Understanding and fellowship, always present in a marked degree in Brownsville, has increased and spread through the Valley owing to the humanness of the beloved tall figure stooping to greet or caress every urchin he passed in the street, the man who taught those of us fortunate enough to have been in his spiritual charge to begin our prayers with the words "Beloved God."

A solid house with personality reminded me of the Vivier family, long identified with building in the town, the original builders of the lovely old Opera House. I remembered Mr. Vivier passing by our house early every morning with his huge, laden market basket. He was one of the few men who clung to the old custom of selecting every item of food for his family himself.

"I used to wish he wouldn't do it," his son said to me. "It always bothered me, because it was different, something everyone else in town didn't do. Then Father explained the significance of the tradition to me. The market basket was the symbol of authority: in a society of matriarchs, he was now officially the head of the family."

I have often wondered, no matter how independent a thinker, how unique a personality one is, at exactly what age does the immense desire for conformity make itself felt as a need in the child? Breast of pheasant under glass won't do when the gang is eating hot dogs. Best's Lilliputian Bazaar clothes hang detested and unworn when blue jeans are the order of the day. Mr. Vivier carrying the marketing home was a fixed part of the day to me. It was interesting to me to have his son's point of view on the matter forty years later.

We talked of the charm and devotion of the old Mexican servants. Neither we nor they would have balked at the words "servant" or "Mexican." We had never heard the word "Anglo" applied to ourselves, but we knew from experience that there were all classes and ranks of Mexicans just as there were all classes and ranks of what we in our naïve way called "Americans." The old Mexican servants ruled the families they worked for with a firm, but subtle hand.

"No one has the ability to uphold the dignity of his people so unobtrusively as the Mexican," Joe Vivier said. "My grandmother was highly intelligent and interested in what went on in the world. She read many periodicals and made a hobby of clipping articles for her scrapbooks. She was systematic about it, and at a certain hour each day retired to a shaded porch to clip. She was not to be disturbed for any reason. One day the housemaid broke all rules and appeared on the porch.

"*'Un hombre* is at the door and wishes to see you.'

"'You know I have forbidden interruptions when I am clipping! What man wishes to see me? And about what?' my grandmother asked.

"'Just a man,' the maid replied. 'He didn't say about what.'

"Exasperated, my grandmother went to the door and found herself face to face with William Jennings Bryan.

"About a week later a similiar interruption took place.

"'There is a *señor* at the door who insists upon seeing you,' the maid said.

"'I have spoken to you about these intrusions before. Who is this gentleman and what does he want?'

"'Just a gentleman to see you.' The characteristic shrug disclaimed all knowledge of his errand.

"My grandmother went to the door and saw that the caller was a Mexican countryman with a load of firewood to sell."

William Jennings Bryan was an *hombre* but the wood-vendor was a *señor*.

Someone has said that the characteristic difference between the Spaniard and the Mexican is that the Spaniard will offer you his common everyday fare and say: "Isn't this wonderful *cocido?* Do you not find this wine superior in every respect?" while the Mexican will mortgage his salary for months in advance, go into debt in every way, to regale his guests with costly viands, and when complimented on the excellence and abundance of the fare will say: "*La comidita de todos los días* — just our everyday fare."

A houseman in Brownsville in my youth had apparently held to the Spanish school of thought that what was good enough for the family was good enough for anybody.

R. B. Creager, State Chairman of the Republican Party, was host to Warren G. Harding on his visit to Brownsville in 1922. Fernando, the Creagers' chef and houseman, had his hands full with so much company, distinguished or not. Mrs. Creager, so runs the legend, had hoped to have an electric bell in the dining room for the President's visit, but had not had time to get it installed. She thought that instead of tapping the button on the little call bell she always used, it would be less noticeable if she put it down on the floor and tapped it with her toe when she summoned Fernando. After the soup, she rang for him to remove the plates. Solemnly he stooped down, picked up the bell, and put it back on the table where it belonged. When he left the room Mrs. Creager slipped the bell back onto the carpet, near her foot. The rallying back and forth continued with a love score until dessert, when the defeated hostess conceded the victory to Fernando.

The Creagers' lovely French Provincial house with the slate roof was no longer there. I had spent many happy days there in the big upstairs playroom with the girls, not playing dolls but peering out the window, spying on the private life of Charlie Combe's gardener next door.

But palm trees still waved in the front yard of a gray painted brick house with a slate mansard roof. The yard was still brick paved — as it had been in my childhood, so delightful for playing jacks. Our music teacher, Miss Anita Kowalski, lived in that house. In the third grade we had begun the study of Music Appreciation. We had it one hour a week and Miss Anita came in with a boy wheeling the big Victrola behind her. She kept her hat on during class. It gave her a certain glamour in our eyes that set her apart from our regular room teacher, although we loved gentle Miss Addie Lou.

I have no way of knowing how much my classmates remember of a certain lesson in music appreciation, but I know that at the time, the audience response was devastating. Miss Anita told us the story of *Madame Butterfly,* how Cio Cio San had been left with a baby, thinking all the time she was married, and then Benjamin F. Pinkerton's American wife had paid her a visit. Miss Anita explained that Cio Cio San had no further desire to live and described how she blindfolded the baby and put an American flag in his hand. Then she played Geraldine Farrar's recording of the death scene and when the anguished Cio Cio San plunged the dagger into her heart, she might as well have stabbed the entire front row of nine-year-olds, for their heads went down on the desks, sobbing in mass heart-break.

In the light of years, *Madame Butterfly* seems very red meat for the third grade. Yet we lived close to reality; the facts of life and death were well known to us. We knew that the secret ambition of many Mexican girls was to marry an American soldier. We knew how many had gambled, lost, and been left with a half-breed baby. Many years later and half a world away I talked, apropos of the same moving story, to a native of British Samoa, an unmarried mother who convinced me of the universality of the truth behind the drama. She said: "It is a chance we take to hold these men. Sometimes we lose."

In a search for a common interest, a meeting ground for the minds of the readers of these impressions, my personal sense of what has happened and what is happening in Texas, I have arrived at one more paradoxical conclusion: for something to be of universal interest, it must be personal in the highest degree.

In the final analysis, it is in the deepest, most basic emotions that we are all kindred. I feel a deep reticence and diffidence about writing down intensely personal emotions where all who run may read, in a kind of spiritual nudism — yet my feeling and emotion toward the place I know best in Texas will account in some measure for my feeling toward the other portions of my "country." So strong is the association of ideas that

I never hear the Puccini score without feeling the hard top of the desk against my wet cheek as Butterfly took her life. I see Miss Anita in her neat tailored suit and trim hat standing quietly in front of us, filling our minds with drama and forming impressions that will never die.

"I heard that you asked for me," Miss Anita said to me on the telephone a few hours after my arrival. "I've followed your life with interest and am proud of you. I have my third-grade record book here beside me, for 1914. You always made good marks in music."

I knew she was ill and asked if I might see her, for she was an important figure in my sentimental journey. Her reply struck me as courageous in the extreme.

"My dear," she said, "I am a wreck from the pain. If you love me, don't come."

I remembered the day she had come in anguish to my mother: their family history was as old as Christianity itself. A devout Roman Catholic Spanish mother and a Jewish father. One of the great Spanish novels of conflict, *Gloria,* by Pérez Galdós, is based on the same theme. Miss Anita, a few weeks after her father's death, came to my mother in her distress, asking if it were true that she would not see her father in Heaven, that they could never meet again because he was a heretic. I see the parlor now and hear my mother's voice.

"Your father was the truest and most devout of men. He was just and honest, kind to every human being, a devoted father and tender husband. You, who have seen him bless the bread and the wine and read the Hebrew words . . . can you believe that the God who made him and made you, would bar from everlasting life anyone who believed in Him and kept His law?" There was faith and an uncritical lovingkindness in our block.

A few houses away Miss Nora Kelly was starting her Charity Home, now Mercy Hospital, the work of her untiring hands and heart. She washed and dressed the village idiot every day, and daily stood by while Willie Baboso, poor, slobbering creature, turned the hose on his clean clothes and rolled in the dust in front of her. But she never gave up.

As the remembrance of things past surged up in my mind, it occurred to me that the lawn parties and church socials were events that were characteristically American and were probably taking place under the spreading elms in parts of Missouri and Connecticut at the same time as those I remembered so vividly in Brownsville.

Aside from the duality of language, what made life different at the edge of the narrow river? The hours and customs, the siesta and *merienda,* the four o'clock treat? I knew that civilized people the world over had these customs: the British their tea and the Germans their coffee. There was something deeper than surface custom: it was a manner of thinking, a kind of working democracy.

At that particular golden age, it seems to me there was a harmonious rendering to God and to Caesar in the lives of most of the inhabitants. On Sundays the Roman Catholics complied with their duty early. Many of the Protestants did also, and left right after church was out in the heavily laden rowboat that was the only means of access to Mexico. They went for the day, taking the family with them. In our own family there was an acute schism: my mother went to the bullfights and my father's ruling passion was cockfighting. He bred, fought, and sold many of the Border champions. His stock was known in cockfighting circles both in the United States and in Mexico. On his deathbed the only thing that could bring a gleam to his eye was a copy of the magazine *Grit and Steel,* the gamecock breeder's Bible. We spent the day at the sport of our choice and at night order was restored and civilization got the upper hand at Daroset's French restaurant where *músicos* played "Angel's Serenade," fountains tinkled and caged mocking birds sang as we ate fried quail with green sauce of avocados.

But in June, 1913, the idyllic Sundays came to a terrifying end: Brownsville *was* different from other towns in America at that period! The smoke that drifted from Matamoros through the open windows of Brownsville in early June, 1913, was not freighted with the pungent scent of mesquite wood. It was thick, yellow, and fetid. It rose from the funeral pyres of dead and half-dead Mexican soldiers after the capture of Matamoros by the forces of General Lucio Blanco in the name of the reform Constitutionalists of Mexico. The dead and the unconscious were piled up, crisscross, drenched with gasoline and burned.

Adults and children climbed telephone poles and clung to the roofs of houses on the boardwalk down by the riverbank to watch the battles until the bullets came too close for comfort, or as in my own case, they were dragged home by the ear. For over two years this horror of carnage was to be a daily part of life for any sensitive person living in Brownsville. There was no escape from it.

Mexican citizens and American residents of Mexico poured across the Rio Grande, at official crossings — and elsewhere — in an unending, terrified stream. Every vacant house, room, shed, barn, and chicken coop in Brownsville housed refugees of some sort or condition. They were largely people of refinement and education, with the poise and sweetness of manner that is peculiarly Mexican.

Gentlefolk escaped only with their lives, many of them disguised in the clothing of their servants. A few managed to conceal a piece or two of jewelry. Most of them were penniless and nearly all unequipped in any way to earn a living. To know the beauty of their characters and the charm of their minds was a privilege that many of us shared. What they received was nothing in comparison with the cultured ambiance they carried with them and spread in some degree upon those fortunate enough to have known them. Everyone who came in contact with them could have learned two things: that considerateness is the infallible sign of the aristocratic person, and that while the fatuous may noise their woes abroad, the well-bred seldom inflict their troubles on anyone, even when asked. They were great souls and have left an indelible mark on Brownsville and its inhabitants. Forty-four years later I saw three distinguished white-haired women near the Plaza in Matamoros, Mexico. Something, perhaps the noble carriage of their heads, struck a chord in me. They were three of the refugees that I had known as a child, in those years young and beautiful women, who had taught me Spanish songs and poems.

Relations between the United States and Mexico had been good since the late eighties when raids by privateers, such as Cortina, had come to an end. In 1910 President Taft and Don Porfirio Díaz, President of Mexico, shook hands in broad daylight across the international boundary in a gesture that must have been one for the gods: Taft in his tentlike frock coat, and Don Porfirio, gauded up with medals and jewels, clad in black satin knee breeches, long silk stockings, and evening pumps. The meeting was arranged by Archie Butt, aide-de-camp to President Taft. I remember the picture of Captain Butt with his military cape beautifully draped about him in our book about the sinking of the Titanic on which he lost his life.

The assassination of the President of Mexico, Francisco Madero, on February 22, 1913, let loose a chain of events which affected American citizens in Mexico, all inhabitants of the Border, and residents of Brownsville in particular. Violence and terror reigned right up until the United States' entry into World War I.

When President Wilson took over the reins of government from Taft in 1913, he refused to recognize anyone who ascended to the presidency of Mexico through assassination, and ordered all Americans out of Mexico. Another influx of refugees came to Brownsville, Americans this time. One striking red-haired Irish beauty I remember well: she had eleven children and was expecting her twelfth, and arrived accompanied by only one small Mexican houseboy. She lived in a Mexican hut, and was never seen to do anything but sit in a rocker, fanning and drinking one pitcher of cold beer after another. Where are they now? Do they ever come through Brownsville, center of the Airways, and think of the starvation days and anxious nights when no word of hope came across the Rio Grande?

Even to children there were amusing sidelights to the revolution. A cartoon published in a Mexican newspaper just after American intervention in Mexico showed a native funeral. Friends of the family, sort of honorary pall bearers, are each given a wax candle to carry in the procession. They take it home and light it in memory of the dead person and say a prayer for the repose of his soul. In the cartoon that became famous, typical *peones* carried the coffin on their shoulders. President Wilson in cutaway and striped trousers was one of the mourners. One of the pall bearers turns to him and says: "Who gave you a candle in this funeral?"

The games of children are often cruel, especially when they reflect the talk of their elders, preoccupied with the political brutalities of the times. We had no comic books, no radio, no TV, no Superman. Anglo children (we had never heard the

expression) used to stop Latin children at the point of broomstick rifles with the question: "*Quién vive?* Who are you for?
Huerta or Carranza?" The poor starveling carrying home
somebody's two-bits' worth of wash didn't know or care what
particular brand of brigands was throttling Mexico at the moment. She wanted only to escape her tormentors, deliver the
washing, collect her *centavitos* and get home before her mama
lathered her.

The amount of property, livestock, jewels, *objets d'art*, and
artillery that changed hands during the melee was staggering.
Guns, especially Winchester rifles, were at a premium with the
revolutionaries. Several sizable Anglo fortunes in Brownsville
were founded upon the trade. One house is still called "The
House of Blood." In 1956 I observed the substantial home —
still in prime condition — of a gun-runner who used to load his
touring car with rifles, concealed under the removable cushions
of the front and back seats, then fill the car with little girls anywhere from five to ten years of age, all decked out in their
frilly white Sunday dresses, and drive across the river to Matamoros ostensibly to treat the little girls to ice cream and candy.
While the little girls were being regaled, the guns were
unloaded discreetly, until one beady-eyed brat caught on.

On the piano in the home of this man stood an autographed
photograph of Pancho Villa, inscribed to the gentleman's wife.
The lady was, however, extremely fastidious in one respect:
she would not let her daughter take piano lessons from the best
piano teacher in Brownsville because that young lady, tall and
willowy, had been seen to play ragtime at a party with her legs
crossed.

The United States put an end to the treasonable and lucrative business. One of the outfit went to Leavenworth. I remember my father's choleric narration of his first encounter with
the released convict after he had served his term.

"How did he take it, Doc?" someone asked.

"Hell," my father replied, "he makes a man feel that his education has been positively neglected unless he has been to Leavenworth."

The Mexican popular songs of the day were largely political, if not in the original, most certainly in the parodies at which the Mexican people are unequaled. Children learned history without realizing it. In "La Cucaracha" we sang about the failure of Don Venustiano Carranza's Morelos convention. And when Francisco Villa's troops captured Matamoros, we all sang "What a pity to see Matamoros in such a situation! Poor Little Federals, those locked up in jail!" We knew the songs "Adelita" and "Valentina," the theme songs of the Revolution in fact and in fable. The philosophy of "drunk today and dead tomorrow" was in the life and songs of the people.

In 1914 the Brownsville High School had not yet been built and classes were held in a building, a kind of storeroom, that was part of the Brulay estate. The main house was a miniature French château, charming and stately like its owners. The Mexican refugees who crowded the neighborhood were justly proud when the graduation exercises were held: the high school building may have been makeshift, but the scholarship was not. May Dickens, the high school principal, discovered the unusual intellectual endowment of Carlos Castañeda, a youth who was to make a lasting impression not only on Texas but on the entire scholarly world. He was valedictorian of that class, over the protest of an unpopular county superintendent who hated "Mess-skins" and picked his teeth with a pocketknife.

There must have been a birth of new hope in the other refugee families when they saw the opportunity in Texas for those capable of seizing it. Dr. Castañeda, a distinguished and much loved professor at the University of Texas, is the author of many works; one outstanding achievement is *Our Catholic Heritage,* a seven-volume history of the church in Texas. Not the least among his attributes is his inspired sense of humor. True to his Spanish language heritage, he has never lost touch with the rich colorful talk of the people.

As I picked up the threads of the years that I spent away from Brownsville, I found many former playmates teaching school and struggling with the same old sixes and sevens. Just as used-car lots had replaced once lovely dwellings, and filling stations occupied the corners where modest churches once stood, new schools had sprung up, but the problem, certainly in the primary grades, was the ancient and ageless one that had contributed so much gaiety to our life in two languages.

Now that progress had come, modern methods surely would have taken over in the classrooms. The State Board of Education insisted on permanents for the teachers, and in Brownsville a permanent is not ever to be confused with a chemical process for curling the hair: it is a State Permanent Teachers' Certificate, the nemesis and albatross, the Old Man of the Sea to most of the old-time teachers. Now there is another poltergeist snapping at their heels: the dhee-gree.

This new bogey man haunts aged teachers night and day. Most of them had little formal training in psychology or pedagogy, but they were, and are, good teachers. They know all — and more — than they need to know to teach primary grades full of children coming in contact with the English language for the first time. Most of these teachers are bilingual and many are Latin Americans, or of Latin American descent, and are therefore capable of understanding the complexities of teaching English to the non-English-speaking child. They are intimately acquainted with the foreign background the child comes from — an important point frequently overlooked.

In order to get a living wage, the teachers have had to go to school to get "hours," "credits," "units," or whatever the fetish of the moment happens to be. They have learned to satisfy the requirements with a Latin practicality that is characteristic of all their dealings. "Take the hard subjects here at the college at home where everybody knows you. Then take the easy ones, like education and psychology, off at summer school. Pretty soon you get the dhee-gree. Then you don't have to worry." One ancient teacher, who taught many famous men and women in her day, was retired after nearly fifty years of teaching.

"Well, Mema, you never did get your permanent."

"Pués, Saint Peter will give me the permanent."

After a lifetime of giving up my spare time, clothing, food, books, money, whatever happened to be in the process of being commandeered by my mother at the moment for her beloved "children" (she was frequently known to resort to blackmail to get food for her school children during the Depression), I know that the finest product of the most modern and scientific school of education would be a total loss and waste of the taxpayers' money when confronted by a roomful of howling *huercos*, lovable as the brats are, such as is the daily lot of a teacher in the Fourth Ward Elementary Schools of Brownsville, or any Border town. The women who teach these interesting children have to be mothers, diplomats, referees, and nurses. They have to deal with slang in two languages. Now they have the added jargon of the television commercial to cope with.

Recently a friend gave her first grade a few exercises to do on paper: color the light that means Go. Color the light that means STOP. When the forty-odd squirming morsels finished, she marked the examples that were correct with the standard check mark and gave the papers back. She noticed that there was much comparing of results on the test. Then one sprite rushed up: "Loook, Mees! Looook my HYGEIA!" pointing to the check mark. "How many HYGEIAS you got, Enrique?" A local ice-cream firm advertises its products on TV with a check mark. Hygeia, a seemingly impossible word for infant Latin Americans, meant "check mark" to them, thanks to ice cream and TV.

In cutting out pictures for the scrapbooks, magazine photographs of Lucille Ball and Desi Arnaz are favorites for "Mother and Father" pictures. "Do you know who this is?" the teacher asked. "High Low Lucy!" (I Love Lucy) the children shrieked.

The ice-cream company, for reasons which are obvious, runs a TV program daily. Girls and boys who have a birthday on a particular day are invited to the studio to sit on the knee of Ranger Jim, an inoffensive "cowboy" who sings banalities to the accompaniment of his guitar. On special days, Ranger Jim is sent to various sections of Brownsville in a big sound truck to give out free music and ice cream. He selects a certain store and announces on his program the night before that he will be at, say for instance, Sánchez's Sweet Shop at five o'clock to give a party.

There is one certain shop in the Fourth Ward where it is unlikely Ranger Jim will appear for some time. The much touted day arrived and the little ones were on hand, en masse. They ranged in age from six to twelve. They loved Ranger Jim and his songs and had been waiting for hours to see him in person, to shake his hand and pay their respects to their "old pardner." They paid them so warmly that inside of a few minutes they had treed Ranger Jim, pulled his boots off for souvenirs, and were working on his trousers when the police arrived with a ladder to rescue the Man of the West from the Primary School.

Forty years after my grammar school days, Brownsville showed such signs of cleanliness and progress that I felt discouraged about entering a schoolroom. I feared that all the fine frenzy, the *joie de vivre,* the demoniac inventiveness of the tiny first-graders would be gone: crushed or inhibited. But I went, anyway. An old friend was getting them ready to go home.

"Look how clean, Mary! Aren't they sweet?"

They were indeed. Four to a table. Little chairs. Curtains on the windows. A piano was the final elegance.

"Wait. See how nice they dance, Mary." The teacher played a chorus of "La Raspa," a Mexican dance that was popular everywhere a year or so ago among the active, and the children beat time with open palms on the little tables before them. "They dance sitting down."

"Times have changed," I said. "No more 'This is Will. Will is a dog. How do you do, Will?' "

"No more Will." We went off into a conversation about family matters, catching up on the many changes.

A sly rogue came preening up to the teacher with a sheet of paper in his hand, winking his dimples in and out at me.

"See how nice he makes his ABC's, Mary? Now go make them double."

He was back in two minutes, tugging at her skirt.

"See how nice he makes his ABC's double, Mary? Now go color them."

Before he could color them, a green-eyed Quisling came sidling up and whispered in the teacher's ear, feeling the material of my dress at the same time. My friend jumped to her feet; in the language of Cervantes she trumpeted *"Quién anda diciendo maldiciones?* Who's saying bad words?" The question was purely rhetorical, since the *chismoso,* the talebearer, had got the attention he craved. I collapsed on a small chair and howled. Nothing had changed: the more it changes, the more it is the same. There were dozens of them tugging at teacher's sleeve, all talking in Spanish, all talking at once. The harassed teacher was banging on her desk with a ruler shouting in Spanish, just like in the good old days.

"Ah, Mary, *qué de huerquerío!"* she laughed. *"Quién anda diciendo maldiciones?"* Just as though the culprits would raise their hands and say, "*I'm* saying bad words, Teacher."

It takes a lot of love to handle those kids. What a *huerquerío* indeed! How would I put into English that priceless, untranslatable word? Slangiest of slang, salty, and fitting. The closest I could come to it was brat-ery, and I knew that wasn't it.

Some process of indirection seems to favor me, and I ran into Dr. Castañeda. I related the incident, one certainly not foreign to him, and said: "How would you, *Insigne Doctor*, translate *huerquerío?*" All I had to do was ask a genius: "Why, urchinry, of course," he said. All his titles, including one from His Holiness the Pope, his degrees and honors paled into insignificance in my mind when compared to that instant and perfect response without one single academic hem or haw.

I blessed the geographical accident that had made it possible for me to be reared amid two living languages: everything is twice as much fun.

In Brownsville the school system is excellent and the high jinks of the First Grade in the Fourth Ward are not intended to represent the whole picture by any means. It is a unique situation which is particularly charming to one who has worked among baby Latin Americans. Once I led a kindergarten band with sixty of them in it, all under six. Perfect pitch and natural rhythm made them a joy to work with. Their manners had not yet become *agringado* — yankeefied — and they were utterly obedient. I shall never get used to a Latin American child yelling "Hey, Ma" when he's not singing "Rudolph the Red-Nosed Reindeer." It was nicer when they played "Indita Mía" and "Pajarillo Barranqueño," and could sing three-part harmony by ear — at the age of six.

I pray that a wise Providence will dispose of the boneheads who would stir all the colorful cultures of the world into one grismal, gray gruel.

As I looked at this Texas-of-the-now through the eyes of Texas-of-the-then I wondered how many of these children were hungry, really unfed, like Rufino? The teacher explained that the eagle sitting on the cactus plant on the Mexican flag was a symbolic bird and asked if anyone knew what he had in his mouth. Rufino's hand went up: "*Chorizo?*" In his hunger he mistook the serpent for a sausage.

Down the street, a modern, ranch-type house with a picture

window looked odd to me sitting next to a house which I know at one time had a waist-high fireplace in the kitchen which was the only cooking facility in the house. Charcoal and mesquite chunks were the fuel. Soon the bulldozer, that product of a very real and personal devil, will have pushed down all the old, lovely landmarks. A few of them have fallen away naturally, but the bulldozer accounts for most of them.

The little white bungalow on Elizabeth Street that we lived in for years had been painted tan and converted to a Baptist Bible School. The reseda, that tall fragrant shrub mignonette, beloved of Latins everywhere, and even of the Victorian English in their conservatories, was gone; so was the nacahuitl, the gray-leaved, white-flowered wild olive.

Are the Bible students ever disturbed by the fumes of fine bourbon whiskey, the ghostly rattling of poker chips, and the crowing of game roosters?

Poker and fighting cocks . . . man's last stronghold in a world of matriarchs.

I think Texas men have defied their womenfolk on those two issues, more firmly than on all the rest put together. Certainly on the cockfighting and breeding, the mildest of men, the most uxorious, have turned savage and ordered their squaws back to the tepee when they have tried to interfere with the sacred fighting game birds. It seems to have represented to them the entire male principle, the one realm that was safe from female intrusion. The last opportunity to show who wore the pants was not to be passed by, and the clinging to the male prerogative accounts for the passionate love of cockfighting by the Latins. It was not, at that time, illegal in Texas, and was approached and entered into in a spirit of utmost reverence. It was a serious, ritualistic performance: elemental, primitive, evenly matched, where the noble birds had literally foemen worthy of their steel.

In a race of men where courage and endurance are admired

almost to the point of worship, it is understandable how such a sport could become symbolic and color the thinking of the people. An individual of the highest courage is a thoroughbred, he is game; he never turns tail or shows the white feather . . . a dunghill bird has some white feathers under the wings and they show when he spreads them to run away.

I saw many cockfights in my childhood and they are inspiring and stirring sights. Bird pitted against bird: the steel gaffs are a man-made refinement not really necessary, for one gamecock often kills another with only his own spurs for weapons. I do not think it is possible for the human heart to contain without bursting any greater emotion than I felt when at the age of ten I saw one of my father's famous Clarets slaughter his opponent, stretch himself to his full height, crow triumphantly, and fall over dead. Wealthy Mexicans, civilians and military, came frequently to the small house on Elizabeth Street to look at the beautiful birds, and often to buy. The prices they paid seem incredible for that day and time, but they were the ruling passion of the Mexican race. General Lucio Blanco, a handsome cultivated gentleman, bought several birds from my father. How much of the purchase price of the birds, in that epoch, came from the loot and spoils of the Revolution I have no way of knowing. A friend from Mexico City recently told of seeing my father win a ten-thousand-dollar bet with one of his birds. Until the day he died, my father always had a few gamecocks, come hell or high water. Some of his stock was sold to the King Ranch, but most of the birds were given to his friend Dick Kleberg.

There was an abrupt halt to the cockfighting across the river when the Mexican bandit trouble started in 1915 and lasted until 1917. The forty intervening years seemed very short to me. The revolution and the bandit trouble are now only memories. Many of my childhood friends, Anglos and Latins, now live across the river on the Mexican side in La Colonia Hipoteca, Mortgage Colony, an elaborate modern residential district. International relations are good, life is relatively safe — if you can dodge the traffic. The Mexican exchange is favorable to Anglo-American dollars and rent is very low.

Gasoline pumps stand now where a charming church, the First Presbyterian, used to stretch its tall spire up to the blue sky. That was the church where we first heard of Mexican Protestants. It is the church where Henrietta Chamberlain married Captain Richard King in December of 1854. My mother was once asked to give a talk there on sanitation to the Mexican women of the church. She understood the indifference of the Mexicans to flies and insects of all sorts. It seemed sensible to her to lecture to them on the connection between the flies buzzing busily between *la casita* out back and the dinner plates on the table. She wanted them to understand that these insects had much to do with the great number of the Mexican children that died yearly. Posters on stands, charts, and a pointer arrived from Austin's Public Health Department. The drawings of flies were greatly magnified, they were perhaps thirty inches long and a foot wide, their pernicious and disgusting habits shown in great detail. One highly intelligent Mexican woman in the group studied the chart gravely and then said: "No wonder, señora, those flies carry disease! The flies in Brownsville are only little things, *animalitos de Dios!*"

In 1955, sad-eyed, mournful men on bicycles, ironically known as Good Humor Men, trundled little carts ahead of them peddling tasteless ice cream bars to the monotone jangling of a little bell. How different the joyous shriek of the *raspa* man, precursor of the vendors of snow cones, who still operates in the less sanitary and more interesting sections of Brownsville. The shaved ice in dirty, streaked glasses with violently colored syrup poured over it cost a penny in the days when I ate it. The ice had probably served to pack around a coffin on its way home from San Antonio to rest in the Brownsville cemetery but then, as now, what we didn't know didn't hurt us. But always the good manages to survive somehow: prowling F. W. Woolworth's store in 1957 I found a *raspa* stand, complete with bottles of colored syrup and a homemade sign saying: RASPA.

Signs everywhere in the town and part of the country are in Spanish, including the very sensible one: IF YOU DRINK, DON'T DRIVE. IF YOU DRIVE, DON'T DRINK.

Spanish signs in Woolworth's reminded me of the only family, three quarters Mexican, I ever knew who refused to learn to speak one word of Spanish. They lost all their money, and went to San Antonio to try to find work. They couldn't get jobs in Woolworth's because they didn't speak Spanish!

I saw the same old movie theater where Mama used to raise not round, but square goose bumps on the natives with her recitation of "Lasca," whenever the ladies' choral society, The Treble Clef Club, gave a concert. In 1896, in Glasgow, Scotland, my Scottish mother got her teeth into that durable saga of "life, and love, and Lasca; in Texas down by the Rio Grande." Her dramatic gifts were considerable and she regaled Glasgow with a hair-raising rendition of her war horse.

Always she began the old way, the real way: "It's all very well to write reviews, and carry umbrellas and wear dry shoes." The poem was written by a man named Frank Desprez and for some unknown reason, many people got the idea fixed in their minds that he was a French Canadian. No one had any knowledge to go on, but that was the accepted theory of the day. Not to Mama! She insisted he was British and British only. The umbrella and rubbers clinched it for her. How she would have gloated to know, half a century later, that a persistent scholar, Dr. Mabel Major of Texas Christian University, tracked Desprez down to his final resting place in Bristol, England. Dr. Major got in touch with the remainder of his family through writing to the public library and, sure enough,

British he was. His family could not account for the surname; it had been acquired too many years back to trace, but the lyrical British subject had most certainly made a pilgrimage to Texas and left an undying testament to that fact in "Lasca."

It's all very well to write reviews,
And carry umbrellas, and keep dry shoes,
And say what everyone's saying here,
And wear what everyone else must wear;
But to-night I'm sick of the whole affair,
I want free life, and I want fresh air;
And I sigh for the canter after the cattle,
The crack of the whips like shots in a battle,
The mellay of horns and hoofs and heads
That wars and wrangles and scatters and spreads;
The green beneath, and the blue above,
The dash and danger, and life and love —
And Lasca!

Lasca used to ride
On a mouse-gray mustang close to my side,
With blue *serape* and bright-belled spur;
I laughed with joy as I looked at her!
Little knew she of books or of creeds;
An *Ave Maria* sufficed her needs;
Little she cared, save to be by my side,
To ride with me, and ever to ride,
From San Saba's shore to Lavaca's tide.
She was as bold as the billows that beat,
She was as wild as the breezes that blow:
From her little head to her little feet,
She swayed in her suppleness to and fro
By each gust of passion; a sapling pine,
That grows on the edge of a Kansas bluff,
And wars with the wind when the weather is rough,
Is like this Lasca, this love of mine.

She would hunger that I might eat,
Would take the bitter and leave me the sweet;

But once, when I made her jealous for fun,
At something I'd whispered, or looked, or done,
One Sunday, in San Antonio,
To a glorious girl on the Alamo,
She drew from her garter a dear little dagger,
And — sting of a wasp! — it made me stagger!
An inch to the left, or an inch to the right,
And I shouldn't be maundering here to-night;
But she sobbed, and sobbing, so swiftly bound
Her torn *rebosa* about the wound,
That I quite forgave her. Scratches don't count
    In Texas, down by the Rio Grande.

Her eye was brown — a deep, deep brown;
Her hair was darker than her eye;
And something in her smile and frown,
Curled crimson lip and instep high,
Showed that there ran in each blue vein,
Mixed with the milder Aztec strain,
The vigorous vintage of Old Spain.
She was alive in every limb
With feeling, to the finger-tips;
And when the sun is like a fire,
And sky one shining, soft sapphire,
One does not drink in little sips.

Why did I leave the fresh and the free,
That suited her and suited me?
Listen awhile, and you will see;
But this be sure — in earth or air,
God and God's laws are everywhere,
And Nemesis comes with a foot as fleet
On the Texas trail as in Regent Street.

The air was heavy, the night was hot,
I sat by her side and forgot — forgot:
The herd that were taking their rest,
Forgot that the air was close oppressed,
That the Texas norther comes sudden and soon,

In the dead of the night, or the blaze of noon;
That once let the herd at its breath take fright,
Nothing on earth can stop their flight;
And woe to the rider, and woe to the steed,
Who falls in front of their mad stampede!
Was that thunder? No, by the Lord!
I sprang to my saddle without a word.
One foot on mine, and she clung behind.
Away! on a hot chase down the wind!
But never was fox-hunt half so hard,
And never was steed so little spared;
For we rode for our lives. You shall hear how we
    fared
        In Texas, down by the Rio Grande.

The mustang flew, and we urged him on;
There was one chance left, and you have but one —
Halt! jump to the ground, and shoot your horse;
Crouch under his carcass, and take your chance;
And if the steers in their frantic course
Don't batter you both to pieces at once,
You may thank your star; if not, good-bye
To the quickening kiss and the long-drawn sigh,
And the open air and the open sky,
        In Texas, down by the Rio Grande.

The cattle gained on us, and, just as I felt
For my old six-shooter behind in my belt,
Down came the mustang, and down came we,
Clinging together, and, — what was the rest?
A body that spread itself on my breast,
Two arms that shielded my dizzy head,
Two lips that hard on my lips were pressed;
Then came thunder in my ears,
As over us surged the sea of steers,
Blows that beat blood into my eyes;
And when I could rise —
Lasca was dead!

I gouged out a grave a few feet deep,
And there in Earth's arms I laid her to sleep;
And there she is lying, and no one knows;
And the summer shines, and the winter snows;
For many a day the flowers have spread
A pall of petals over her head;
And the little gray hawk hangs aloft in the air,
And the sly coyote trots here and there,
And the black-snake glides and glitters and slides
Into a rift in a cotton-wood tree;
And the buzzard sails on,
And comes and is gone,
Stately and still, like a ship at sea;
And I wonder why I do not care
For the things that are, like the things that were.
Does half my heart lie buried there
    In Texas, down by the Rio Grande?

It strikes me as almost supernatural that my mother, even as a young girl, loved with enduring passion the poem that was to be practically her life story. How much of our destiny is shaped by the poems we learn and the songs we sing in childhood?

Glasgow was a long way from the Orange River Colony of South Africa, where she went as a teacher for the British government, and a still longer way from Brownsville, "in Texas, down by the Rio Grande."

In 1902 at the close of the Boer War my mother became a Texan when she married William Robinson Lubbock of San Antonio, in South Africa, where he was selling American farm implements to the Boers. In 1910 when my mother and father came to live in Brownsville, the young Scotswoman's wheel of life had given the full turn.

Now as I studied the town, I saw that Fort Brown, where Gorgas experienced yellow fever personally, had become bustling Southmost College. The library combines college, city, and county! The charming little French brick cottage in the Fort, where we once lived, has been torn down, but Robert E. Lee's ghost still sits on boring other-world Courts Martial, and Old Rip Ford's phantom still fights the redheaded Mexican Robin Hood, Juan Nepomuceno Cortina, even as he did after Cheno Cortina had roundly whipped the Brownsville Tigers and a motley assortment of Texas Rangers. In the blue border dusk, these wraiths out of the past still speak to those who have ears attuned to hear.

Fort Brown

In Brownsville the word *árabes* had and has nothing to do with Arabia or the desert. An *árabe* is a peddler. They drove buggies, then *fotingos*, their venerable Model T's, selling sleazy bedspreads, gaudy yard goods, sewing machines, and fancy coal-oil lamps to the Mexicans. All that has changed about credit buying is the terms. These "Arabs" have introduced the terms Lay Away Plan under the guise of *"Use Nuestro Plan de Separación."* The word *enganche*, the "hooking on" is their graphic word for down payment. A few years back, the lead-pipe cinch in their stock was a highly colored, elaborately framed enlargement of a photograph provided by the customer, usually a picture of some deceased and much revered member of the family. The *difunto,* or as Evelyn Waugh would have it, The Loved One, was hung in a position of honor in every jacal from Brownsville to Roma, regardless of whose eyes went blind or whose belly went hungry to pay for it. The *árabes* appeared regularly to collect and were almost never disappointed.

Edelstein's Furniture Store is one of the few surviving firms founded over fifty years ago that started out selling parlor tables and stiff straight-backed chairs to Mexican farmers for a dollar down and a dollar the rest of their lives. The old sign looked homey and good to me, until I found out that a sop had been thrown to progress, and that Edelstein's now operates a "Studio of Interior Decoration" in the graceful old Armstrong house. *No hay remedio.* There just isn't any remedy. Demand has to be supplied. But no matter how many deep freezes are sold, there are still many families in Brownsville who stick to the old custom of buying only sufficient food for each meal, fresh from the municipal market each day. It pleased my reactionary heart to see that the stalls in that market were bare, picked clean, by eleven o'clock in the morning and the owners stretched out enjoying a nap, even as in my childhood.

Before me stood the New Bridge, new in 1924. Back of me and to the right, the Old Bridge was still in use and favored by many of the natives. More relatives working there: more consideration! I recalled the day I first rode over the International Bridge in 1914; the name filled me with pride. After crossing, we boarded a Mexican mule-drawn streetcar. At the foot of the bridge in Matamoros is a slight hill. The brakes of the overloaded streetcar gave way, and the car crushed the little mule to death. That for the new bridge!

I saw the Charles Stillman house, built by a New York banker who had considerable to do with the founding of Brownsville. Its lines are good, and suggest the life of the times when Richard King and Mifflin Kennedy were active on the Border.

There is considerable interest in the Stillman house as a museum, but I was surprised to hear that there was also opposition to the project, on the grounds that the used-car dealers of the commercially zoned section would suffer! The Stillman family in New York offered to put up part of the purchase price, Brownsville to raise the balance. The Treviño family had owned the place ever since I could remember. The two brothers, Abelardo and Mariano, died bachelors and the estate went to distant relatives in Mexico. When the State of Texas wanted to put a historical marker on the property, the Treviños made them put it out on the sidewalk, and there it stands.

Abelardo Treviño used to ride out on a fine horse on Sunday, a real *caballero*. On windy days he would stand on a street corner to watch the wind toss the skirts of the pretty girls as they crossed the street.

One story about him delights me beyond all explaining. Perhaps it is poetry, or maybe just the words to a song that he made up without knowing it. At any rate, it is cavalier, and simon-pure Brownsville.

Abelardo got in touch by mail with an unnaturally blond lady in Dallas and invited her to come to Brownsville by train to be his guest at the Miller Hotel. She arrived on schedule and Abelardo, about to telephone her, became uneasy about the fluency of his English. He beseeched a friend to speak for him, like Christian in *Cyrano de Bergerac*.

"But she will be expecting to hear your voice," his friend said.

"No," Abelardo insisted. "She has never heard my voice. Your English is far better than mine. You must help me."

"What shall I say to her? How shall I address her?"

Abelardo thought for a moment and then said gravely: *"Háblale con dulzura, y de cuando en cuando, le dices*

'Honey.' Speak to her with sweetness, and from time to time, call her 'Honey.' "

Brownsville still "speaks with sweetness" to those it likes. The natives appear reserved although they are still friendly and uncritical. Under an apparently aloof exterior there is warmth, and a solid foundation of common sense. They understand human motives and frailties, and possess a vast lore of tales and yarns, personal histories in two languages. The Latin attitude has rubbed off on the Anglos and they, too, take their time before extending the hand. Once they do, it is for keeps. The best way to make friends in Brownsville is not to let your effort show. It is best to wait for the green light, and it will surely come on if given sufficient time.

Society, *la gente de razón,* still frowns on breaches of manners rather than on breaches of morals. There was and still is enormous curiosity, but little censure. The curiosity is a form of participation, for a community more given to the policy of "live and let live" never existed — now or at any other period. In any illicit affair, the interest of the nonparticipants is in what happens. "*Qué pasó?* What's the latest development?" The Wheel of Life has been turning so long, each person shrugs and thinks: *Mañana a mí me toca!* My turn may be tomorrow. The wheel will turn — and the bottom will be on top. Be charitable.

In less than thirty years I have seen some of the fences of old Brownsville change. In many cases, the bottom rail is on top now. But the natives still believe in "who you are," not "what you have."

"The old order changeth," architecturally more than otherwise. It was a shock to me to see the high brick walls of the Incarnate Word Academy torn down and the convent standing right out in the middle of the street. I remember when the cloisters were officially opened by the Vatican in 1918 and two nuns, Sister Clare and Sister Paul, saw the outside world for the first time in thirty-two years. They were both sisters of Judge Jim Wells. Sidewalks and streetcars were sources of great wonder to them.

Bluebells

The home of Judge and Mrs. Wells was directly across the street from the Federal Building and Post Office. The first nuns that came to Brownsville from France were lodged in that house. Mrs. Wells would never allow it to be changed in any way during her lifetime. Commonplace commercial buildings stand there now. I inquired of an old-timer about Robert Wells, their youngest son.

"*Anda por ahí en un rancho de esos.* . . . He is out on some ranch or another," was the reply. It developed later that Robert Wells was in charge of Public Relations for the King Ranch. So much for modern methods in the eyes of old Brownsville. I do not think even Queen Victoria could have managed a better understatement.

I felt like the old woman who had had her "petticoats cut off all round about" by the peddler whose name was Stout when I saw the orange trees of the convent garden standing out in the open for men to see.

Forty years before, my brother, Commander Clyde Grayson Lubbock, U. S. Navy, Retired, then aged seven, was allowed to receive piano lessons from the nuns as a very special concession. Since he was a male, he could not be taught in the convent, but out of affection for my parents, a compromise was reached and the infant "Don Juan" learned his *do, re, mi* in the high, closed-in wooden bridge that connected the convent with the parochial school across the street.

The pupils in the convent were brought up in strict modesty. It was a modest era. The nightgown was slipped over the head before other clothing was removed. The Sisters of the Incarnate Word went one better: alone, locked in the bathroom, we bathed wearing a long, unbleached domestic shift, soaping and scouring underneath its clammy folds. At no time were girls allowed to "gaze on beauty bare."

And on my return, I saw girls in Bikini bathing suits. However, in spite of the change in dress, the old Spanish grip on modesty has not lessened its hold very much. In 1956, 824 babies were born in hospitals, 94 delivered in homes by doctors, and 1095 delivered at home by midwives. Casa Maternidad, a small maternity home for Latin Americans, charges very low fees, and Mercy Hospital has even lower indigent fees.

But it is not the cost that influences Latin American women to have midwives at their confinements. It is centuries of Spanish tradition, making it painfully embarrassing for an uneducated woman to have a doctor attend her at such a time. Many Mexican husbands still insist on having a midwife in attendance!

Under Texas law, the licensing of midwives cannot be enforced, and there is no way of telling exactly how many are practicing in Brownsville. The encouraging aspect is that infant mortality, once appalling, has dropped markedly.

Once I got my bearings in Brownsville, I was ready to solve the mystery that had bothered me for twenty years: where *was* the Port of Brownsville, number one cotton-shipping port in the United States? I had read about it, and had jumbled together a picture in my mind, with the Port down somewhere by the International Bridge! I could understand Point Isabel being changed to Port Isabel. That made sense, for there was enough salt water there to float sizable boats, and dredging could make it into a fine harbor. But the Port of Brownsville! My structural imagination was not equal to the task of mentally locating the harbor.

When I finally got my first sight of the Port, I sneaked up on its blind side and saw a great ocean-going vessel, loaded with cargo, seemingly aground, resting crazily in the middle of dry land. Jackass Prairie, a vast green meadow where I had as a child chased wild burros with my brother, had a freighter in the middle of it, apparently becalmed like a painted ship in the middle of a canvas field.

This optical illusion is due to the fact that the man-made harbor has no waste space of shallow beaches that would require ships to anchor away from the piers. It is dug out deeply all the way to the docks, making it possible for the six licensed pilots to bring the ships up close for loading. At last I was satisfied that the port really existed. It is well worth anyone's time to drive down the Boca Chica road and look back at the channel as it runs between two arms of land. The water is not visible and the illusion is something like what a drunkard's dream might be. The clear Gulf air and the perspective coming up the road from Port Isabel play tricks, too. I wondered what the *square* concrete oil tanks were for as I approached them in the car. On coming nearer to them, all the people in the car remarked on the *trompe l'oeil* effect: there were several groups of perfectly round tanks, placed in such a way that the perspective, owing to turns in the road, made the spheres appear to be perfect cubes.

I told Fritz Hofmokel, the man responsible for what my eyes were seeing but not quite believing, of my perplexity.

"I know," he said. "We got the land and built the Port. It's very simple." He flung an aerial map down on the desk and gestured with his cigar. "We own and control twenty-four thousand acres of land on and near the channel. The man who owned the land wouldn't sell at first. I told him I'd go ahead and dig out the harbor anyway. I did. He had me over a barrel. But he sold."

Fritz Hofmokel has a somewhat Prussian manner; he reminds me of Erich von Stroheim. But he gets things done. I began to see how the man with the land would sell, once Hofmokel set his mind on it. I was overcome at the size of the operation. In 1955 the waterfront storage space was to be increased by 50 per cent at a cost of $3,000,000. The length of the turning basin will be increased again this year. All this improvement and enlargement is financed out of revenue bonds without a penny of tax money.

"Up until 1918, and perhaps even later, the funny, antiquated Point Isabel train still ran to the Point and back every day. The old freight depot stood right there." I pointed to the picture on his desk, and another memory came back to me. The little train was a perfect delight, with its huge hopper-shaped funnel and tiny wheels, like a child's wooden toy engine.

The schoolteachers rode it twice a day to the district schools they taught. My mother and brother rode it five days a week. Tommy McGovern, the obliging engineer, used to stop the train when someone wanted to take a shot at a fine flock of ducks feeding among the salt grasses. Whoever had a gun would shoot his birds, get out and pick them up, and board the train once more. Tommy would pull the string for the whistle, and *El Trenesito* would be on its way. Sometimes he'd stop the train to cut a mesquite and shove it into the firebox. Every afternoon on the return trip he used to blow the whistle about five minutes before he reached each district schoolhouse, Mesquite and Las Matanzas, so that the teachers could be packed and ready, standing by the track waiting for the train to take them back home to Brownsville. Miss Viola Egly and Miss Manuela Longoria are 'train regulars,' who still teach in the Brownsville public schools.

I was glad the little engine was safely enshrined in a special shed built for it by the Chamber of Commerce, but I began to feel older than Noah. The train cars had the seats placed lengthwise against the sides. The aisles were not thirty inches wide.

Once my father was riding to the Point with Lon Hill, a Cherokee Indian pioneer with a long black bob. A woman had hung a pasteboard ice-cream bucket above Papa's head. Something dripped on his bald spot: "Pickles, madam?" he said, starting his finger up to his mouth. "No, Mr. Lubbock," she said, "puppies."

When the two gentlemen and their traveling companion got off the train at the Point, they helped her unload her luggage including a tiny Mexican hairless dog in a shopping bag in addition to the bucket of puppies. She let the little beast run loose while she thanked the men, but Mr. Hill, an enormous man — tall and heavy — was patently nervous. He kept backing away and fidgeted from one foot to the other.

"Don't be nervous, Mr. Hill," she said. "He won't bite you."

"I ain't afraid he'll bite me, lady! I'm afraid he'll kick me."

The march of time has brought money and prosperity to Brownsville and the Valley, but I could not help feeling that more than Lon Hill and Papa had gone to the Happy Hunting Grounds — some of the old simplicity was gone. Labor unions were now a factor where the only labor law had been "from can till can't." Merchant sailors reeled through the streets and brawled in the nightspots. Shrimpers spent their wealth loudly and lavishly, but the shrimp fleet was still blessed

by the Bishop in a ceremony that goes back to the Sea of Galilee.

According to the University of Texas' Institute of Marine Science, 70,000 extra mouths to be fed come into the world every day. The sea must provide! The miracle of the loaves and fishes is a hardy perennial. The new shrimp beds will help bolster the diminishing food supply of the world. The Institute, at Aransas Pass "where the fish bite every day," tag the shrimp in order that the travels, rates of growth, and morality of the shrimp may be followed! Good Heavens, Lasswell, do get those glasses checked! I said to myself. Not even a marine scientist wants to tag a shrimp to check its morality: *mortality* is the word! But it's good to know the shrimp are being looked after.

Everywhere I saw bustling commerce. Two nations were involved. Leviathans loaded with cotton zoomed down in long caravans over the International Bridges from points in Mexico to the Port.

Brownsville is the southern terminal for the Intracoastal Canal, just as it once was the beginning of the Chisholm Trail. The Rio Grande International Airport is the border-crossing point for half a dozen international airlines. In order to facilitate private plane traffic, Mexico has recognized Brownsville as an international airport and established an inspection station there with customs, immigration, public health service, and civil aeronautics inspectors. Private planes can be cleared and on their way to Mexico in five minutes.

Cotton, oil, shipping, and the airports have brought many young, active people to Brownsville. They are building suitable homes and already show signs of becoming "naturalized." They have brought oil burners and air conditioners with them, all nice to have, but to the natives not really a necessity. They raised large families, went through spectacular lives in health and comfort without ever having owned an electric fan. They didn't build the hot west walls of their houses out of glass. The gardens and patios are shaded, and they know the physical and psychological value of a cool trickle of water. It is significant, in a way, that the "natives" — and I mean Anglo as well as Latin — have electric mixers, but cling to the old lava-stone *molcajete,* the mortar and pestle, to grind *chile verde,* pungent and tasty. It is an imperishable symbol of the elemental and primitive in their culture.

I saw that progress would never go to Brownsville's head, making her cheap and gaudy. No onslaught of chain store civilization, no desecration by neon or nylon newness would penetrate her heart. She is the serene Old World town she always has been, taking the best of the new, still maintaining the beauty and comfort of the old. The ambiguous bustle may deceive the newcomer. Commercial buildings have pushed the old residential district almost out of existence. The lovely old Opera House is to be the next to go, but they can't kill the Phoenix, old Brownsville.

The natives have accepted the added prosperity philosophically. They are realists. Modern methods bring money. In order to have money, they know they must sacrifice a little of something else: perhaps a little quiet, a small measure of repose, and permit a speeding up in the tempo of life, but not one particle more than is absolutely necessary. Much they flatly reject, such as large factories and smelly industries. They keep out gamblers and racketeers, the petty gangsters who follow big payrolls. Natives still observe telephone hours, and it is possible to take a siesta without Mr. Bell's butting in.

Not everyone, of course, can hold out against the attraction of novelties. I was putting in a long distance phone call in a hole-in-the-wall café when two young Mexicans came in and asked for a certain waitress by name. I imagine the girl made all of ten dollars a week, plus tips. The older, a salesman, made his pitch. "You want to be modern, don't you? The interior decoration of your home must be up to date if you are to maintain your prestige," I listened shamelessly from the open phone on the wall.

"You will feel inferior unless you get at least one of these wall telephones, in color! The very latest! There is no color that you can name that I cannot supply, nor any combination of colors . . . for I make them! Special. Pink and green? Red and yellow? Only ten dollars . . . two dollars a month. And the dial is chrome."

"I am planning to redecorate my living room and have not decided on the color scheme," she said. "It should match . . . and my furniture is green . . ."

"Ivory goes with everything." The salesman placed a rose-pink phone on the table.

"What exactly is ivory?" the girl said.

"It is a tannish cream, a betch (beige) color, only more elegant."

"You'd better ask my mother first," the girl said. "Phone and see if she is at home."

"No need," said the salesman, "I've already been there. She told me to ask you."

"Well," the girl shifted her weight, "the phone they sold me at the company doesn't ring loud."

"Aha!" the salesman reached in his bag. "For two more dollars, you see this switch? It controls the bell, loud, regular, or soft! Chrome!"

"That makes twelve dollars?" the girl said. I could see she was weakening.

A barber in a white smock came up and asked the salesman to make him a black-and-white phone, trimmed in red, with the dial, of course, in chrome. The salesman produced the order book and signed up the volunteer instantly. Shooting fish in a bucket!

The waitress was doing mental arithmetic. The satchel carrier put his two cents in: "You can tell what kind of family it is by the phone they use."

"My brothers monopolize the line," the girl said.

"Ha!" shouted the salesman, and dived into the black bag. "You see this loudspeaker? This apparatus hooks on the phone. Only five dollars, and everybody in the house can hear everything the other person is saying at the other end of the line, just the same as they can hear what you say!"

"Is that an advantage?" the girl asked.

I almost shouted out that it was an invasion of privacy, an invention of the devil, and should be forbidden by law.

"The best! Seventeen dollars, total!" The girl signed the order and the salesman ordered two cups of coffee. When the waitress went for it, he leaned on his elbows and addressed his partner: "See what I tell you? You gotta see 'em face to face! You can't do nothin' over a phone!"

With or without telephones — colored or plain — the days are sunny and the nights, almost without exception, breezy. No native would dream of going to bed without a light blanket within hand's reach. Living is reasonable and retired people like living so close to Mexico. They love to go dancing to the open-air night clubs across the river, and to bring back low-cost liquor. Some customs officers state gravely, upon inspection of the bottles: "And, of course, *nobody* in this car has brought anything across in the last thirty days!" The answer comes in chorus, no matter how many bottle-buying trips have been sneaked in during the month, "Oh, no sir! No." I never before suspected any civil servants of possessing a sense of humor.

Point Isabel and Padre Island are a little over twenty miles away. Hot white sand, golden tropic sun, and deep blue water with snow-capped waves. The shells are famous for their variety and quantity. Padre Island is being eyed now as a possible National Park. It is described by the National Park Service as the "longest undeveloped seashore remaining in the United States." May God keep it so! Children, those forthright realists, recently refused the books of free tickets for "rides," on Ferris wheels and other Coney Island atrocities, given them by the owners of commercial entertainment concessions at Isla Blanca Amusement Park on Padre Island. The kids wanted the beach "wild," natural as it always was, where a fellow could play Robinson Crusoe and Swiss Family Robinson till his empty belly drove him back to the food of the present.

And east of Brownsville lies that wild wonderland, the meeting of waters, where the salty blue of the Gulf of Mexico meets the turgid water of the Rio Grande at Boca Chica. They meet, the two waters, but do not seem to mingle. It's a grand spot to stand and fish.

On this beachcomber's paradise, I spotted some wonderful boards, brand new, apparently washed loose from a freighter. The tide brings in lots of loot for anyone having a touch of junk-loving Mrs. Feeley in his blood. I went back, ready to carry off the prize, but a pick-up truck was ahead of me, well loaded down. It made its way leisurely along the hard-packed sand, stopping whenever a particularly tempting piece of plank lay on the beach. The occupants of the truck worked with the slow tempo of long habit. Later I saw a second-hand lumber-yard where the treasures were offered for sale. The cost of the boards was only the cost of the gasoline to drive out and pick them up. The men got the beautiful *brisa,* the *paseo,* and maybe did a little surf casting into the bargain.

Not a signboard nor a hot dog stand in sight. Nothing but the ocean and the river, sand hills and beach, blending into that characteristic quality of the Gulf Coast country: warm and cool, sweet and salty, calm and breezy. One of the few places left in Texas that can still say: As it was in the beginning! About the "And ever shall be, world without end" part, I cannot say. I can only be grateful for small mercies, and leave bewitching Brownsville without heartache for the first time, knowing her to be secure in her serene beauty. Timeless and of all time, eternal as Roma, that dusty city that rises out of a chalky hill to guard the other entrance to the Rio Grande Valley from the west. Those guardian cities, Brownsville and Roma, keep faithful watch over the golden resources that lie along one hundred miles of palm-lined pavement, encompassing a region unique in Texas, a fruitful winter wonderland, horn of plenty filled with fruits and vegetables for the snow-bound sections of the United States.

My anticipation was high as I left Brownsville and the compass on my car pointed west, for there was not an inch of that highway that did not hold rich associations and memories for me.

Beginning at Brownsville, the towns of the Southmost Valley of the Rio Grande are linked up along the highway like charms on a bracelet. Together, they might be called a city. Not far apart, all hang onto the main artery, with the exception of Edinburg lying to the north.

The Valley structure, geographically and socially, is unique.

It is a gigantic Main Street of a hundred miles, with 300,000 families living along its palm-lined splendor. For that reason it is treated here as an entity, not town by town.

There is a close-knit family feeling up and down the Valley, a remarkable solidarity among the people: they have a single telephone book, gas system, and power system. They combine into one regional Chamber of Commerce. The newspapers give valley-wide news coverage, as do radio and TV broadcasts, and they share library facilities.

A card party will bring players from perhaps fifty or sixty miles away. Progressive parties are still popular, cocktails in Harlingen, hors d'oeuvres in Weslaco, dinner in McAllen, and dancing across the river in Reynosa. Someone in the crowd may suggest scrambled eggs and a nightcap in Mission, or a swim at the lake at Sharyland.

The land is flat, and I was twenty-three before I knew what an emergency brake was for. Speed limits are reasonable and well enforced. The cool nights, delightfully fresh, make driving a joy. Most people arrange parties at the end of the week in order to sleep late next day. The Valley is a very special way of life.

From Weslaco on, the effects of the last devastating freeze were all around me. The loss of citrus groves was appalling. The sight would have been depressing to one not accustomed as I am to the eternal quality of resurgence of the Valley. I know so well what an indestructible phoenix she is: time and time again I have seen her almost destroyed, always to rise gloriously from her own ashes. Irrigation and the building of Falcon Dam has very nearly conquered drouth, but for years the Valley has risen triumphant from drouth, floods, sleet, ice, hail, "plagues of locusts," and sacking by crooked politicians. Labor problems have assailed her when the crops were richest. Fruits have hung heavy, rotten-sweet from the trees for the lack of pickers.

Wet-backs? Like the poor, they are always with us. There is nothing new in that situation. Wherever there is a river or an invisible dividing line, an international boundary between two nations, one of which offers a better standard of living than the other, there will be wet-backs. The situation will endure until human nature changes considerably more than it has given any evidence of doing in the last twenty-five hundred years.

The people, like the crops in the Valley, are, of necessity, resilient and adaptable to sudden change in temperature. Any old-timer will tell you that truer words were never written than "The Texas norther comes sudden and soon, in the dead of night or the blaze of noon." The poem "Lasca" keeps running through Texas like a scarlet thread through a tapestry. It belongs. It is Texas.

The Upper Valley, beginning according to my reckoning, at San Benito differs considerably from Brownsville, a city apart, because of the varying types of people who settled it.

In the early 1900's, trains loaded with homeseekers, known rudely to the natives as "homesuckers," came from the cold North, North Texas and northern United States, seeking warm climate and fertile land. The land companies loaded up all-Pullman trains with likely prospects, most of them well-heeled and tired of wrestling with snow shovels in Minnesota, or trekking out to snowbound barns in Iowa. If the train was scheduled to stop by a desolate stretch of unimproved land, the canny impresarios arranged to have the stop made during the night.

Land companies laid the foundation of several large fortunes at that time, and their salesmen stopped at nothing. A common sales technique is illustrated by the story about an old German couple from Milwaukee who trudged all day through a bearing citrus grove, wiping the fat drops from their sweating brows, listening to the harangue of the salesman. Momma was cagey, but Poppa was ready to sign. The land man got them into big comfortable rockers on the gallery of the clubhouse.

"Let me get you a nice glass of fresh grapefruit juice," the salesman said. Momma's dim view had communicated itself to him, so he laced the tall glasses with a triple shot of tequila, totally imperceptible when served in grapefruit juice. The couple were dizzy from the unaccustomed walking under a blazing sun, and the cool drink hit home. It had been a long time since breakfast, too, and a skimpy one at that, minus the usual sausages and fried apples and pancakes. Momma's glass got down to about one third. She leaned her head back against the rocking chair and sighed: "Sign, Poppa, sign!"

Hidalgo County was famous in the late twenties and early thirties for its political scandals, and its Nickel Plated Highway to Hell. A. Y. Baker was sheriff at the time. The shenanigans of the "Ring," as it was called, make the current Duval County pilferings look like a benevolent meeting to raise money for Foreign Missionary Societies. No one could say it was not exciting and different, whatever the moral aspects of the dealings. Illegal Mexican votes sold for five dollars a head, and many a truckload of them were "horse-shedded," taken out and "instructed" how many lines to count down on the ballot "and then make the sign of the cross."

The Good Government League, or the Bolies, as they were known, finally won out and the gravy train was derailed. Many of the lasting improvements in Hidalgo County in the way of schools, colleges, and highways were the work of the Ring. True enough, they cost considerably more than they should have, but I have observed no measurable lowering of the taxes since the Bolies got in.

Westward from Brownsville a hundred miles lies Rio Grande City, once called Carnestolendas, the three carnival days before Ash Wednesday. It is old, silent, and severe. There is new-found oil money. New money to blend with the old, hard-earned Spanish peso, ground out of sweat, hides, and tallow. Out of trade, legal and illegal. But of an oldness, a quality inherent in the close-mouthed, tight-lipped natives who water the flowers of Our Lady in the grotto, a Rio Grande replica of Lourdes, a landmark on the Oblate Trail that runs through the stronghold of the faithful.

Modern ranch houses, built with oil money, are going up daily. New political organizations flourish and are in the process of overthrowing a machine that has held the county in a boa constrictor grip for years.

The land remains dry, with crumbling adobe structures blurred at the edges by time and neglect, nibbled away by oblivion. A few stone and brick houses keep the graceful, primitive lines of their shape; they stand in melancholy opulence like an aged statesman in a battered top hat.

The new life is the highway, the courthouse, the oil wells, and the neighboring dam. Water is still the prize. The old and new, so closely entangled, "as rich as sudden," what interior conflict and schism they must bring.

The courthouse on a high gravel hill overlooks the Valley for many miles in all directions. From this hill can be seen the Sierra Madre ridge of mountains, even those surrounding Monterrey. The mountains of Cerralvo, Mexico, forty-five miles away, present a beautiful landscape.

Dusty Spanish cliffs, almost chalky in the white sunlight,

buildings that would be landmarks anywhere but in Texas —
side by side with modern chain stores, blatting radios, and
squawking TVs in a town where all freight was delivered by
oxcart as late as 1917. Permanent waves. Air mail. Filling
stations. Delivery trucks speeding up and down the roads with
frozen ready-to-heat dinners for the grocers' shelves.

Next door the soft-soled shoes of a black-robed priest make
a gentle swishing sound in the corridor of the house of the Oblate Fathers, "The Mounted Cavalry of Christ," as he paces silently reading his missal. The young Mexican girl who is the
secretary to the Reverend Fathers is very polite and efficient.
She does not mind the heat. There is plenty of water for the
gardens, she says. "From the wells, of course. It has not rained
in a very long time." Her eyes wander off after a *chamaco* driving a grapejuice-colored Pontiac trimmed with pink.

As Sam Hargrove of Rio Grande City used to say: "Miss
Mary, it's the encroachment of civilization."

To the west lies Roma. As in eternal Rome, religion is strong
here. It might as well be Spain. Sparseness and drouth. At
every turn you expect a brown Franciscan. The austere beauty
of the old Spanish houses, the iron grillwork on the windows
and doors, the church at the top of the hill, the Sisters' School,
the dust, and the numberless urchins that hang about the street
speak more of Spain than of Mexico. In 1951, Twentieth Century Fox, filming *Viva Zapata* by Steinbeck, shot scenes for
three weeks in front of the picturesque church.

Lads of teen age stand over in Mier, on the Mexican side,
fishing, calling filth back and forth across the river to their
friends on the American side. Closely shuttered houses nearly
three centuries old hug the edge of the cliff. Abandoned? Perhaps. It is a tempting location; they are stout storehouses for
wares to be delivered or removed under cover of darkness. The
river can be waded in many places — no need to wet the back.
There is a saying in Texas that the river corrupts.

I cannot look across at Mier without thinking of the dangerous and cruel Mier Expedition by Texans into Mexico in 1842 in the days of the Texas Republic — probably their most dangerous foray into that country. One hundred and seventy-six Texans were captured and ordered executed. The decree was modified to call for the execution of every tenth man. They drew beans from a bag, and those who drew black beans were stood up against a wall and shot. Seventeen black beans were drawn. Seventeen Texans executed. Ewen Cameron, for whom Brownsville's Cameron County was named, drew a white bean, but was ordered shot anyway.

One of the old houses of Roma fascinated me beyond all decency. I walked around and around it. Finally a little boy came out. I asked him who lived there. I knew the family name at once, an Anglo name, yet I knew that in that house no word of English would be spoken or understood. I rang, and after a long wait, huaraches scuffed down the corridor. An Indian woman with long black braids and copper skin opened the *mirador* and looked at me questioningly.

"Tell the Señorita on the part of Mrs. Lasswell that she would like to pay her respects."

A slim forefinger went to her lips and wordlessly she disappeared down the shadowy hall. In a little while she re-materialized with a slow-motion beckoning gesture.

The Señorita sat in a rocker in her bedroom. She had long snow-white braids, delicate pink skin, and wore two green leaves of fresh sweet basil pasted to her temples. Her white dressing sacque and ruffled white petticoat were fresh, and of good quality. In her hands she held a rosary of Job's-tears.

"Yes. I remember when my father put the second story on this house. I am almost ninety. I am the last of my family. You see, I have everything here," she indicated her saints and holy pictures, her pot plants, electric stove, and icebox, and two small enamel chamber pots by her rocker. "There are many changes, but of course nothing really changes. No one has paid a call for many years. It was good of you to come."

I chatted of her family for a few minutes and said goodbye. The silent dark one ushered me out.

"It is fortunate that the Señorita has one so devoted as you. She is in good hands."

With no change of expression, in the deadest voice I have ever heard, she looked through me and said: "Nor even any need to say it."

The hot sun felt good after that. I joined Bob Pool and we went into Guerra's store to find out if any of the Guerras, who had been friends of my family for years, were still around. We explained our mission in Roma, the fact that we were gathering material for a book.

"A writer?" the man said. "We've *got* a writer. Mr. Lott. Go to see him."

Roma has an economy of words, a dispatch that would do credit to Vermont. There is a lean, spare quality in the very air of the place. None of the swarming yeasty overflow that is Mexican life — with the one universal exception, the swarms of kids.

"Writing a book about Texas?" Mr. Lott beamed. "I'll give you one." Mr. Lott was in his undershirt watering the yard. He is a retired Customs Officer, a charming, outgoing person. He presented a copy of *The Kingdom of Zapata,* a history of Zapata County which he wrote with Don Mercurio Martínez, at the request of the County Commissioners.

As we chatted we gazed off toward Hebronville, "the great horse ranch, El Randado. . . ."

"It's right over there," Mr. Lott stretched out his arm. "At one time it contained forty-five thousand acres of land, was well stocked with horses and mules which were marketed in San Antonio and Mexico. It is now the scene of major oil production. The present Randado, however, is at least six miles from the original Randado where Robert E. Lee camped and where the *randas* were manufactured. The present population is thirty-five." Mr. Lott sighed for the old days.

Artistically trimmed lassos! Where are they now? I did not know then that in less than a week I should learn the romance of Randado from Tom Lea!

The dusty streets of Roma were almost deserted though it was early afternoon when we went into a tiny *fonda*, clean and charming. The *patrona's* face was the pure oval of a Murillo, the same delicate olive skin with apricot cheeks, and eyes like a doe. She spoke no English.

"Business is slow?" I said after we ordered.

"Terrible. There is literally nothing. Especially since they started the Falcon Dam, at Zapata."

"I should think there would be trade from workers and tourists; the dam is only forty miles from here."

"Nothing. *Absolutemente nada.*" She pointed next door where her husband and a friend were extending one of the rooms of the house practically onto the sidewalk to hold a white enamel refrigerated showcase.

"But it is not worth the trouble, *las tiendas de cadena . . .*" It was the first time I had heard the literal translation of chain stores.

"Your patio is extremely beautiful." I got up to look at the tastefully arranged little roofed courtyard.

"Everything has dried up," she said. "We cannot spare the water." The flowers were quite lovely in spite of what she said. Rare vines and ferns climbed the walls. At either end of the patio she had wooden posts on top of which were mounted antique hurricane lamps of enormous size and great beauty.

"You like the globes." She smiled. "You see the rat wire I have around them . . . and you know why."

There are plenty of stones in the streets of Roma, and small boys are one breed the world around. She pointed to an ancient ox yoke hanging under tropical vines; two small oil lamps were mounted on it.

"The yoke is very old — and very good," I said.

"The lamps . . . I saw a picture in *Mejores Hogares y Jardines.*"

Better Homes and Gardens. In this scrap of Spain!

Great God of Printer's Ink! What that man Gutenberg started when he invented the printing press!

I wondered what I should find at Zapata, one of the two towns swallowed up by the Falcon Dam. Now I say "Viva Zapata!" — not Emiliano Zapata, that storied brigand-hero brought back to the public eye by John Steinbeck and Marlon Brando. Say rather "Long live the people of old Zapata," who with no choice but Hobson's had to pull themselves up by their two-century-old roots, watch the bulldozers and scrapers move in, and the Rio Grande roar down upon them, drowning memories and hopes, all they held dear, in the name of progress.

I suppose the good of the many must take precedence over the suffering of a few. Stout hearts and stoic faces; fortunately they had them, those descendants of the *conquistadores,* who got the word — "Move! The Rio Grande is taking over." There was nothing new about that. The river had taken over many a time in their lives. Families had fled before the raging torrent of the flood, a bundle of clothing over one arm, kids and a couple of chickens in hand. The floods came and went, in their own sovereign time, leaving the land deeper, richer, and blacker for the river silt; leaving the stout rock houses standing as they have for two hundred years.

This was different: deliberate destruction. For a cause, like most systematic destruction. The floods and drouths would be stopped by the construction of the Falcon Dam. Out of the wild brush country of the Rio Grande the United States and Mexico built this huge retainer at a cost of $60,000,000 — and many heartaches.

Co-operation and progress, desolation for two entire towns, one on each side of the river. The mayor of Guerrero, on the Mexican side, lived in a house that was built in the year that George Washington won our independence from England. On the American side, the pioneers whose homes were drowned received their land grants as prizes from the kings of Spain to daring adventurers, the conquerors of the New World.

The flooding of the two towns, Zapata, Texas, and Guerrero, Mexico, formed a lake forty miles long, a joint venture of international co-operation by the United States and Mexico.

The dam is supposed to be insurance against the disastrous floods that periodically wipe out thousands of acres of cotton and other crops in the Lower Rio Grande. It is sound government insurance against the killing drouths the Valley has suffered over the years. It has the capacity to limit the discharge of the greatest of floods that have rolled down the Rio Grande during the past fifty years, such as the one in 1932 when 190,000 cubic feet of water passed Rio Grande City each second.

By treaty, the United States and Mexico divide the water equally. Power is allotted on the basis of 58.6 per cent for the United States and 41.4 per cent for Mexico.

Greater benefit for the many at the expense of the few. This is progress.

What of the people on both sides of the river, whose ancient home were drowned by the dammed-up flow of the river and the rainfall? The shrines of generations of people who had the toughness and resistance to fight for survival over encroaching brush, Indians, bandits, Comanche slave traders who captured and sold their sons in the slave market at New Orleans, the river itself, and all the elements?

The Latin Americans, resigned and used to suffering for generations, were still hard put to keep themselves within bounds when they saw relics that were sacred to them ripped from the kindly arms of the earth where they had slept in safety for centuries. A race profoundly religious, and of a religion which believes fully in the "resurrection of the body and the life everlasting, amen," had to stand by with silent tongues and powerless hands while trucks came with shovels and winches and tore the slabs from the graves, scooped up the coffins from their resting places, and dumped them unceremoniously in trucks to be hauled off to a "new" cemetery.

All Souls' Day is a serious business to many of us, especially to Latin Catholics. It is more to them than just Memorial Day. Their dead are close to them, they visit them with flowers, in Mexico even with food. I am sure they tell them their troubles and ask for help and guidance. It is a warm and beautiful thing . . . not cold and fearful. Memories are kept green. The finest flowers are grown or manufactured for the decoration of the graves. Life goes on after death, to these people. They are more than mouth-Christians. In a bleak November mist the graves were moved to a bare spot three and a half miles away on a shifting, sandy hill.

Some of the tombstones bore birthdates of 1832, 1846, 1871. Some bear a later date, such as the stone that says "Pfc. Arnaldo Gonzales died Feb. 13, 1945, fighting with the 108th Medical Detachment."

The land appraisals were done by teams of qualified United States appraisers. The prices for lands where tomatoes, onions, and other crops furnished the livelihood were fair on the basis of present values.

All very fine in theory, but who does not know that kissing goes by favor? The wily, and political-minded, the people with pull, got the choice locations on the highways. They knew the only hope of Zapata's survival lay in the lake's becoming famous as a fishing center, bringing with it free-spending sportsmen, and the tourist trade.

In the new town it will cost much more to build dwellings comparable to the old. There is little irrigated land around the new Zapata, although an irrigation district has been formed. The rich bottom lands yielded heavy money crops in tomatoes. No matter how many new electric lights they have, and good, clean tourist accommodations with modern sewer systems, fine roads, nice breeze from the lake, New Zapata is not home to the old-timers. I cannot feel it ever will be.

There is a fine new school — but they were holding school in shacks when I visited Zapata, because the school building had not been accepted officially — some hitch in the final inspection contracts. Many residents refused the new land given them in lieu of the old. It was inferior in every sense. Unless they hit oil, how would they live?

"Come," said the restaurant proprietor, "tomorrow I will take you in a motorboat and you shall sit on top of what was once the courthouse of Zapata. The water is low now and the concrete top is visible. You can sit on it and fish." I declined with small thanks. I had seen the mesquite trees raising their drenched but still feathery heads out of the lake that covered them. The dam, a masterpiece of construction, looked like a menacing monster to me.

Mexican philosophy and Latin thinking have conditioned me. The daily risk of man against the elements, death by fire, or tornado, or flood is something I understand and accept. Extinction by mechanical contrivance, by slow strangulation of the heart and emotions, by poverty and despair, is a living death that makes me wish the men of science had left the lid shut on Pandora's box.

As they say in Zapata and Guerrero: "*No hay remedio.*" I am afraid there is no remedy. We have reached the point of no return.

The people in Guerrero, Mexico, were given homes of comparable value to those they were forced to abandon; again an opportunity for favoritism. The *pipero* with his little barrel of water mounted on wheels is out of business. Fine! Progress, says everyone but the *pipero*.

In the tower of the city hall there was a magnificent French clock, bought by José María Gonzales fifty years ago as a gift to his city. It is a complicated affair of cogs and gears and wires. It was dismantled and moved, piece by piece, to its new location, for it kept perfect time.

The church was built in 1747 at the cost of four bulls. Of this the natives cannot speak, the wound is too deep.

At San Ygnacio nearby there is a beautiful old ranch house and fort, built by the great-grandfather of the present owner. The walls of the fort are nearly two feet thick and over the *portón* on an arch stands a quadrant, a noble timepiece that for centuries has marked the hour. The arrow that slants through the quadrant is designed so that time can be read from inside the fort or from out in the street.

"Will you come in?" The owner and his wife invited us to the cool interior. "A gentleman took a photograph of our house for a guidebook, he said — but we have never seen it."

We showed them Dr. Rex Z. Howard's *Texas Guidebook*, and they were delighted to see their home in it.

"How is it you speak so much Spanish," they asked.

"My early days were spent in Brownsville."

"I, too, am from Brownsville. I attended the Incarnate Word Academy," Señora Uribe said.

"So did I. Do you remember Eva Yzaguirre?"

She put out her hand: "I *am* Eva Yzaguirre."

As we looked at pictures of her taken during her school days, I saw that it was indeed the girl whose long chestnut curls we had admired. It looks incredible, set down cold on paper. But this is Texas!

"My home was in Falcon," she said. I hesitated to ask questions, for I knew how she must feel.

"It is no use," she said. "We are better off than most, for we had this ranch on the higher land. What they gave us in exchange . . . it is laughable. We will never be so poor or so hungry as to sign for what they gave us. They were magnani-

mous when we had to leave our old homes. 'You may take anything you wish.' What can you take? A stone? What use to
loosen a brick? The doorsill of your birthplace? After all, we
had nothing there but our living — and our dead. We try not
to be bitter and hope only that our daughter will be saved such
an experience in her lifetime."

I know the century-old devotion to the soil; the love for the
birthplace of the Latin. The melancholy of the place seeped
into my heart, and I could feel with the Zapatans the muddy
waters rolling over the homes of their ancestors, washing above
their empty graves, while fish and turtles swam in and out of
doorways of windowless houses that stood with staring, empty
eye sockets.

The crashing roar and surge of the water flooding over
houses and churches, setting the bells into helpless crying made
me think of Debussy's "La Cathédrale Engloutie." The only
thought that consoled me was that these victims of progress
are good Christians, and the Christian religion is based on
sacrifice. Old Zapata and Guerrero. *Requiescat in pace.* The
Rio Grande had its own Sunken Cathedral.

But it is hard to sadden youth for long.

The courthouse crowd, unmistakable in any border town,
was having a coffee break at the highway café. The sadness of
Zapata had taken hold of me deeply and I had no joy in their
musical Spanish chatter. An old man with elaborate manners
but soiled and whiskery approached the group. Apparently
they all knew him. He was not mooching or cadging. I saw he
was not going to annoy them in any way. He wanted someone
to talk to. Nothing more. The young people greeted him politely, but did not ask him to sit down. He seemed neither
disappointed nor hurt. He walked over to a group of ranchers
and spoke for a minute. They received him courteously, but
did not pull up a chair. Finally, he went to the counter, and
drank a cup of coffee, standing up. All alone. He adjusted his

battered felt to the proper angle, swiped the back of his hand across his whiskers, clutched at the frayed rope that served to hold up his pants, and started for the door.

As he passed the table where we sat drinking coffee, Bob Pool looked up at him with a smile and said:

"How're you, sir?" in English.

Don Anybody stopped in his tracks. He looked at Bob with utmost gravity for several seconds.

"*Vd. me conoce?*" he said at last.

"What's he saying, Mary?"

"He says, do you know him?"

Bob shook his head.

The old man still stared at him. Slowly and stiffly, amost indignantly, he turned to me:

"*Porqué me saluda si no me conoce?* What does he mean by speaking to me if he doesn't know me?"

"*Ganas de saludarle, nada más.* Simple desire to greet you. Pure respect. Nothing more," I said.

He pondered for a long time, then with immense earnestness and dignity, said: "Very well. In *that* case, tell him I once spent twenty-seven months in Sedalia, Missouri, working on the railroad."

He made the ghost of a formal bow and shuffled off.

Twenty-four months later, Falcon Lake, created by the dam, is dry. There is no need to sit on the roof of the courthouse to fish. There is nothing to fish in. The youngsters and wild burros run in and out of the buildings, where what grass there is creeps up in its effacing kindliness. Jonah emerging from the belly of the whale could have been no more of a defiance to the believable than old Zapata resurrecting herself from the waters where she had been drowned, held under until the last air bubble reached the top. Once more, man proposes and God disposes. The floods will come again—and after that, who knows? *Viva Zapata! Viva Dios!*

Mother Spain had provided the religion that made this Texas land habitable — surely her saints would preserve it!

All along the River Road the influence of many saints was felt, and I began to wonder how many people really appreciated them.

What is a saint? I think saints are people who have lived exceptionally full spiritual lives, intensely human — yet divine beings who can never die. They help us in Heaven, as they did on earth, if approached in the proper spirit. Naturally, the petitions must be made in good faith, since the saints are sensitive souls — human enough to want us to respect their foibles. James Thompson says: "The Saints are they who know, and live up to the knowledge, that love is the one supreme duty and good, that love is wisdom and purity and valour and peace, and that its infinite sorrow is infinitely better than the world's richest joy."

Life among the Latin Americans has brought many Texans this added cultural and spiritual richness, which they might otherwise have missed. Non-Protestants have realized for years without end the great spiritual benefit the saints have to bestow, if they are asked to intercede. Many Protestants, far removed from Spanish religious influence, go merrily ahead and name their churches Saint Anne's, Saint Margaret's, Saint Mark's, and Saint Martin's. But most of these same Protestants would faint stone-dead away if someone suggested that they kneel down calmly and reasonably to talk over their troubles with the particular patron saint of the handsome church to which they contribute substantially and which they attend with considerable regularity.

The prosperous "executive's wife" with her station wagon parked out in front of Saint Martin's accepts with gratitude and complete faith the idea of Alcoholics Anonymous. Very few of them would bow their Lily Daché hats before Saint Martin — patron saint of the drunk and insane: "My husband is drinking too much. He was venomously insulting at the party last night. Nasty, fighting drunk. Won't you help me to help him? You know what a problem it is. Say a word to God in his behalf. I believe in your power to intercede for mortals, and the prayer of the righteous availeth much. I will light this candle in your honor to show you I am thinking of you, and will make a contribution to the poor — since you ask nothing for yourself — as a token of my gratitude."

Ah, San Martín! What things you have seen. On the Texas Border, San Martín not only looks after drunks and lunatics, but is good for horses, their health and healing. He rides a horse, in most of his representations, wearing a pied cloak of scarlet and white to symbolize the fact that he tore it in half to share it with a beggar who had none.

Saint Martin is also the patron of one of Texas' lucrative but plebeian crops: garlic. A farmer pulls a stunted head of garlic from the ground and asks: "*Ajo, por qué no medraste?*"

"*Porque para San Martín no me sembraste.*"

(Garlic, why didn't you prosper?

Because you didn't plant me by November 11th, you didn't dedicate me on Saint Martin's Day.)

To some of his ardent devotees, he is a great bringer of money. One woman I know prays to him regularly to help her financially. She places a small glass of water in front of his image on her altar and drops a dime in it. Then she places a blade of grass in the glass: "For your horse, San Martín."

After the good man has had a chance to work his miracle, my friend takes the water from the glass and sprinkles it around the doorstep of her house to make money grow. And somehow it does. Then she fills up the glass with more water. Same dime, however.

My own belief in Saint Anthony of Padua as a finder of lost articles is unshakable. When I was a child, our cook used to paste red tissue paper over the eyes of the image of Saint Anthony that stood on her little altar in the kitchen when she thought he was not using his eyes industriously enough in her behalf. One awful week that I remember, she hung the Good Man of Padua head first down the well for some imagined breach of contract.

Many years later, on a certain bitter day, at my wit's end, packed, ready to leave for a long, arduous journey — the keys to the safe deposit box could not be found. Both keys were fastened together, against all laws of common sense and the bank's instructions. The bank would have to blow the box open. That would cost a lot of money. All arrangements had been made, including some very close connections, for my departure that night. It was Friday. The bank could do nothing until Monday, if then.

Wailing, I called the Latin American friend who was giving me dinner and taking me to the train that night.

"Don't act like a *gringa*," she said. "Offer Saint Anthony thirteen of anything — thirteen cents, thirteen dimes. You'll find the keys before five o'clock. I'll come for you at six."

It had been many a year since I petitioned Saint Anthony to help me find the key to my skates: I wasn't sure he would co-operate with a Protestant who had been off among the Yankees for so many years. I should have known better than to doubt his broadness and efficacy, for it is just such charitable behavior that has given him so many converts to his credit. Led by an unseen hand, I found the keys in the most unlikely spot imaginable, in a place where I should never have dreamed of looking except for supernatural help. My relief was so great — and the cash saving so considerable! — that in view of the inflation that had overtaken the earthbound, I raised Saint Anthony's offering to thirteen dollars which I paid into the poor box in his own beautiful city, San Antonio, Texas.

Mary Austin Holley was also an admirer of Saint Anthony,

and said that he was a great favorite of sailors. In her "Brazos Boating Song" there is a line that reads: "Saint Antonio, send us a fair wind."

I heard a legend from a Border girl recently, told in a shy and enchanting manner, with utmost diffidence by a devout and reverent person.

"You know, Mary, they say Saint Anthony has the baby in his arms because the Blessed Virgin was embarrassed at having him, and Saint Anthony offered to carry him so nobody would notice anything." The dear humanness of carrying the baby proves my point that saints were superhumans.

An excellent bringer of husbands, Saint Anthony is a special favorite of old maids. He seems to have a special affection for all spinisters left to dress images. The unwed have been heard to beseech him as follows:

> "San Antonio Bendito,
> Tráeme un maridito!"
> (Blessed Saint Anthony,
> Bring me a dear little husband!)

And after they get the husband, they have been heard to say:

> "San Antonio Bendito,
> Quítame este maridote!"
> (Blessed Saint Anthony,
> Take this awful old husband away.)

The caprices of women, human or divine, are nothing new to Saint Anthony.

Many Texas ranchers have a firm belief in San Roque, the patron saint of dogs.

Farmers believe in San Ysidro Labrador, the tiller of fields and bringer of rain. Especially after a prolonged drouth the backsliders remember him. Just as no one remembers Santa Barbara until the thunder and lightning starts, too many farmers forget San Ysidro until the crops toast to a crisp under their stricken eyes. Then they kill snakes and hang them on the fences to bring rain — and drive the *fotingo*, the jaloppy, into town to see the saint-seller about a nice, new San Ysidro.

My friend the saint-seller tells me that modern methods have affected this generation of customers very greatly. A man appeared not long ago asking for a "pretty, new-style San Ysidro, riding on a tractor, with a nice striped umbrella over him to keep the rain from fading his pretty clothes and streaking his nice colored paint." San Ysidro Labrador is usually depicted plowing with an ancient Egyptian plow, drawn by a yoke of oxen. The younger generation demands progress of the saints. Modern methods, soil conservation, terracing, they are all very fine. But when the chips are down and the year's work is hanging like a pound of butter in a dog's mouth, then the old saints and the old ways are resorted to. If the young customer gets a San Ysidro, ancient or modern, ten to one he will fasten him to his own tractor as he goes on *calavereando*, a delightful play on words, meaning in Spanish to play wild practical jokes, and by its similarity in sound to the English word "cultivator" that implement is called a *calavera*, or prank. *Calavereando*, aided by San Ysidro or lone, is practical but it is no joke.

"These youngsters!" the saint-seller, who is a gifted writer, groans to me. "They don't care what they say. A *bonche de Tarzanes* (bunch of zoot suiters) came in here the other day asking for a nice statue of El Santo Niño del Hampa . . . the Holy Infant of the Holdup. They were pulling my leg."

There is no end to the number of saints whose good offices are known to Texans; they already have a bigger and better book of their own. But one more must be mentioned: Saint Rita of Cascia, the Sicilian Patron Saint of the Impossible. I shall be forever indebted to her if I succeed in finishing this book before it finishes me. The Mexicans have a story about her that is proverbial, and is applied to any person who is continually leaving things behind.

Saint Rita's history as a married woman was one of eternal strife and misery with her husband. Her patience under his diatribes and blows was great. Finally she could support life with him no longer. She took her scanty belongings and left.

"Get out and don't come back," her husband shouted.

The next day she returned to the house.

"What do you want?" her husband growled.

"My Blessed Virgin, hanging on the wall."

"Take it," he said.

Saint Rita took the picture down off the wall.

The next day she came back to the house again.

"What do you want now?" her husband yelled.

"The nail for my picture," she said.

"Take it out of the wall," he cried.

Saint Rita took out the nail.

"What are you going to do?" her husband asked.

"I am going away," Saint Rita said.

The next day she came back to the house again.

"What in the world is it this time?" her husband said.

"I am going to stop up the little hole left in the wall by the nail." Saint Rita produced a little ball of putty.

"What are you going to do now?" her husband asked.

"I am going to stay," Saint Rita said and took off her shawl.

When a guest on the Border comes back for his hat, and then for his pipe, and fifteen minutes later for the basket of oranges he was given and forgot to take home, the family smiles, exchanges looks and says: "Saint Rita's nail."

The same beneficent saint brought in the Santa Rita oil well that provides much of the black gold for the University of Texas. A nun in New York gave the driller the notion of dedicating the well to Saint Rita. She gave him a white rose and told him to cast the petals to the wind when he plunged the core of the well. Saint Rita and the rose did it. Roses are blessed on Saint Rita's Day, May 22.

With 9,300,000 people in Texas and more pouring in every

day, the saints in the Calendar are going to have their hands
full . . . especially watching over the old Texicans who love
and venerate them. You've got to have a warm human understanding between yourself and your saint before you can hang
him head first down the well. They add color and gaiety to
life, and inspire by their joyous example. We can push through
the thin paper leaves of the Christian Calendar very easily
and find relics of the old pagan gods, smiling and ready to help
as they were thousands of years before a solemn, rather lachry-
mose religion disciplined the humanity out of them.

Much of Texas was built in the name of the saints. They are
part and parcel of the scene and were meant to be enjoyed and
appreciated along with the inspiring missions and the jubilant
cathedral bells.

A land rugged and smooth, sinful and holy, violent and tender needs the saints.

Such is the land that formed my thinking and philosophy.
Drouth and flood. Changing weather and fluctuating finances.
Feuds and friendships. Ancient Spanish ways and modern
American methods. Holy Rollers and High Masses. Bullfights
and church bazaars. Bach and "El Abandonado." Bandits
and Baptists. Fighting cocks and May fêtes. Interscholastic
League Contests and international disputes.

The life of the time and place was a blend of the mystic and
the picaresque, colored with the romance of roguery. I am glad
that I had the opportunity to be awake and aware during so
exciting a period of life in Texas, for the memories of childhood
are deeply graven on the "smooth tablet" before the frenetic
lines of later experience have been scrawled in a tangled web
on its surface.

It all seems incredible to me now, as I look back in perspective.
In the vein of the old school of "they'll never take you alive"
novels, my father took me to one side, in 1917 when there was
an imminent possibility of being murdered during the Mexican

bandit trouble, and said gravely and calmly, "Don't try to run. It would only be worse. I'll save one shot for you and one for Mama." If I read that line in someone else's book, I would shriek at the melodrama. It was no laughing matter to my father, or to a twelve-year-old girl still wearing short socks, but a woman just the same. The saints had their hands full that year. I read again, in Walter Prescott Webb's *Texas Rangers*, the incredible story of those bandit raids. The sick feeling I had when "they sent word" of Mrs. Austin, sitting in the field by the bodies of her murdered husband and son to keep the coyotes off them, came back in full force. Judge Kleiber and Harry Wallis, fathers of my playmates, shot — and Dr. McCain, our beloved friend, killed. And to confuse youthful thinking even further, one of the bandit leaders, Aniceto Pisaña, had been a friend of my father's.

When brighter days came, I recall my mother lining up the thirteen pupils that made up the total enrollment of the Blalack District School she taught. Out in the middle of the trail that served as a path in front of the little rat-trap school in the heart of the *monte* she marched us. Heavy brush closed in on all sides of the one-room schoolhouse. To Mexican marauders on a raid, it would have been like finding a bird's nest on the ground.

We were lined up at stiff salute, heels together, toes out, to greet General John J. Pershing and his staff as they passed on their way to maneuvers at the old sugar mill a few miles away. The fine horses stamped to a stop in the thick dust, and Black Jack looked puzzled.

My mother thanked him for his service to Texas and its people in putting down the bandit trouble, and expressed the wish that he receive a suitable decoration from the government.

General Pershing's lantern jaw was steely and his eyes stern as he looked at the invitation to ambush that passed for a schoolhouse.

"Madam," he said, "it is you who should be decorated. Not I."

This was my Texas.

As I compared the present with the past, I saw that I had lived through a series of events in the evolution of the Valley not quite far enough back to be of much importance to the historians, but far enough removed for the present day to be unknown to many Americans. Looking back I thought: What an air of an epoch all this has!

Particularly along the River Road I pictured the brown-cassocked barefoot friars who had plodded its weary, dusty miles, taking no thought for their comfort nor even their personal safety. How deeply they had burned their brand on Texas! The Cross and the Crown are symbols, the everlasting imprint of the Old World on the New.

Along the nine-hundred-mile meander of the Rio Grande, the border of Texas, the landmarks were Hispanic in character from little Santa María near Brownsville to ancient Ysleta, and the inspiring Cristo Rey on the mountain peak at El Paso.

The craggy grandeur of the Big Bend of the Great River, an unknown and alien Texas to me, would be awesome, I knew, but the silver ribbon of the Spanish language would unite me to it speedily. How quickly and how firmly I would be captured by its glory, I could not guess.

4. THE BIG BEND

EVEN THOUGH fact and reason reassured me, when I saw the grandeur of the Big Bend, I kept saying to myself: Can this be Texas? Have I not fallen asleep and wakened in the high sierras of Mexico? Here was a Texas beyond anything dreams could produce — and the dream a reality.

Where is the Big Bend?

That is a controversial question. There are as many answers as there are inhabitants. Each Big Bender feels that his own boundary description of the region is the official one. And why not? You can stand on any peak and look over your shoulder at yesterday or look ahead of you into day after tomorrow. In the desert section, centuries of sand and dust swirl around you. When the gray eddies and whirlpools die down, it would not be surprising to behold the Sphinx.

A Mexican vaquero of nearly a century ago described the Big
Bend Country something like this:

You go south from Fort Davis
Where the rainbow waits for the rain,
Where the river is kept in a stone box
And the water runs up hill,
And the mountains tower into the sky
Except when they disappear to visit other mountains at night
There is nothing down there for the cows to eat.
So they have learned to live without eating.
There is room for a thousand cows.
But not for ten thousand.
And how far is this?
One hundred miles. Possibly two.
Quién sabe?"

The soul of Spain is here. Santa Elena Canyon is the stone
box and the mountains in late evening light do appear to
double-up for night. The distance is roughly a hundred miles
if you go by Alpine and was surely twice that a hundred years
ago, by the tortuous path the vaquero must have taken from
Fort Davis. The Big Bend region gets its name from the great
dip to the south made by the Rio Grande about fifty miles below Presidio. The broad arc of the river cradles a region un-
paralleled in the United States in that it is an almost unaltered
area of mountainous Mexican Border wilderness. The solitude
and ruggedness deepen as one winds into the heart of the Big
Bend National Park in the Chisos Mountains.

Most of Brewster County, Texas' largest with almost six thousand square miles, is considered Big Bend Country — yet the
population is so sparse that rarely are more than fifty votes
cast in the lower Big Bend.

Laura Gilpin's book of photographic studies, *The Rio
Grande, River of Destiny,* contains superb photography of the
Big Bend. To look at the pictures is the next thing to being

there, for her camera reproduces not only the face of a mysterious region, but its heartbeat as well.

How many times did the unknown vaquero-poet see in the black, volcanic evening a ghostly full moon rise over the jagged rock of the sierra on his right, while a blood-red sun low down in the west dipped into the purple sea of the horizon at his left?

This I have seen, and like Joshua, commanded the sun to stand still, and with as little success.

Along the side of the road, in the rocky chips, wild mint and creeping sage send out puffs of incense. A bell rings silently inside the beholder, and he begs: "Thy blessing, Lord."

The ritual ends. An unseen hand snuffs out the cathedral candles and the traveler pushes on, restored. Warm, enormous stars stand out, almost close enough to touch.

From mysteries such as these the ranchers, men and women, gather strength to face the unequal struggle with the capricious seasons. They call up a more fortunate rancher who has grass, tell him how many head they want to run, and ask, "How much?" Then they nail up the doors and windows, put the brake on the windmill, and start "riding the chuck-line route": visiting more fortunate friends.

"We'll go back when it rains," they say calmly. "We're drouthed-out. Might's well admit it."

"When did you last have grass?"

"Nineteen forty-one. It rained good. Not enough to flood, but enough for grass."

"When was another good year?"

"Lessee. Nineteen-fourteen was fine!" They turn their backs on what has been home through fat years and lean, and go into town, some to do carpentry, or drive buses, or some to write books, a few to work on magazines and newspapers, or to fry steak in roadside cafés. The spiritual strength and beauty of these men and women matches the great region that produced them.

"The atomic fission boys might knock off a few chips and splinters, but by the Almighty God that made them, they won't make much of a dent in them rocks." So runs the sentiment in the region of the Big Bend. What could the atom split that extremes of temperature had not done long ago?

The A-bomb or the H-bomb might reduce the Santa Elena Canyon to rubble, but they could never carve out anything comparable to the grandeur produced by the bold strokes of violent and sudden temperature changes. Rocks and mountain fastnesses were split asunder as though with a giant wedge, by the molten fire of noontide and the deadly freezing drop at night countless aeons ago.

The glory of the Big Bend National Park starts at Persimmon Gap, the northernmost entrance to the park, and to my mind, ends only when the beholder dies. Maybe not even then. I make no comparisons to the other natural wonders of the western United States. What I saw was entirely within the picture frame of Texas, and contrasts only with other parts of this state: that is to say, from sea level at Brownsville to eight thousand feet at Guadalupe Peak. The mood was set for me outside of Marathon on the way to the Park: five antelope of indescribable grace bounded along in gentle parabolas parallel to the car, leaps Nijinsky would have loved. The soaring of the antelopes was contagious to the human spirit, and I had that same feeling of primordial peace that comes from Rousseau's paintings of animals.

In the Park itself, my main impression was much the same: unspoiled, natural beauty. Grandeur, not just bigness. Great craggy copper-rose cliffs rise sheer and majestic on every side. The rosy red of the mountains is brocaded with the deep black-green of the vegetation clinging to a precarious toe-hold. The effect is of a heavy rust-colored silk with an exotic pattern of blackish-green cut velvet superimposed on it. High soar the peaks in shapes to stagger the imagination. Cathedrals, palaces,

Valhalla. Those and many more: one the unmistakable image of the Alamo, high in the clouds, immortal as its history.

Colorful immensity and primeval magnificence fill the beholder with a great sense of upheaval, a feeling that gods older than ours clapped their hands to command the canyons into sudden glorious being. The pedestrian mind of man is linked for an instant with the force that created man and mountain.

Up among the craggy cliffs and precipitous ledges there is a sense of gigantic turbulence. One feels that the gods are still engaged in a primordial rough and tumble, an Olympian roughhouse that gouges and rends chasms through the heart of the mountains.

The scene before me, like much of Texas, was simultaneously my inspiration and despair. How should I attempt to picture such vastness of space and spirit? Beethoven, in a super-symphony, might have succeeded in communicating the glory. Fate would need to knock loud and long before this majesty would open the door.

A year after this section was written an article on Texas by Ludwig Bemelmans appeared in the *McCall's* Magazine, in which he too expressed the thought that only Beethoven could capture the essence of the Big Bend. It was interesting to me that two practicing gourmets whose writing has been largely of a humorous nature should reach into the roster of the Immortals and seize upon the same genius as the only one who might have captured and put into imperishable form the Big Bend of the Rio Grande. Unless a titan endowed with musical power, imbued with melodic nobility emerges from the amorphous cacophonists of the present, the symphony of the Big Bend will never be written. Beethoven has no more of a successor in sight than has Shakespeare.

The haze-crowned beauty of the Park is awesome and ennobling. Here *genus homo*, the litterbug, has not yet left his spoor. His ugly, mendacious signboards have not marred the pristine spaces of the Park and Chisos Basin.

The wild garden of the Big Bend is exciting. Where have the enterprising textile designers been all these years? Instead of hideous wagon wheels and cattle brands, twisted wooden ropes, and beastly, abnormal blossoms in garish colors, a whole related series of prints, drapery materials, upholstery fabrics, and carpetings could be worked out combining the natural colors and designs of the rocks, plants, and flowers, against various backgrounds. The century plant, seemingly carved of antique green-bronze iron beautifully corroded by age, holds up its branching candelabra to the sky. The waxen bells of the yucca, the giant Spanish dagger, are all begging for some sympathetic hand to set them to work, to bring them inside our houses.

Throughout the Park, the cinnamon-pink bark of the madrona and the Texas persimmon trees, their lovely round dark blue-green leaves, and intriguingly shaped trunks, twisted

Century Plant

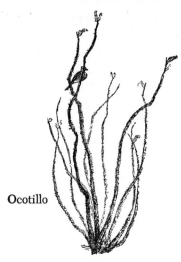

Ocotillo

and gnarled stand out as colorful accents in the landscape. Here and there clumps of ocotillo rise in breathtaking splendor, their great dark green stems reach out like slender fingers clutching bunches of red firecrackers, holding their scarlet bursts of flame against the sky. There is no end to the intricacy and beauty of the plant life in the Big Bend.

The Park, and most of the Big Bend region, is little known because of inaccessibility. I think there is something in the atmosphere that is more than a little frightening to hot-shot extroverts, so the Park is unspoiled. So far.

Those who love and respect the Big Bend suffer a feeling of ambivalence toward publicity: they want everyone who can to come and enjoy the Park, but at the same time they want to preserve the primeval quality that sets it apart. There is nothing there that will attract the undesirable tourist. If the Park Boards, National and State, maintain the same high standards of taste and ethics they have shown up to date, there will be small danger of week-end hell-raisers appearing there in numbers large enough to matter. They want liquor and honkytonks. The drive is too long for them in the first place. Scenery, nature trails, riding, exploring, and the creative arts of writing, sketching, or photography hold no appeal for them.

"Seems like I've heard of the Big Bend National Park," Texans have been heard to say, "but if I was gonna drive that far, I'd wanta go some place where I'd feel like I'd bin somewhere: Las Vegas or the Carlsbad Caverns!"

Castalon and the Canyon of Santa Elena — these I would see. The Chisos Mountains' wild wonderland would be the background.

Where were the human figures? There were not too many in sight. I felt certain that those we might ferret out would not be disappointing. Man and the way he has stacked up against the combined beauty and malevolence of the country would give perspective and contrast, add to the meaning of the scene. The mountains are higher, the sky farther away, and distances more vast when the forked radish draws himself up to his full height against their background. Man is magnified or dwarfed by the canyons. He is tried in the crucible of unpitying and implacable nature. No man has altered that country, but it has altered many a man.

Over the chalk-white, dusty roads full of ruts we drove to Castalon, pretty much the end of the world. The river flowed serenely by a lush cotton field. Across it rose the great Mexican cliffs. Castalon Peak stood out in bold relief. After seemingly endless jolts we came to La Harmonia, to the store that is one of the three buildings in the town: ranch owner's house, manager's house, and the store. It is post office, drugstore, drygoods emporium, grocer shop, hardware store, filling station — the works.

They had sold the last huge bear trap in stock. That was a disappointment, as I had heard of the size and businesslike quality of the trap. They still had wooden wheels better than five feet in diameter for oxcarts; rope made of *lechugilla,* strong and beautiful. All the appurtenances of life in the outposts, for two nations. There were patent medicines for every imaginable ill, saddle blankets and sewing thread, shoes, scythes, and hemp *bosales,* hackamores, halters for leading horses and donkeys. Oil lamps and candles. A few artificial flowers. Cosmetics, and the candy that is universal, hard and tasteless, but highly colored.

Two Mexican men stared at me and discussed me as though I were in the next county, just as they did when I was a child. I conversed in Spanish with Mr. Uranga, manager of the store. The onlookers listened and commented on the color of my skin, hair, and eyes with all the freedom in the world. "This *huera* has stolen our idiom," they agreed. "It is a marvel, these women of writing. I have seen one in Mexico. But brunette." The store smelled ancient, and of the Border: coal oil, dusty seed corn, and loud candy.

I felt a great desire to pitch a tent by the river, under the cottonwoods, and stay in such a peaceful region until I was glutted with quiet and repose. "How lovely," says the Mexican, "to do nothing and then rest." Castalon is the place for it.

Down the dusty, choking roads again to catch the sun just right on the Santa Elena Canyon. My hair felt as though it had been in a plaster cast overnight. The cementlike dust has an adhesive quality, a kind of inanimate perversity. As I fought the chalky powder, I could scarcely believe that between the hours of sunrise and sunset I could drive from due West to deep East — to a woodland of lush, velvety pines, growing out of thick sandy loam covered with pine needles and ferns, myrtles and hollies. Later, I did just that and fixed forever in my mind the two major divisions of Texas: climate, scene, and way of life. Brown West. Green East. And each with its own charm. The West Texan, inured to hardship, tough as a boot, his hide cured to the color and texture of jerked beef, and his heart as big as Brewster County. The East Texan, an easygoing old Plantation person inhabiting the replica of the Old South he has created, can afford to let nature take its course with fifty inches or more of annual rainfall. He can lie under a tree, move his chaw of terbaccer from one cheek to the other, grin up at you and say: "I'm too lazy to hit a lick at a snake!" As I studied the chasms and gorges, I kept reminding myself that there was another side to the Texas coin.

In the late afternoon, without having seen another living soul, we drove up within walking distance of the river. I picked up a good sized stick and charged off through the underbrush of willows and *tules* to see the famous canyon.

Just as I got my first glorious sight of it, something crashed through the brush behind me and I froze in my tracks, expecting a dinosaur. It was only a bald-faced cow, annoyed at having her afternoon tea interrupted. I waved the stick and shouted *"Huy!"* and she charged off again.

Pictures of the Santa Elena are many and beautiful; adjectives are louse-words to begin with, but the Big Bend makes them excusable. They were all used up. I was fresh out, and a good thing, too. Nothing in the way of description — and I have read some good ones, is adequate. The impact of the first sight is a thing to be experienced. It defies adequate description. It is a little like looking into the nave of a gigantic cathedral, with the river flowing through the middle of it. An old hymn mentions "the beautiful, the beautiful river, that flows by the throne of God." That's as close as I can come, and it's not original.

Since Bob Pool was far off, busy with cameras and film, I indulged a secret yen that had nibbled at me for a long time to try out a real, live rocky echo. What was to stop me? The cows wouldn't mind. I felt absolutely certain that there were no other human beings within forty miles. The first timid, rusty notes of Thrane's "Norwegian Echo Song" came back not once, but twice. Magnified and incredibly improved. Like certain microphones, the echoing crags improve voices, conceal defects, and intoxicate the performer with his own golden notes. I shifted into high gear. It was many years since I had attacked the Queen of the Night Aria from *The Magic Flute;* I knew I should never again have such an uncritical audience nor such acoustical assistance.

As in Robert Nathan's *One More Spring* when the fiddle player shows his old press clippings, and the hero of the book says, "You should have stayed in Albany. In Albany you were 'adequate,'" coloraturas should stay in the canyon. The echo was flattering enough to lure me on and on. The time lag between the emission of the notes and the return of the phrase by the echo allows the performer to hear himself. A crashing sound behind me almost stopped the music. I brandished the sick behind my back at the cows, who must have been responding in classic fashion as they did to Orpheus' lute. I kept swinging the stick wildly behind me till something made me turn. A man of about seventy, his decent gray-haired wife, and their son and daughter (or so they looked to me) — neatly dressed tourists who might have come from Des Moines, were gaping at the Laughing Loon of the Big Bend. There was nothing left to do: I waded into the river and sat down on a rock looking like the Misogynist Monkey on the cover of *Life.*

Not even tourists could mar the canyon. I thought again of the vaquero and his line in the poem: "Where the river is kept in a stone box"; Santa Elena canyon is the stone box, part of the Eternal Mysteries.

Jouncing along in the jeep, I remembered all I had read about the formation of so fantastic a region. The reasonings and reconstructions of geologists seemed less theoretical and improbable to me as I looked at the Chisos area at close range.

The Rio Grande, cutting its way to the sea, formed a great lake at the southern foot of the Chisos until it broke through the barrier of the Sierra del Carmen at Boquillas Canyon. Proof that this area was once a great tropical swamp, dominated by enormous trees and inhabited by prehistoric reptiles of great size, is found in the fossils uncovered by the scientists. Near Castalon we had seen a petrified tree stump fourteen feet in diameter — one of the largest known to science. Anthropologists as well as geologists are interested in the region because of the extensive and well-preserved Indian remains discovered in the caves of the Chisos.

The name of Chisos Mountains is one that invites the student of language and the lover of words to delve into the mysteries of adequate translation. Chisos is translated and accepted commonly as meaning a ghost, or phantom. It is supposed to be Indian, and refers to Alsate and his squaw who escaped from their captors and returned to their mountains to die, the last of their tribe. Early Spanish records reveal that one of the predatory Indian tribes first encountered at Junto de los Rios (the site of the present town of Presidio, Texas) was then called Chisos. There is little doubt that the word is a corruption of the Spanish word *hechizo,* meaning a sorcerer's spell or an enchantment, a malevolent condition brought about by supernatural means. Magicians and sorcerers did conjure up ghosts and phantoms. Perhaps the Indians were under the spell of the wizardry of the mountains. They may have called themselves the Hechizos, the Wizard Indians, soon shortened to Chisos, the Casters of Spells. The name fits the Chisos Mountains: the great craggy peaks often look in the late evening like ghosts, or weird double exposures.

It would be good to be able to ask D. H. Lawrence what the word meant to him, for he knew more about the Mexican Indian by some intuitive process than most anthropologists learn through research. He was a Chiso himself. All through the incredible region I kept thinking of *The Plumed Serpent*, especially where I saw the pink rattlesnake. There is no liquor in the Park, but there are pink rattlers of a particularly venomous kind.

The Big Bend is a biological island, on which various flora and fauna have taken refuge. The isolation of this area is due to the climate, ranging from subtropical to Canadian, and to the position of the region. Cut off by the desert from the rest of a world in which they could not survive, plants, animals, and insects survived in this island fastness. There are certain forms of life found in the Big Bend which exist nowhere else in the United States. An outstanding example among the trees is the weeping juniper, a species discovered in 1924 at an elevation above 7000 feet. The tree is certainly a rarity, but it only looked wilted to me. The Colima warbler is one of the American birds found only in the Big Bend.

Aside from the Chisos Mountains Basin and Santa Elena, Mariscal, and Boquillas Canyons, the chief points of interest in the Park are the fossil beds, the Badlands, Indianola Peak, Mule Ear Peaks, the Talley (Cow Heaven), Chilicotal and Mariscal Mountains, Glenn Springs, Hot Springs, San Vicente, and Boquillas.

The only improved and state-maintained highway in the area skirts the Chisos on the north, with a spur leading into the basin in the heart of the mountains, and terminates at the mouth of the Santa Elena Canyon. There is a state highway from Alpine which enters the southwestern corner of the Park at Study Butte, over a desert expanse totally different from the approach via Marathon.

The National Park Service has kept man-made construction to a minimum. The roads are good and there are carefully marked low-water bridges in the area. The signs may seem unrealistic or unnecessary to the inexperienced traveler during most of the year, but there have been tragic happenings in the Chisos Mountains, largely owing to failure to heed the warning signs. It is not safe to ignore them. On the measuring posts is printed: Do Not Attempt to Cross When Water Reaches This Mark. The floods, like the Texas norther, come sudden and soon. It is not fun to run at full tilt ahead of a rushing wall of water churning over what a few seconds before was a parched, cracked creek bed. All markings are plain and plentiful. Water for boiling-over car engines heated by the steep climb is placed at strategic points along the road leading into the Basin. There are the fewest possible buildings in sight. The Park Service deserves the gratitude of the American public for its unflagging effort to preserve the primitive, natural integrity of the Park.

The joint project of a State, Federal, and International Park was set in motion by the depression. The Mexican government set aside some 400,000 acres on the Mexican side for the creation of a smiliar park for their people to enjoy.

The work of the CCC camps in the Chisos Mountain Basin in helping preserve the primal beauty of the scenic areas for future generations is too often overlooked in the avalanche of criticisms that have fallen upon the whole WPA system. The memory of man is short, but I remember droves of young civilians, hungry and easy prey for hoodlum gangs, ready recruits for the thugs of the day, who got wholesome constructive outdoor work under the program. Every one of them, man or boy, who lifted a rock, helped build a monument to himself and to the program.

The accommodations in the Basin are simple and in full keeping with the elemental surroundings. There is a passable concession restaurant and an excellent stand where postcards, books, pamphlets, and printed matter of various kinds may be purchased. The rates for accommodations are fair, as is true throughout the State and National Park Service.

Maggy Smith at San Vicente was somebody we ought to see, a figure to be reckoned with on the river. She used to run the bathhouse concession at Hot Springs, but the government refused to renew her contract. Maggy says politics. Others say unsanitary premises. Between midwifing, postmastering, and general activities at her "trading post" in San Vicente, Maggy seems to put in a full day. We saw her mail box on a post about two miles from her store: Margaret Smith, San Vissenty, Texas.

I wanted to see her because of a yarn I had heard about her. Her son, who is a jockey, took a small tank and put it on a shelf outside the house. A few feet of pipe were threaded in and Maw had running water. A day or so later somebody asked her how it felt to have running water in the place.

"Lord," she said, "I bin seasick all day!"

Down the road over hummocks and hollows, with no regard for car springs or sacroiliacs, we drove till we reached a small adobe building, a brush arbor, a chicken shed, and one mud hut with a goat tethered nearby. For the irreducible minimum, it took the cake. You couldn't call it a wide place in the road, because it was the end of the line.

"Maggy's gone. You passed her on the road in the new pick-up. Her sister's sick and she's bein' drove to Uvalde," a young woman we took to be Maggy's daughter told us.

One of the grandchildren was making hay with the brightly colored nylon panties, tearing them from the glass showcases and strewing them over the floor. The office, where the big safe is, had iron bars across it. *Candelilla* wax is outlaw traffic, but on the river a dollar is a dollar and damn hard to get. The Mexicans trust Maggy and spend money with her. She gives credit and charges outlandish prices. The back room had rocking chairs and two nice electric refrigerators in it. You could buy votive lights and beer.

"How do we get to San Vicente?" Bob Pool asked a white-haired grandmotherly-looking woman who was talking to a young man in the back room.

"This is San Vissenty," she said.

As we went out the door, she lifted her voice and said in edged tones: "Imagine anybody not knowin' where San Vissenty, Texiss, is?"

Having seen the Park from the northern approach to the center of the Chisos Basin, we made another run on it coming in from Alpine this time. We converged on the central portion in a kind of pincers movement, although we had to operate one side of the pincers at a time.

In that natural fortress there was bound to be good hunting and fishing; for characters, I mean. It's always open season on humans. I do not know the "legal limit" on the bag in the Big Bend, but those I stalked were certainly rewarding. There were none in evidence small enough to "throw back."

The road from Alpine into the Big Bend National Park, leading to the Chisos Basin and the Park proper, is in good shape, but I was feeling cross for the first few miles. A tourist in Alpine was standing by the car when I came out of the drugstore. He mentioned the Rhode Island license — always a conversation piece in Texas. "I see you're a writer; I've just been looking at your notes." The clipboard was on the seat. One of my many quirks is detesting people who peep at my notebooks or paw over material. I cannot bear to have it clapper-clawed by anyone. He could see I wasn't listening to his catechism of "Do you know So-and-So in Providence?" and finally shivered off, smiling timidly.

"Well, write pro-Texas!"

I hadn't made a pun in a week and was feeling extremely virtuous. The heat and sign on the lumberyard across the way, "We Put the Pine in Alpine," weakened my resolve. I am afraid I shouted: "God pro-Texas."

The road was hot and powder-dry, and the pun lay on my conscience, heavy as a country dumpling. The strength and beauty of the mountains, the sun bouncing back on the white, winding road soon restored my joy. The grasses and small low mats of dog fennel that edge the road, starred with their golden discs, grow elegantly along the sides of the highway. The taller shrubs seem to fall naturally into a graceful grouping.

The weeds in Texas are artistic. Mary Austin Holley observed in her voyage over a hundred years ago the elegance of the natural plant arrangement. Landscape gardeners would do well to copy the subtlety of nature's own method of facing-down. The mats of creeping *Zinnia pumila,* white-daisy, gold aster, tansy aster, blackfoot, and *limoncillo* that smells delightfully like fresh lemons grow among the rock chips at the edge of the roads with a noble disregard for drouth.

There is an old saying that in Texas everything either sticks, stinks, or stings. Maybe so, if you have no better sense than to try to pick up things, or get too close to them. I do not find it true. No tame herb garden can equal the fragrance of the various sages, mints, and germander. The clean invigorating air breathes of leaves and flowers. "Here shoots the healing plant," just as in Haydn's *Creation.* The whole atmosphere is charged with newness and freshness, as though a new world washed by the sun and the wind appeared every morning. That is one reason the natives love the region. Dry desert, white alkali dust over everything. Ghosts that once were towns. Relics of former activity, mining shafts rise against the purple mountains. Charitable night cloaks it all every evening. And every sunrise, a fresh start. Nothing else seems to matter much. There is no possibility of growing food for man or beast, so the lush growth takes place inside the spirit of man. He loafs and invites his soul. There would never be time enough to fight the dust or keep things cleaned up. But there is time to let the mind soar.

Study Butte looks like the quintessence of all the Alkali Ike sets in the silent movies. It is the jumping-off place, the back of beyond. Bleak. Powdery. Dry. One wooden store, Poke

Hinson's "Night Club" & General Store, like the granddaddy
of every store in the Western movies. A covey of adobe one-
room houses clusters round the mother-house. But you can
see Santa Elena Canyon and if there is any breeze, you will
get it on the gallery.

"You Poke Hinson?" I said to the man with a quid of tobacco in his mouth.

He nodded: "Sit down."

He wore a cap just like Popeye's. He had a rakish air that
reminded me of Barnacle Bill the Sailor. His sport shirt was
unbuttoned all the way down and his belly got full benefit of
whatever breeze wandered by. He wore a low-cut sneaker
of maroon hopsacking on one foot and a high-cut tennis shoe
of navy blue on the other, both well slashed to accommodate
his bunions. A younger man in khaki sat across from him.

"I'da stood up when you come in, but I got a bad knee." He
put his beer can down politely.

A lady was sitting on a cot with her back turned to the assembly. There was a stack of books in front of her, and she
was reading a newspaper, oblivious to everything else.

"Barry Scobee over at Fort Davis told us to come to see you. He said you were a sociable man."

Poke Hinson grinned.

"Now this Doubleday Dollar Book Club isn't bad at all." The lady turned around and entered the discussion. She handed me a membership blank. Her intelligent eyes were the blue of old-fashioned blue glass beads and her expression gentle.

"You like book clubs?" I said.

"Saves a lot of trouble, living out here," she said. I began to wish I had brought in a pad and pencil, but didn't want to make a move to break the current.

"That's a big ditch." Bob Pool gestured to the narrow gash that is formed by the Santa Elena Canyon.

"Yeah," Poke Hinson drawled. "That's when I brought them Indians into this country, to dig that ditch and dreen off the great sheet of water that covered all this. Lost money, took the contract too cheap . . ."

"My right leg is already two inches longer than my left one," I laughed.

"That's right, Poke," Mrs. Hinson said. "Go ahead and shoot your big face off and land in the papers again. I'll have another batch of those letters to answer." Some sixth sense carried a whiff of printer's ink to Mrs. Hinson.

"You are the smallest Chamber of Commerce in the world, aren't you?"

"Feller down at Alpine wrote a piece about me bein' the President of it an' Ollie the Secretary. The wire services picked it up and all hell busted loose." His use of newspaper jargon delighted me.

"We got hundreds of letters inquiring about Study Butte, what business opportunities were here, and how housing conditions were. All that kind of stuff. And I had to answer them all." Mrs. Hinson looked rueful.

"I notice you say Stoody Butte."

"Feller named Study founded it," Poke said.

"What you building?" Bob Pool asked.

Poke turned to look at two Mexican laborers who were fiddling with a pile of adobes.

"Clint's puttin' up a buildin'," he said.

Clint Fulcher was the man in khaki. He joined the conversation.

"Poke put a fire under the washpot an' burnt his courthouse down. I didn't pay no attention to it, just figgered Poke was fixin' to wash again." He turned to the two Mexicans who had come up on the gallery. "*Pasen a tomar una.*"

"*No más una?*"

"If you get more than one beer, you'll pay for it yourself. I gave you one at noon." The Mexicans grinned and went into the store.

"They bought them a surveying gun, then went an' bent the barrel to make it go in the case."

"Wouldn't you like me to get you some beer?" Bob Pool went into the store to get a Coca-Cola for himself.

"I'll take anybody's money." Poke Hinson got up and took care of all three customers at once.

"Many dudes come by?" I asked.

"Yeah." Poke had returned to the box he sat on. "They sidle up to you, tryin' to impress you, like. After they get their nerve up they shove one o' them two dollar and seventy-nine cent Geiger counters in front of you. 'Ever see one o' these?' they say. 'Yeah,' I tell 'em. 'I take *True West Magazine.*'"

"One man had a scintillator worth four hundred and seventy-five dollars. Plus tax," Mrs. Hinson said.

"Plus freight," Poke added.

"Much uranium around here?"

"Naw. Just a trace," Poke said. "They make you so tired, never let the damn thing outa their hands not even when they . . ." His eye wandered to an adobe building out to the rear. Mrs. Hinson fixed him with a look.

"We got rooms," Poke said.

"They're not fancy like up at the Park." Mrs. Hinson motioned toward the adobe houses.

" 'Course we don't stick you like they do neither," Poke said. "Reckon what would happen if the Geiger counter started ticking while . . ." I looked over my shoulder at the small adobe structure out back.

"I saw some Uranium Sittatoriums over around Brownwood. Two dollars an hour to sit with your feet in the dirt," I said.

I could hear the Geiger counter, plus cash register, clicking in Poke's head. "Be a boom in real estate," he grinned. "Now these doctors . . ."

Poke broke off and went in to serve the two Mexicans who had decided to have a beer at their own expense. He came back in a few minutes. "Now they got all kinds of 'em. Five of 'em out here lookin' at the rocks and pokin' an' pryin' . . . every one of 'em was a doctor. When I ast 'em what kind they was, they was doctors of rocks, an' oil, an' minerals an' stuff like that. I looked at 'em an' sez: 'Doctors! All five o' you. An' not one o' you can do nobody no good!' "

"Not too long since there were Indians depredating around the Big Bend Country, was it?" I asked.

"Back in the eighties, one man turned loose twenty thousand head an' got back eleven hundred."

"I'd certainly like to talk to some of those old-timers. That man's dead, isn't he?"

"Too dead to move," Mrs. Hinson said.

"Skin's the word, Ollie! Too dead to skin!" Fulcher said.

Seemed to me it was pretty descriptive either way.

"This is my idiot sister," Fulcher added.

"Reminds me of the story Barry Scobee told me about the time four Mexicans got drunk over in Fort Davis," I said.

"Three of them decided to shoot the fourth one. They did, and threw his body in a clump of cactus over by his house. A bunch of Boy Scouts found it, badly decomposed. They buried him and forgot about him for several months. Then someone in his family started wondering about the cause of death. The authorities decided to exhume the body, provided they could find a Disinterested Observer.

"Barry Scobee was out on the highway when the Law drove up. 'Scobee, you're the Disinterested Observer. I'm appointin' you as such!'

"Scobee said it was one of those freak July nights in the Davis Mountains: windy and icy cold. The investigation had to be carried on at night and the police car picked him up rather late. He wore a heavy leather jacket.

"When they arrived at the graveyard, three Mexican grave-diggers were hard at work, opening the grave. The doctor who was to do the official examination and two police officers got out of the back seat. Scobee and the driver remained in the front seat watching the gravediggers raise the coffin out of the dank earth.

" 'I believe they've got it,' the driver said and hunched himself forward over the wheel for a better look. An unearthly wail, as of a thousand tortured souls, split the air, only to taper off in a wild shrieking cry. The Mexicans dropped the box and set a world sprinting record through the brush. The driver had leaned forward on the siren of the police car without realizing it. The place, the time, and the mission were all distasteful to the Mexicans. It was against their religion in the first place, and they were afraid of ghosts. Finally the police got them stopped long enough to reason with them and induced them to go back to opening the coffin. They set it in front of the car lights and took the lid off. Scobee said a most horrible, unbearable odor filled the air, utterly indescribable, as though the nauseous odors of the charnel houses of the earth had been forced into one foul flask. The doctor took hold of the head of the corpse and two men took hold of the feet. As they were lifting him, the head came off in the doctor's hands. The men dropped the rest and jumped back.

" 'There stood the doctor,' Mr. Scobee said, 'in the glare of the headlights, holding the head in his rubber-gloved hands, shaking it until he heard the bullet rattle inside. Then he shook it until the bullet dropped out. I examined it and marked it for identification. Long after I returned to my home — for days afterward, in fact — the dreadful, horrific odor clung to my person. My leather jacket just never was much good after that."

"Let's have a beer," Poke Hinson said. "I read his story, *The Steer Branded Murder.*"

"Scobee's title is intriguing."

"Peregrinations, is that how you pronounce it? *Peregrinations of a Pioneer Printer* is a book I like," Fulcher said.

"It is a collector's item today," Bob Pool said.

"Well," Poke Hinson spoke up, "if you want some real high class litrachoor, you read that there *Suds In Your Eye.* I got it in case you ain't read it."

He got up and went into the house while I stared at my collaborator accusingly. He shook his head. Poke came back bearing battered copies of *Suds* and *High Time.*

"How would you like to have the author autograph them for you?" Bob Pool asked.

Nobody turned a hair.

Finally Poke said, "You write that book? Lemme shake your hand."

Mrs. Hinson got up. "We love it," she said. "We've read both of them over and over and loaned them to everybody we know, including the Mexican girl that lives in one of the adobe houses."

Fulcher got to his feet. "I read it in the Army. I'll tell you

we used to swap those books. We'd trade 'em back and forth
to other outfits, and *Suds* was always the favorite."

"Do you still read much?"

"Everything we can get hold of, at night after my monsters
go to bed."

"How did *Suds* get here?"

"My wife," Fulcher said. "She's postmaster at Terlingua."

"She was an Army nurse in the Philippines and brought it
home. Passed it all around," Mrs. Hinson said. "You've got to
go by to see her. She'd never get over it if you didn't."

"I never felt well known until this minute," I laughed, "and
I am certainly not going to miss meeting the one responsible
for that state of bliss!"

I went into the store to get some beer and to have a look-
round. Shelves, floor, icebox — all spotless. There was a handsome juke box in the position of honor. I saw that one of the
pieces was "La Nueva Adelita." After I dropped my coin in
and Poke opened the juke box two or three times to make certain that it played properly, also to be sure no one swiped the
money, I found her to be the same old "Adelita" — the battle
hymn of the Mexican Revolution, without too much face-lift-
ing. Clint Fulcher and I began to sing it Mexican style: close
harmony in thirds.

"I'd love to be here some Saturday night when the Mexicans
come over to spend the money they get for the *candelilla* wax,"
I said.

"We could sing 'Una Noche Serena,' Fulcher said as we
lined up to get our pictures taken. "You gotta stop by to see
my monsters. I got a hunk of petrified palm tree I want to give
you. For your giggles."

I looked blank.

"All the giggles that you've given people when they felt
low."

Mrs. Hinson pressed something smooth and cool into my

hand. It was a charming little pack-saddled donkey carved out of white and yellow quartz.

"I'll call him Aristotle." He goes with me everywhere. Best pet in the world: no plumbing problems.

"You know, my brother that died never was satisfied with the translation of Chisos. They say it means ghost and he always said it didn't."

"He's a man after my own heart," I said. "It doesn't mean ghost at all. It is an Indian corruption of the word *hechizo*."

"I wish he were alive to hear you say that, Mary. It would have done him good. He had an old, old dictionary in Spanish, on kind of parchment paper; the esses looked like f's . . ."

"Over at the University Archives I've been studying just such a book, and the dictionary of the Royal Spanish Academy makes me certain I'm right. These are really Wizard Mountains; they bewitch people and cast an enchantment on them."

"Bear down hard on it in your book. You will, won't you, Mary?"

Here at the end of the world was a living interest in language, both English and Spanish. Mrs. Hinson is a college graduate and correspondent for a regional newspaper. She knows a great deal more about what is happening in this changing world than many closer to the sources of so-called knowledge.

Books are a big part of the lives of the people isolated from most other sources. The mountains prohibit TV and sometimes interfere with radio reception, adding another charm to the region. My mind went back to a newspaper article Barry Scobee had written about young Dr. Albert Myer, who "invented the signal corps" at Fort Davis in 1860. In it he quotes a letter of Dr. Myer's in which he says: "I am in comfortable quarters; I have my books, some old acquaintances as associates, no one can interfere with my sovereign pleasure and I should be thankful."

Poke and Ollie Hinson should be thankful, and I know they are, for if I ever saw two people who do not allow nonessentials and the Joneses to "interfere with their sovereign pleasure," it is they. Their sharp minds, unruffled dispositions, their sense of values, and the knowledge that they would be loyal friends in a pinch drew me to them quickly. All pretense is stripped away. That did not take long, for I cannot picture either one of those originals ever having had much of it. Whatever shred of "preserving appearances" they might have had is all gone, melted away in the "fining pot" of the Big Bend, leaving only a great, vital sense of humor and immense human dignity.

The dash over to Terlingua was not nearly long enough to suit me. Mrs. Fulcher had just shampooed her hair, one half was in pincurls and the other half hung down wet. She knew we were short of time and marched out like a trooper facing the firing squad to have her picture taken in a Which-twin-has-the-Toni pose. Three little girls, Emory (called Squeak), Palomina, a sorrel-top, and the youngest, a charmer with gold-flecked green eyes called Prieta (the Dark One), came out to be photographed.

"These are my monsters," their father said.

They are bilingual, self-reliant, friendly children. The combined store, post office, and house was interesting — especially the excellent collection of books, *War and Peace* alongside the latest thing from The List with the paint hardly dry on its dust jacket.

Mrs. Fulcher did not tell me so, but I know she is a godsend in a region where there are no doctors or nurses within a hundred miles. I hated to leave, because I am like a certain kind of air plant. Pin a leaf of it to a window curtain and in a few weeks roots will appear. They don't garden much out in the Big Bend, but they make friends as gardeners do, who make only two kinds: instant and bosom.

"I always thought whoever wrote *Suds* had to be crazy to do it," Fulcher said as he presented me with the chunk of petrified palm trunk. "Now that I've met the author, I'm certain of it."

Up the twisty dust-deep road, there was an abandoned mining center — a few old buildings were all that remained of the once prosperous Terlingua, a quicksilver mine, named for the three Indian tribes who spoke three different tongues and were called in Spanish *Tres Lenguas.*

One long, low house looked like the ghost of an ancient tourist court. An erect figure stood out in bold relief against the dark solitude of the place. A slender, regal woman with copper-bronze skin, pure Arab features, and short, naturally wavy silver hair stood silently waiting my explanation.

When I spoke to her in Spanish she smiled, displaying "two strings of fine pearls."

"María Florez, to serve you." Her voice was music itself. "Yes, this was once the lodging of the officials of the mine. My mother and I live here all alone. See how comfortably off we are? We move our cots outside and sleep under the stars."

A small cur dog barked steadily. "I must call my mother. She is always scolding this dog because he doesn't bark when people come. I must tell her how well he barks. See, Mamá? *Es fiel!* He is faithful!"

"Where do you get water?" I asked.

"They bring it from town in the *troca.*"

I have seen the gender of the word "truck" change in my lifetime. It started out as *el troque,* and ended up as *la troca.*

"You see we have everything! My brothers work in the mines. I am not married. Are you?" We smiled and swapped a proverb about the state of single blessedness. She touched the spec bands I wear to keep my glasses within reach.

"That's what I need more than anything: spectacles."

Bob Pool had a pair of extra glasses. He said they were just plain magnifying glass and María was thrilled.

"It's exactly as though I had new eyes," she said. "God will repay you!"

"Juana Gallegos de Flores." Her mother put forth her hand with a queenly gesture. She was at least ninety. "Where have these angels come from to restore eyes to my daughter? Have you no photograph to leave us?"

We told her that we must drive all the way to the Park.

"But be sure to come back, if not before, at least in time for Christmas."

We stopped for a moment at the Hinsons' on the road to the Park. They were still on the gallery. Poke was lying on the cot and Mrs. Hinson was sleeping in a hammock, both fully clothed. It is the way I used to sleep at Point Isabel as a child, except that I wore a bathing suit, for an early start in the morning. When your bedroom is a goldfish bowl, part of the only store in that part of the world, and droppers-in expected any hour of the day or the night it is the only solution. And so handy in case of fire!

"Nearest bank's a hundred miles away, but we'll take your money." Poke grinned.

"I don't know what I was thinking of," Mrs. Hinson said. "I meant to give you that Doubleday Book Club selection. Take it."

I thanked her and told her I had one at home. Poke went inside the store and it reminded me of a yarn a friend told me about stopping there and trying to get some water from Poke.

"No water."

"Cokes?"

"No cokes. Ain't come."

"Well, you're bound to have some ice in that Frigidaire that you can sell us. We've just got to have something to drink!"

Poke opened the door of the electric icebox. "Don't you see? Not a bit of ice . . ."

The customers threw themselves on the box with shouts.
What he hadn't told them was that it was filled with what they
wanted more than anything and had despaired of finding: ice-
cold beer!

"And Poke wants to apologize for what he said about your
book," Mrs. Hinson said shyly.

"Apologize? He said it was high class literature, didn't he?"

"You'll come back soon, won't you?"

I looked down at the rare devil's-head cactus growing in a
bucket by the steps. She followed my gaze.

I kissed her goodbye and ran before she could try to give
me the plant.

The first person I talked to in the Park proper was Peter
Koch. Naturalist, explorer, and photographer, chief of the
photographic department of a Cincinnati newspaper, he came
to the Big Bend National Park in 1950 on an assignment. He
brought his family and stayed. Here were riches in his field
greater than the riches of Lost Nigger Mine or the fabulously
rich mines the Spaniards once worked. For his is living gold:
the desert, the sun, the golden eagles against gold cliffs. Koch
has captured in symbolic photography the spirit and psychic
essence of the Big Bend of the Rio Grande. His travel adventure films are labors of love.

Koch's work is the outgrowth of knowledge and intensely
individual research. Like the artist he is, he uses indigenous
material in every possible instance.

I think of the lines of the Venezuelan, Andrés Eloy Blanco:
"Painter of your native land, why do you paint with a foreign
brush?" Koch's knowledge of the plants and animals of his
region is the firm base on which the pyramid of his success as a
photographer rests.

Prior to our meeting I knew little of Koch beyond his photographs. "In what specific way can I be of the greatest help to
you?" These were his first words to me, and he echoed the

spirit of the warm, generous confraternity of creative workers I have met in Texas.

The century plant, or *Agave scabra,* had just passed the peak of its bloom in July. Koch noticed that I was smiling as I saw the graceful stalks bending low to rest after completing their cycle. "It's on account of my birthday," I said. "A highly original and witty friend in Austin tried to buy a century plant on my last birthday, so that she could cut it in half for me."

We know that it doesn't take a hundred years for the *Agave scabra* to bloom. They take only ten to twenty years to prepare the great golden-green stalk of bloom, which often reaches fifteen feet in a very short time, by using the great amount of food stored in the fleshy leaves of the plant. The plant blooms but once. After the seeds mature, the mother plant dies. But there is no loss in nature. This I have seen proven again and again, and have tried to build my personal philosophy on such a sound concept: the idea that everything is useful, even outworn ideas, discarded habits, and old ways of life. As these dead leaves fall from our tree of life onto the ground, they form the lifeblood of new thought and food for the mind and soul. The century plant knows that it does not die, that it only disappears to emerge in a new and perpetual resurgence by the offsets that form around the mother plant as it approaches maturity. Nothing is wasted. A new set of leaves takes the place of the old worn-out ones, to furnish flower and fruit, food and lodging to the birds of the air.

As I looked at the glorious candelabra of the agave, its symmetry of living gold and green, it was hard for me to realize that it belongs to the same family as the dainty, fragrant evening star rain lily that appears by magic after a rain, and the delicate zephyranthes that take so kindly to our tame gardens.

Peter Koch watched the woodpeckers at work on the stalk of the century plant, pecking at its softish interior to dig out holes to nest in. I wondered if the woodpeckers got a little

buzz on while they worked, for I had seen old Mexican women
cut a little door in the bark, hollow out the stalk of an agave,
and place an earthen cup inside to collect the sap, *agua miel,*
the juice from which pulque and tequila are made.

"I discovered that the stalks of the agave were very light
and buoyant," Koch said. "For a long time I had been casting
about for material for a raft in which to explore the three great
canyons of the Big Bend." I began to get the variety of goose
flesh I am subject to when a really good story is coming up. I
felt as though I were talking to Father, in *Swiss Family Robinson.*

"I didn't want to cut into any living thing," Koch continued, "but since the stalks were finished with their cycle, I selected three of them. I cut and trimmed them to the length I
wanted for my raft and bound them together with cord. In
the whole job I spent only twenty-three cents, for three metal
screws to strengthen the structure. The weight of the raft was
such that I could carry it. That was my idea in making it, for
I knew that I should have to proceed through many parts of
the canyons on foot, carrying the raft. I hollowed out the middle section where I was to sit in such a way that I could just
squeeze into the opening, and the raft itself would rest on my
hipbones when I carried it. The weight was the irreducible
minimum: fifty-five pounds.

"I rigged a seat underneath and a brace for my feet
stretched out in front of me. I would propel myself along over
the rocky river bed when the water was shallow. The varia-
tion in depth of the water allowed me to use my feet just like
a person sailing a boat with a centerboard, lowering or raising
them as the depth demanded." On this frail craft which he
called *The Broken Blossom,* he transported himself, cameras,
food, water, bedding through the vast and mysterious canyons, Santa Elena, Boquillas, and Mariscal. He kept the cameras in a large galvanized milk can with a tight-fitting lid, the

weight of the cameras carefully balanced and calculated in such a way as to keep the milk can upright should it wash loose from the raft in the treacherous water.

The story fascinated me, and that night a considerable number of guests at the Big Bend National Park had the privilege of seeing the color film of Peter Koch's voyage aboard *The Broken Blossom*. He gave the lecture that accompanies the film in a poetic fashion, unique in my experience. The film included plants, flowers, birds, and insects in a magnificent progression of fully integrated shots presenting the fullness of nature on the stoic frontier. The stories and legends unfold logically and with drama, climaxed by the sequence of Koch scaling the yellow cliffs to capture a golden eagle.

"How could you scale that cliff, aided only by your rope, capture the fierce eaglet, and take the picture?"

"What I usually did was to set up the camera at a given point, start it, and then go on to act out whatever part of my script I had planned to photograph."

There is a smoothness and absence of artifice throughout the film that inspires admiration and respect for Koch's technique — and for his integrity.

At dinner I had gazed through The Window, that spectacular gap in the mountains, the only place in the United States where the Rocky Mountains and the Appalachians are seen to converge. I knew that next morning on the South Rim of the canyon I should sit on a horse and look into the Sierra del Carmen Range, the jagged, impregnable mountains that at one time sheltered Pancho Villa. I thought of the legends that surround him in that region — I felt I was living one myself.

"Have you ever heard of Pancho Villa's *dorados?* His golden men, a personal escort that he never allowed to go into battle without his express permission?"

Koch had not, and I told him that they played an important part in an oft-repeated folk tale of Mexico that I planned to use in this book. "I don't feel that the non-Spanish-speaking reader gets the full force of the expression *dorados* if I translate it as 'golden ones.' I plan to translate freely and use the phrase 'golden eagles.' "

Koch's eyes lit up. "It's perfect," he said. "You will see some tonight."

I had read what I could about the eagles, but was totally unprepared for their majestic appearance in flight against the true-blue sky of Texas. The eagles often have a wing spread of over six feet, and can fly at the rate of two hundred miles an hour when swooping down on their prey. Seton Paul Gordon says in *Days with the Golden Eagle:* "The downward rush of of the golden eagle is the swiftest thing, as it is the most magnificent thing in the bird world." When Koch captured the baby eagle, it was evident from remains in the nest that it had not eaten for days. It had never seen a human being, yet it reared back and glared at him fiercely and imperiously, pecked at him balefully and fought like a tiger. The eaglet was covered with white down that stood out in bold relief against the cliffs.

The sequence that followed, showing the rearing of the eaglet, was a parable in the dependence that comes with civilization. The Koch family were kept busy finding food for the greedy youngster. They brought rabbits to it, and other small game. At first it did not know how to feed itself. But the knife-edged talons soon learned what they were made for. The shots of the eaglet devouring a rabbit are realistic in the extreme. Hair, hide, meat, bones, and entrails all go into the maw of the growing bird. Color film makes the viscera stand out shockingly; this is nature in the raw.

Once the eagle had learned to depend on man for food, he imitated man himself. "Is this all?" was soon his attitude. The Kochs then had to teach him to fly. He lived in a tree stump and frequently got lost when he wandered off afoot. The film shows the patience of the artist in capturing every stage of the process of growth until at last, with a triumphant, graceful dip of the wing, the King of Birds flies off, monarch of all he surveys — so long as he soars aloft within the confines of the Big Bend National Park. If he flies outside its limits, the King of Predators becomes the legal prey of eagle exterminators operating sawed-off shotguns from small planes. His depredations among sheep and lambs make him the natural foe of ranchers.

I sighed when I was finally able to bring myself back to the world around me. Like the eagle, I thought: Why wasn't it more? If every child in the United States could see the film, he would learn what he must learn sooner or later: that nature created both the predator and the prey, and that each living organism in this complex world has a place and a purpose. The picture emphasizes the fact that there is no monotony, save inside a human head. Every creature fulfills its destiny, that spirit which is born in him: the eagle to prey and the rabbit to be preyed upon.

This is much the story of life in the Big Bend itself: man smashes himself against the mountains, or learns to love his jagged fortress, and eventually ceases to bruise his battered self against the rocky walls of his voluntary prison.

"You really haven't seen the Park till you've ridden the Rim Rock trail. And with Bert Beckett," George Miller, Superintendent of the Big Bend National Park, insisted.

"Thirty years is a long time between horses."

"They're gentle, and you'll be with one of the personalities of this region who shouldn't be missed."

"When this project was started, I took a silent oath to charge hell with a bucket of water if necessary. I'll make the Rim Rock ride. When do we start?"

By ten o'clock in the morning I was riding a bay mare named Bob. The saddletree was too wide and the stirrups were too long, as I was to discover before the day was over. The ride took a little better than eight hours and is roughly (I do not use the word loosely) sixteen miles.

Beckett, the horse concessioner, makes every effort to have his customers mounted comfortably and safely. In my haste to get under way, I took the first small-looking saddle they brought out. Later in the day, as the stirrup leathers got longer and my legs got shorter, it turned out that the holes for adjusting the length of the stirrups were simply not in the right places for my kind of architecture, so I let my stems dangle. It wasn't the first time. Bert Beckett and Bob Pool looked agonized whenever my mare Bob broke into a jolting trot. They didn't know the number of times as a child I had caught a horse by the mane and crawled on his back without so much as a rope around his neck.

What counted was Beckett's choice of surefooted mounts on those precipitous trails and steep climbs. Some of the curves are sharp, and it's a long way from them to the bottom of the canyon, especially if you fall off a horse and take the express. There is no danger with those horses: they are sure, gentle, and patient as Job.

The beauty of the trails, going up, and coming down, crowned by the breathtaking panorama at the top, is more than enough compensation for any slight stiffness that might result from the use of unaccustomed muscles. I recommend that anyone visiting the Big Bend National Park, who is sound in wind and limb, take the Rim Rock ride, all the way, if possible.

The guides take every precaution for the rider's safety, keep an even, easy pace, and stop frequently. Perhaps someday the miniature jeeps that are used so much by the housekeeping staff of big motels through Texas will be able to navigate the trails for those who cannot possibly make it on horseback. Part of the charm is in wearing old clothes, feeling the strong animal carrying one along, hearing the creak of leather, and enjoying the good clean smell of horse sweat. I had on a pair of hiking boots, a blue denim riding skirt, and a red flannel shirt. In July, it was a comfortable outfit.

Instead of seeming less impressive close to, the sheer walls of the mountains were more awesome than ever. The beauty of the rock formation, variety of colors, shapes, and textures are all fascinating. To a total "floragoof" like me, there was a temptation to stop every foot of the way. Ferns abounded; varieties I had never seen, not even in books and encyclopedias. Yuccas of every type. The century plant seems to thrive at any altitude. Along the way, within hands' reach, were great quantities of *Lobelia cardinalis,* loaded with blossoms. Eupatorium and wild ageratum. My neck went round and round like an owl's trying to look in many directions at once. Nearly every picture of that botanical dream world that is engraved on my memory was framed by a gap or gorge of some sort in the mountains.

"Any alligators around here?" Bob Pool asked Bert Beckett.

"'Bout all caught out," he said. "Gotta know how."

"What do you use for bait?" Bob asked.

"We don't use nothin' but a trombone, a spyglass, a dull book, an' a matchbox," Beckett said.

"How?" I bit.

"Well," Mr. Beckett twisted round in his saddle and rolled a Bull Durham cigarette, "you just pick you out a alligator and get him near a little one-room shanty, close the windows, and leave the door open."

"Will he go in?" I asked.

"When you start playin' the trombone real loud, the alligator gets disgusted and goes inside the house to get away from the noise. Then you shut the door. When he gets in there, he don't have nothin' to do, so he sees this here dull book an' he starts readin' and first thing you know, he's snorin' away like he was sawin' wood. Then you open the door and slip the spy-glass in. Not the big end, but the little end. You look through the big end and you see the alligator gettin' littler and littler. Then you reach in, pick him up, an' put him in the matchbox."

The good bay mare, Bob, made the best comment on the whole thing.

"Trouble is," said Mr. Beckett, "some people ain't happy unless they're unhappy."

We were climbing steadily, and by noon I could feel the altitude a little, especially after two cups of real cowboy coffee, boiled in a tin can. There is nothing in God's world to equal either the altitude or the coffee for sheer flavor. It carries a Texan back to hunting season. During the white-wing flight season, hunters used to carry a big iron skillet with them, clean the birds on the spot, fry them in bacon fat, and eat them then and there, with crispy Mexican loaves . . . and cowboy coffee.

"You'd never think," Bert Beckett turned around as we started up the second half of the steep trail, "that right there was a cow ranch one time, back in my folks' lifetime. There's the remains of what was the corral." Sure enough, there was evidence of fencing. "When my father was a young man, he told of his father driving cattle along the Chisholm Trail to market in Kansas City. There wasn't no communication for nobody livin' in the Bend in those days. When he got back, nearly five months later, my grandmother told him that one of his sons had died of erysipelas, and one had died of snakebite while he was gone. Now you get day after tomorrow's news before it happens."

All along the trail he pointed out plants and trees because he saw I was interested in them. He showed how the woodpeckers had pecked holes in a Ponderosa pine to store acorns in them. His conversation was enormously informative. Bert Beckett is a fine guide because he knows the Big Bend. He is a man of native tact and courtesy; knows when to talk and when to keep quiet.

"After this next curve in the trail," he said, "look back. You'll see the clumps of quaking aspens. They have white trunks. You can't miss 'em. Then you'll know how high up in the mountains you are."

The quaking aspens are exquisite trees that look very much like the white birches of New England, but belong to the willow family. The slightest breath of air makes the jade-green leaves seem to tremble with delight. The aspens are found in the Big Bend National Park only on a limited area on the upper slope of Mount Emory. I expected music to come out of them, tinkling like Japanese wind chimes.

Around two I began feeling rather weary. My wilted condition must have been noticeable, for in a few minutes Bert Beckett got off his horse, came and helped me dismount.

"Get down and rest a minute," he said as he threw the reins on the ground. "In just about another mile, I'll show you something you'll never see anywhere else." The rise we stopped on was covered with good grass growing up through pebbles and chips. The horses munched contentedly. I sat down on a rock for a minute, combed my hair, and cleaned my sun specs.

"Okay?" Beckett ground out his cigarette. "Come over here a minute." I followed him and my knees almost buckled at the grandeur before me. I decided I better sit down and take it slowly.

We were standing on the thin edge of the world. This was the South Rim of the canyon, nearly eight thousand feet in the blue air. I felt as the First Woman must have felt when she awoke, rubbed her eyes, and beheld the splendor before her. As far as my eyes could see there was nothing but beauty . . . beauty on a bender, gone wild, intoxicating the senses with her prodigality.

Beckett had arranged for the sight to burst on our eyes with the greatest of stage management. I didn't "drink in little sips," and the splendor would have gone to my head, even if I had. The violet-blue Sierra del Carmen spread out in front of me until it was swallowed by the horizon. I gazed until my sight was withered with looking. I wished for a thousand eyes like the night, to take it all in. Wonderment filled me, and I felt a great kinship with the Mexican who sat one whole day on the porch of the store at Castalon looking at the mountain before him repeating his litany: "I wonder who made it? I wonder who made it?"

"See that little bitty gold-lookin' road down there?" I followed Beckett's gesture with the field glasses and finally caught a thin thread that might have been a road through the craggy peaks. "I got friends down there," he said. "If you look real good you can see the roof of their cabin."

"How can they live there?"

"That's what I asked them," he said. "Me an' another feller went down there on a pack trip an' visited them folks. I asked 'em how they got all them kids in there an' the furniture an' stuff.

"'Made it, mister,' they said. 'Wasn't but two of us when we come here. Me an' my wife rode in on two horses right after we was married. All them kids was got an' borned right here.'"

The Book of Genesis seemed very close. It was a little like seeing the history of mankind acted out for your special benefit.

"That's Mexico, you know." Beckett pointed to the Carmen. "Villa and his men hid out there. One man with a gun could stand off an army in that pass."

"Could and did," I said. "You know 'Adelita'? It's a song about a girl, the sweetheart of the workers in the struggle between the Haves and Have-Nots that was the Mexican Revolution."

"Sure. Play it at all the dances."

"There's a legend around Durango that Adelita was a real person."

"Lots of women followed the soldiers right into the fightin' durin' the revolution. Camp followers," Beckett said.

"Most of them were the wives of soldiers," I told him. "They carried fifty-pound *metates* on their backs to grind the corn for tortillas. Strapped the baby on top of the *metate* and tethered the goat to the sash round their waists. Some of them cooked on bits of tin on the tops of moving boxcars loaded with horses en route to a battle. They cared about their men.

"I owe you a story in return for the vaquero's poem about the Big Bend. We'll just pretend that little exchange about the alligator never took place."

Beckett rolled a cigarette as he listened.

"According to tales told in the State of Durango where the song started, Adelita was a striking-looking, wholesome girl of the people. Baltasar Dromundo, a Mexican writer-statesman who has won many literary awards in addition to being a lawyer, poet, essayist, memoirist, and congressman, has done some valuable research on the subject of Adelita and tells the story this way. She had no formal education, but was full of charm and common sense. She was around twenty, with ivory skin, loosely waving blue-black hair, huge black eyes and a dashing smile. They say her height was not great. She was well fleshed-out, stocky and firm, a real *norteña*.

"When Pancho Villa had won nearly three fourths of the bloody battles of the revolution, in late 1914 or early 1915 — the legends are vague — the city of Parral gave a banquet in his honor. A very small portion of Mexico stood between Villa and the capital, possibly the presidency. General Villa arrived surrounded by his cohorts and his special guard of honor, his prized young lieutenants whom he treasured and never allowed to enter battle without his permission. They were handsome boys and Villa called them his *dorados,* his golden ones. Ever since I heard the various stories about them, they have been fixed in my mind as his 'golden eagles,' especially the blond one . . ."

"Huero Portillo, wasn't he?" Bob Pool said.

"Yes. Blond Portillo was Villa's *ojito derecho,* the apple of his eye . . . and Adelita's sweetheart."

I told him that the City Fathers chose Adelita, for her wit as well as for her beauty, to make the welcome address to the General at the banquet. They say she was as beautiful as a country festival that day. The local band was playing Villa's favorite piece, a very old, romantic waltz, "La Alejandra." He could not keep his eyes off the lovely girl. When the time came for Adelita to deliver the address, her voice rang with patriotic fervor and she aimed her remarks, so they say, at the space between General Pancho Villa's eyes. She spoke of Durango's debt to the liberator, and of his promise to Mexico that a tyrant should never rule, and wound up by expressing the hope that Durango and all Mexico would show its faith in Francisco Villa by electing him president. The applause was a prolonged rain of palm upon palm. The effect of Adelita's fire and eloquence, coupled with her beauty, were not lost on General Villa, who was at no time impervious to the charm of lovely women.

Late into the day, Adelita and General Villa sat on a bench and talked. That evening they were entering the General's headquarters after a long and deep parley. People believe that Adelita convinced Villa that if he could not win the presidency, no one could.

Blond Portillo came through the door of General Villa's headquarters, clad in the uniform of the *dorados:* riding boots, American riding trousers, khaki military tunic, red silk scarf knotted about his throat, wearing the characteristic Texan hat. He looked up from the dispatches in his hand that he was about to deliver to Villa, just in time to see Pancho Villa clasp Adelita passionately in his arms and kiss her on the mouth. The boy worshiped his chief with fanatical devotion. His hand flew to his pistol and aimed it at Villa, then, after a split-second decision, he turned the gun on himself.

At the sound of the shot, Villa released the girl and turned: his favorite *dorado* was on the floor with his head blown off. Adelita dropped sobbing on the body of her sweetheart. Villa experienced one of his sudden reactions: revulsion to the girl. "Where do you come in?" He shook her. "What do you know about this?"

"He was my sweetheart," Adelita sobbed.

Villa signaled another of his lieutenants.

"Take her away. Out of my sight. Where I'll never have to look at her again."

About three weeks later, to ease the fatigue of battle, Villa sent for his guitar player.

"Play me something new," the General said. The man began to scratch out a lively air and catchy rhythm. The song told the story of a camp follower, a *soldadera* who followed her *juan* onto the battlefield, cooked his frijoles for him over a fire of twigs, loaded his Mauser and handed it to him, then drank pulque with him when they rode into town on the always overloaded victory trains after a battle.

As the song unrolled the ballad of the brave girl who followed her lover amid shot, shell, and machine-gun fire, Villa listened attentively. He even stopped tipping back the chair he was sitting in. "Who wrote that song?" he demanded. "No one knows, *mi general*," the guitarist said. "Some anonymous composer made it up in Durango, they say."

"Durango?"

"*Sí, mi general*. About three weeks ago it began to sift through the troops. Before many days all the Division of the North was singing it. They play nothing else these days. It has become the hymn of the revolution. They claim, *mi gen-*

eral, that among the forces of General Arrieta a girl rides a horse and fights as fiercely as any soldier he has."

"Sing it again."

> "Si Adelita se fuera con otro
> La seguiría por tierra y por mar;
> Si por mar en un buque de guerra,
> Si por tierra en un tren militar."
>
> (If Adelita should go with another,
> I'd follow her on the land and bounding main;
> In a warship I'd search all the ocean,
> Search the land in a military train.)

General Villa was silent a long time. "It's not bad," he said at last.

Many times during the fierce fighting and after, when clearing up the carnage, Villa would send for his guitar player and make him play "Adelita" over and over.

Villa's armies made history with their unprecedented victories. Celaya was one of the bloodiest of the fights. The battlefield was so covered with corpses and dead horses that passage over it was almost impossible. General Villa went over the field himself to make sure none of his *muchachos* were left for dead. The wounded, if left on the field, would be burned along with the dead. His sharp eye spotted a red neckerchief and he spurred his horse over to where a young officer lay. Villa dismounted: "They know, God damn them, that I never allow them to get into the line of fire without my permission! Which one is this?"

He lifted the dead officer up in his arms, gazing at him to know which of his golden men he had lost. The Texan hat fell off and Adelita's black satin hair flowed down over her shoulders. Villa looked at her for a long time.

"She *was* a golden eagle," he sighed.

Filled with the glory of the Carmen, I came back to level land reluctantly — but strangely renewed.

The trail to El Paso led through Sierra Blanca. Mountain breezes cooled the sun-baked plains. The Quitman Mountains, about six thousand feet in altitude, reached southward to the Rio Grande. The Middle Valley of the Rio Grande is an area of extensive cultivation. Water from the river and from the Elephant Butte Irrigation Project is conveyed in canals. The Middle Valley was once famous for its grapes and the golden wine made from them, but the fighting and unrest caused by the "salt war" put an end to that.

I saw the Mission of La Purísima Concepción del Socorro. The first building was founded in 1683, but was abandoned on account of the Indians.

Ysleta, Little Islet, was founded in 1682 — the oldest town in Texas. Ysleta, Socorro, and San Elizario were once in Mexico, but a flood changed the course of the Rio Grande and left them on the American side. Flat-roofed, square adobe buildings stand among the more modern structures. The door and window frames are painted blue to insure happiness and good luck, and to repel evil spirits.

Up the tree-lined highway to the Pass of the North I enjoyed the patchwork of shade from the overhanging trees. Orchards and truck gardens, cotton gins and cotton fields; the flowering desert is rich indeed.

I could scarcely wait to see the city that had stood near the Pass since the *conquistadores* trudged through it nearly four centuries ago.

That city, where I was to meet writers and artists whose work I had long admired, marked the end of the River Road for me, and I found the end of the trail to be a welcome oasis: the air-conditioned lobby of the Paso Del Norte Hotel.

At the end of the River Road, a jagged mountain holds aloft on a rugged peak, Christ, The King, the majestic Cristo Rey of Urbici Soler, an imperishable monument to the *santa fé*, the holy faith that made the whole Southwest possible.

El Paso, home of cattle chutes and smelters to most people, is known to the world of letters as the home of Tom Lea and Carl Hertzog, peerless combination in the art and science of creating lasting beauty. Not since Gilbert and Sullivan blended their combined genius to enrich the world has there been so perfect a marriage of two gifts as the long, fruitful collaboration of Carl Hertzog and Tom Lea. They have restored a lost virtue to art: patience.

Hertzog is slim, sinewy, and intense, taut as an E string most of the time. Infinitely patient when it comes to his work, full of dialect stories and gentle clowning, he loves square dancing and is an authority on the subject. One does not always realize that he is heavily burdened by the responsibility that comes to all who strive for and achieve perfection. To me a Hertzog book is like a Chinese jade fingering piece, something to caress. There is a sensuous pleasure in holding and touching such a jewel.

Lea is muscular and wiry, tough and resilient as one of the rawhide *reatas* that whirl through his lambent prose. Dogged and determined, he seems to court the impossible. There is a kind of ruthless, systematic fury in his work, as though he were scourged daily by the demons of his many talents. Tom Lea's paintings and drawings are full of gnarled, sinewy people with lots of strength in the legs. They seem to stride out of the canvas. Horses and bulls come to life with a vigor that is characteristic of all Lea's work. Prick his paintings and they bleed. The figures of Marines in the Peleliu Landing have a writhing thrust of strength to them that is all action. He paints a wide range of moods and subjects. To my mind, one of his greatest works is the portrait of an ancient Chinese standing in a rice paddy.

His vivid and expressive lettering is part of the writing and painting. Lea's *leitmotif* is a passionate love of his Texas, its age and timelessness. *The Brave Bulls* is perhaps his best-known novel, but every Texan who reads *The Wonderful Country* will end up saying with Sir Walter Scott:

> Breathes there a man with soul so dead
> Who never to himself hath said:
> "This is my own, my native land!"

Texas is Tom Lea's own, his native land. Historiographer, novelist, muralist, painter, illustrator, calligrapher, and poet. The gods threw the book at him. Of his millions of readers, not many know him as a poet, but his poem "Randado," the story of a great horse ranch, has some of the epic quality of the Conquest itself.

Hertzog says, "Porter Garnett, the artist-printer who contended that all fine printing must be done with hand-set type on handmade paper, is the man I call my old maestro. Tom Lea and I teamed up in 1937 and our first big book came out in 1942: the unpublished letters of Adolphe Bandelier, a Swiss anthropologist who made the first scientific study of the Apache Indians. I sent Garnett a copy. The old maestro pointed out two mistakes and sent me a book printed in Venice in 1496 on vellum by Johannes Hertzog. 'Change Johannes to Carl, and you have a worthy printer's mark,' he said."

Hertzog, the wag, has been known to advertise: GET YOUR PRINTING DONE HERE. IN BUSINESS FOUR HUNDRED YEARS. He hates careless printing that looks slick and handsome books that are merely handsome. He cuts back a lower-case letter under a capital for more grace, and shaves the tummies off periods if they look awkward to him. He has been known to make two thousand minute adjustments in a sixty-page pamphlet. Lea and Hertzog believe that in some way a book's appearance must grow out of the subject matter. Each of their books is a story in itself. "Plain man, plain book, plain paper."

The story of the King Ranch which has kept their hands full for seven years is a masterpiece of bookmaking, written, illustrated, designed, and printed by the incomparable team. The off-white cover with the King Ranch brand, the running W in charcoal brown, is a replica of the King Ranch saddle blanket. The charcoal-brown wool in the brand comes from "black sheep" and is not dyed.

"To me painstaking work is not exquisite, it is merely honest," says Hertzog. No pains are ever spared by these men. Michelangelo said: "Perfection is made up of trifles, and perfection is no trifle." Hertzog and Lea are infinitely painstaking in everything they do.

Together they share the attributes of honesty, reality, and uncompromising standards of excellence in any phase of creation.

I am only guessing, but from my own limited experience, I think it would be unrealisitc to suppose for a minute that two such powerful personalities, each with strong convictions as to "how it should be" could work together without ever locking horns.

Over the past twenty years they have eaten their peck of salt together, that ancient Arab method of testing a man's worth. It is through the friction of conflicting views and ideas, the clashing of thought, and the final meshing of the gears of concerted action that creative and highly original work is brought into being. Nothing valid and distinctive was ever cooked up by "yes men." There is always present the one great tranquilizer and adjuster of differences of opinion: the centrifugal force of the work itself. When two or more people are pooling their brains and lifeblood in a piece of creative work, each contributes and will stand up for certain points on which he will not yield a hair. So emerges a strong, unyielding skeleton, the base from which springs all beauty and strength. What makes up a lasting piece of work is the sum of the combined points that neither collaborator would give in on. Such conviction brings out the best that is in each. Sincere workers do not shout, stamp, and pound the table over trivia. Each respects his colleague when the other feels with equal conviction the point he is defending. Each has minor conceits that he cherishes, little fetishes and gimmicks that are dropped without argument. Because they are nice people, good fellows? "For the book" — and because they respect each other as individuals.

With characteristic modesty they say the chapter titles of the King Ranch book are rather unusual and "pretty good" because of a circumstance that seldom occurs in the book world. Lea and Hertzog get together with the manuscript and decide what words to capitalize and display. Then Hertzog sets the type in place before Lea draws the illustrations. In this way he can make the drawing conform to the space and use the letters as part of the whole composition. This is impossible in the production of most books, because the artist may be in Chicago, the printer in New York, and the author in Timbuctoo, where each one must work independently.

"It is the situation that makes this good, not any excellence on our part. Two crafts working together as a unit get results," says Hertzog.

I would like to see that quotation engraved on the hearts of creative workers everywhere. With such men as Hertzog and Lea for inspiration, Texas may very well stage a Renaissance of her own.

One of the promising Texas artists who has been influenced and encouraged by Lea and Hertzog is José Cisneros of El Paso, an illustrator who has had part in several fine books. His work springs from the soil with vigor and imagination. Color-blind, he works usually in black and white. Cisneros paints the outsides of buses in the daytime, and works at his art by night.

The International Museum and the El Paso Public Library also bear evidence of the fine hands of Hertzog and Lea — in décor, furnishings, and the impressive collection of books on the Southwest.

The heading of Chapter XII of the King Ranch book is a

drawing of a mesquite twig, feathery and shadowed; the piercing thorns, capable of puncturing a tire, are cruel in their realism. Gray and green tones bring the black ink to life. Each ferny leaf in the negative was slit by hand with a razor blade to make the paper take the ink. The same design is used for the end papers of the trade edition of the book.

I would rather have drawn that piece of mesquite than to have written *Death Comes For the Archbishop*. An Eskimo who could not read could look at the mesquite and know the feel of the Southwest.

The diversity of Texas must account in great measure for the scope of the two artists at the Pass. Genius, to me, is the power to do something in such a fashion that no one else can do it. Lea and Hertzog have few imitators.

An imperishable tribute to a land that has all but "lost her horseback men," Tom Lea's poem "Randado" tells the story of the Southwest in epic form.

According to tradition the horse ranch and hacienda called El Randado was established in the empty and forbidding brush country of the southern tip of Texas, now in Jim Hogg County, sometime late in the 1700's by a man of horses named Viscaya. El Randado soon became known for five hundred leagues north and south of the Rio Bravo as the breeding ground of the finest Spanish horses. The numberless wild mustang progeny of Randado stock caused cartographers of the early 1800's to mark the region WILD HORSE PRAIRIE. From Tenochtitlán to the Judith, men came to Randado for the hardy breed that carried them best across the vastness of a wild new world. Buyers at Randado merely threw a silver piece, vaqueros say, on an Indian blanket spread by the corral gate each time a mount was roped out of the *caballada*. Nothing remains now of El Randado but the crumbled hacienda, the watering tank, and the name, slurred by all tongues of the *campo*, to the musical name —

"Ran-dow"

Who names the far off music,
Gives testimony, bears witness to the ghost,
The gray dust ghost at dawn and dusk,
The music, the ghost, the name of a dream,
The old dream of El Randado?
"I name it," said the thin cock at second crowing.
"I testify," said the Morning Star.
"I bear witness," whispered the wind in the huisache:
This was El Randado,
The name of a dream like far off music and a war cry,
The song and the hoarse SANTIAGO
Of proud free men and wild horses."

It is true the spur rowels have broken and are lost from
their boxes; the jingles are gone and red rust has eaten the bit
chains. Yes, the fine leather and iron-hard rawhide both have
cracked and crumbled to mould and the saddletrees crumpled
with age. The very stones of the houses have loosened and
yellowed and soured and flaked and fallen back to the dust
and the well is a black weedy hole for scorpions.

It is true the wind has long filled the last tracks of the steel-
limbed stallions driving their wild swift *manadas* to tall grass
and sweet water. . . . And the quick whirring songs of riatas,
deadly as dark coiled snakes, those songs are gone now, Ai, gone
like the gold and the blackened silver from El Randado.

We name the hand of the craftsman Time
At work in the lonely place
Smoothing the shapes of the old days
Into rounded myths and remembrances.
Now in the high noon, beyond the horse-tank,
Over the thin-leafed haze of thorn in the brakes,
In the stillness, in the ghost dance of the empty heat,
Rises the dust of the whirlwind, tall, stinging *ánima perdida,*
Lost soul and ghost of old Viscaya
Leading his lean-faced *cuerados* armoured in rawhide,

Long spurs chinking at the flanks of dun horses,
Dry throats singing the song of the outlaw
Novillo Despuntado, Blunt-horned Steer who could fight.

> Viscaya in the whirlwind
> Riding the black *morzillo*
> At the head of his singing *corrida*
> Northward through slashing thickets of thorn,
> Driving horses to the watering place of the gray stones
> Which he named by the name of El Randado.
> Then it was El Randado:
> Where *carne seca* hung in the sun by the cook house,
> And the smoke curled blue over iron *braseros,*
> And old Viscaya sat in the shade,
> Damping down dust in his leather gullet
> With brandy like the sun on the fire-dazzled side
> Of *El Bolsón de Mapimí.*
> He drank the wine of the New World straight
> And his cup left a ring on the table.
> Old Viscaya —
> When they asked for a horse brand at El Randado
> He sat bemused, then grinned like a wolf,
> And showed them the print of his cup!
> This was the mark of El Randado,
> Round ring of the world, and mark of fire
> On the flanks of ten thousand horses!

We remember you with honor O *caballada,* gray-colored, dun-colored, *grullo* and *bayo coyote,* hue of the earth at El Randado. We know the worth of *cabos negros,* and the little black line on the backs of the amber-tawny buckskins. We have seen the silken lights on the warm gray flanks of the *grullos.* Who can forget the high clean heads with the tapered muzzles and quick nostrils, the small lively ears that talked, the eyes of velvet and of fire, the well-arched necks and tossing manes, the shoulders so deep and powerful, the high croups and the fine spring-muscled legs? Ai we recall how you ran when riatas sang in the dust of the westering light at Randado!

We know your blood and your breed O *caballada*, remembering well the ancient vision of the foals nursing golden mares by the tents of Kedar; our old dreams knew black stallions in the rumble of battle drum and shrilling of Moor's pipe. Long we loved the gray Barb horses on the bare hills of Toledo and at waterings by dark fountains in Granada. None among us will forget you O *caballada*, enduring the holds of the Indies ships, travelling *machete* paths in the sick green heat, bearing the burden, the bloody fetlock of *Noche Triste*. You ran the wide flint ridges, broke the dry thickets northward O *caballada* and your hooves made the heart-beats of El Randado.

> Then sing in the thunder and dust of those hoof-beats,
> Ai sing the song of the *gran caballada,*
> Galloping curvetting caracole song
> Of Randado and its proud slender horses:
> *Color of earth and temper of flame,*
> *Free as the wind on the winter plain,*
> *And strong as the sun in the sky.*

Stilled are the heart-beats, dust is the heart, silent the song of El Randado. Gone are the riders, dead are the mustangers, lost in the years are the ropers, the tamers, gone are the riders from El Randado. Only the wind in the huisache at dawn when thin cock crows and *El Lucero* shows, remembers and whispers the power in the hands, the strength in the loins, the surge in the hearts of rawhide men on wild horses.

> "Ai make you a lazo," whispers the wind,
> "Swing a riata mustanger style,
> And make you a lazo for far ranging ghosts
> of long gone whirlwind riders!"

They spurred wiry horses the color of dust over the rim of the New World's space, along *Comanchero* trails, on *cibolero* paths, into the trackless waste, from salt marsh to thicket to *llano* to sierra and beyond —
Far beyond —
Ai they pinned Polaris on their hat brims
And headed their herds for the dim Northern Light!

Men of fire riding the blood-flecked tracks;
Men of flint and of steel enduring the heat and the cold,
    the hate, the hurt and the love of being free:
Yours is a music that will not die,
The deep unmeasured power of questing men
Laughing and riding the tempering flame
Alone on the edge of the earth.
O land that lost your horseback men!
Remember you the riders, the long gone riders,
The gray dust riders in the far off music
Of the dreams of El Randado.

Lea and Hertzog are in the vanguard of the pioneers —
scouts who blaze the trail for creative hearts and minds now exploring Texas' Youngest Frontier, the frontier of the mind and
the spirit. I realized that wherever there are individuals, there
will always be frontiers, and Texas is "long on" individuals.

It was like being awakened abruptly from a romantic dream
to return from the Pass of the North, in the realm of the Great
River, to tear myself loose from the spell of old Randado and
return to my "home port" at Austin. My feet hit the ground
with a jolt as I came back to the business of everyday, "organized" living.

Some time back, Walter Reuther had announced: "Texas is
the next place we have to take!" Some old boy in a lumber mill
over in the Piney Woods replied: "Tell him to brang his
lunch."

I got back to Austin to find the AFL and the CIO joining
forces in Texas, over at the Coliseum, and not a bad place for it.
Organized labor was trying to free itself from peonage, re-
asserting its belief in the brotherhood of man while slipping
hastily and indistinctly over some passages, like a Doubting
Thomas mumbling certain passages of the Nicene Creed that
he can't quite swallow.

Here at the well spring of productivity, I would watch the new flowering of Texas minds. The roots of the pioneer tree are sound and hale; some pruning, lopping off of dead ideas and withered prejudices, has caused the fine old tree to bear a new and polished crop of fruit. The frontiersman was a great hand to keep records and journals. A little thing like spelling didn't stop him. In his setting down of events in his own language, a simple straightforward prose has been handed down to his descendants, in old journals and diaries, which approaches poetry in its depth and simplicity. The pioneers sired a worthy breed and I was privileged to be at the fountainhead. Ancient Greece and Rome had nothing on Austin. Every day the sage philosophers, Roy Bedichek and Frank Dobie, meet at "the baths," the icy waters of Barton Springs. They alternately freeze and bake themselves while those happy few within earshot have their lives enriched by the conversation coming off the primitive rock I call the Philosophers' Stone.

Boot Springs Trail,
Big Bend

5. THE YOUNGEST FRONTIER

THERE WAS A TIME in Texas that when two men met in the street and plunged right hands into left inside breast pockets, they were reaching for their guns. Today, they are usually reaching for manuscript: "If you read me, I'll read you." If you get on a plane and say to a representative Texan, "How's your book coming?" the chances are that he will look embarrassed and then start telling you.

Many quiet Texan businessmen are diligent writers, amateurs in the pristine sense of the word. They write pieces for trade journals, newspapers, publications of learned societies, historical and regional quarterlies; a few write books, and a handful of them write book reviews.

The heartwarming angle to the whole movement is that these men are realists, seldom expecting to make money out of writing. Their prime aim is, in most cases, to "make a lasting contribution." Each wants to leave his thoughts and memories in permanent form — with his brand on it. A few pay to have their works published privately, but an astonishing number of these Texas writers find commercial publishers. Three or four of the Big Rich have had their memoirs ghosted, and one has had his biography written in advance, ready for the stands when he dies.

One gifted Texan, R. Henderson Shuffler, public relations director of Texas Agricultural and Mechanical College, at Bryan, writes light verse.

> The sand is habitat of fleas
> Where horses sink down to their knees.
> It's long on heat and short on trees
> And makes fat tourists sweat and wheeze.

His "Steer's Lament" is a small classic:

> A cowhand's idea of recreation
> Is a bit of bovine emasculation.

Limitations of space prevent me from attempting to mention even a few of Texas' successful professional writers, or from including a list of her gifted amateurs writing today.

One grizzled old pro stands high with Texas: Stanley Walker, "for years distinguished city editor of the New York *Herald Tribune*," according to the *Saturday Evening Post*, is known for his trenchant wit as well as for his remarkable journalism. His *Herald Tribune* articles on the Texas Seven Year Drouth are masterpieces. To a neophyte struggling to learn some of the technique of non-fiction writing by trial and error, Walker's ability to sling the five w's (who, what, when, where, and why) into a compressed opening paragraph seems nothing short of inspired. His mordant speech is a delight to the loathers of Sweetness and Light. Any writer, amateur, pro, or what Walter Prescott Webb calls a "pen-fighter," would be moved to the marrow at Stanley Walker's inscription to a fellow-writer on the flyleaf of his book *Home to Texas*. It is Biblical in its simplicity: "God help us all! Stanley Walker."

This new frontier of the mind is a sphere still capable of being formed and influenced. There is a plastic, malleable quality present in Texas, a refreshing sense of being able to get in on the ground floor of events, the opportunity to take part in her ultimate cultural destiny, to watch it evolve and, with luck, perhaps even to have a hand in shaping that destiny. It is gratifying to those who have never believed that money and prestige were synonymous to see that like other Americans, Texans are growing up. Creative workers, artists, writers, musicians, and dramatic producers are recognized as the people who provide information, entertainment, and some degree of culture for the money-boys to spend their money on. They have come to respect the mind of the maker, the creative person, because they think he makes something out of nothing, which in a sense he does. The artist doesn't need cows, cotton, or oil. He makes a best-selling book out of pencil and paper and the twenty-six letters of the alphabet, a prize-winning painting out of a piece of canvas and a few tubes of paint, a brand-new hit song out of the same old seven notes of the scale.

"Never cost him hardly nothing!" The tycoon is impressed, thinking of his difference between gross and net. Maybe that dreamy fellow, who never made out a Profit and Loss statement in his life, isn't so impractical after all. The writer and allied craftsmen are daily expanding their territory in Texas and creating a new border to be explored, classified, and claimed.

In the vast conglomerate that is Texas, indigenous culture is evolved from many and varying sources. To treat any one of the sources adequately would require as many pages as Frazer's *Golden Bough*. Texas' physical location, her proximity to a foreign power and language, her history, her ancient and now newly revived seafaring life, the inner fastnesses and empire-within-itself quality of the land make it a bursting Comstock lode of material out of which culture may be mined.

Her very soil harbors material for expression of the natives' own feeling for that soil. "Do you know you can sling Texas porcelain like you sling common clay?" Harding Black asked me in San Antonio.

The "culture vultures" would call him a ceramic artist. Black says he is a professional potter.

"I didn't know there was any porcelain in Texas except the kind brought in by genteel ladies who paint violets and pansies on it 'by hand,'" I said.

"Porcelain comes from Elmendorf, twenty-five miles from here."

The square-jawed stocky man in the canvas apron showed me delicate, fragile porcelain pieces from his kilns, that were comparable to Irish Belleek.

Black is a product of the depression, one of the lads who had to "make do" with what he had. Stubborn and resourceful, he is entirely self-taught. After ten thousand tests he was able to break down and reconstruct the ancient Chinese method of making copper-red glazes. His first wheel was made from an old potato peeler of World War I vintage found at Fort Sam Houston. He makes pottery because it is the only thing he has wanted to do all of his life. It is beautiful and useful, rapidly snatched up by connoisseurs. Here is a truly indigenous art made right out of Texas dirt.

Creative workers in Texas are beginning a revolt against a deeply ingrained fallacy: the exalting of the exotic and ignoring the indigenous. Any monstrosity that came from "away off" was art, and still is to many Texans. All creative workers are learning that, whether they are writers, painters, sculptors, architects, professional potters, or composers, they must create from the inside out and not from the outside in.

They do not need to paint cactus and sagebrush or write

Westerns. No need for wagon wheels and lariats in every regional design. The native life has to be cherished and understood, lived and experienced before it can be shown to others in any art form. Art is always racing to catch up with experience. Experience counts most for the creator. To know life and to know people is of more value to the artist than skill with brush, pen, or chisel. When an artist or creator knows his "country" and becomes part of the traditional life that surrounds him, he creates a truly regional culture that will tend to have a universal appeal because it is recognizable instantly as being intensely personal, and therefore convincing. Modifications of the personality, from any source, foreign or native, will provide originality and individual difference: real distinction. A Texan trying to pretend he is a Cape Codder will not produce a good work about Cape Cod. And certainly not a good one about Texas!

In architecture the pure classic lines of the plantation house, and the poignantly lovely old Texas houses, first cousin to the log cabin, were superseded, when the settlers got the wrinkles out of their bellies, by Swiss chalets, horrible mausoleums dripping with busy, nervous gingerbread fretwork, a reflection of the fidgety owners' own personalities. Lumber had become plentiful. Labor was available — and cheap. It was elegant to be fancy. So they butchered the wood, tortured it into towers and cupolas. The noble simplicity of the pioneer houses was turned over to the slum parts of the towns. Those stalwart dignified dwellings were counterparts of the strong, angular, and open Texans who inhabited them. The sweet beckoning line of the ancient roofs, the gently silvered hand-hewn logs and cypress shakes split with a frow, have an appeal that no other form of architecture holds for me. Derived from the stately, pillared plantation houses, those houses were largely double log houses: two square rooms connected by an open breezeway or dog-trot. A few had brick or native rock fireplaces. If not, mud and stick "chimbleys." Mud and sticks cost nothing. Many of them have been in use for over a hundred years and still draw perfectly. Some of the "Texas houses" have one or two small rooms tacked onto the ends of the gallery. Many of these rooms were just ends of the gallery planked over, and did not have direct entry to the house itself. They were called "Stranger's Rooms," and a traveler could open the door to the stranger's room at any hour of the night, find a bed for himself and feed for his horse. Usually the strangers departed before the family was stirring. If they had anything to leave, they left a gift. The A. B. Hardin family of Hardin and Liberty County got their family copy of Shakespeare as a gift from some unknown traveler who must have appreciated his bed a great deal to leave his treasured book as a token of his gratitude.

San Antonio Archway

Two Texas architects are active apostles in the cause of preserving, restoring, and popularizing once more the basic functional beauty and satisfying lines of the Texas frontier architecture: E. M. Schiwetz and David R. Williams.

Buck Schiwetz's drawings have a special appeal, a striking reality about them that is understandable. A man who designs and constructs houses knows how to draw them. His watercolors have a solid base on which to stand. He has one particularly fine watercolor called "El Rancho Blanco." The background is chocolate-brown and strawberry-pink. "Who ever saw air that color?" an incredulous person asked. Anyone who has lived through a dust devil has seen it exactly that thick coffee color. Wherever an old house survives, Schiwetz goes with his sketch pad to record it before it falls into unrecognizable sticks. He records the flavor of the times along with the pencil sketches of the houses.

"Aren't the plain, economical lines, low ceilings, and thick walls ideal for modern adaptation?" I asked.

"Perfect," he replied. "Easy to air-condition. The old proportions and the characteristic pitch of the roof can be duplicated easily. You have not made a shameful compromise, but a practical one. I agree with you: there is a lot of emotion in an old Texas roofline."

This is Dave Williams' credo: "A logical regional architecture has for its origin the simple, early forms of building native to its own locale, and grows by purely functional methods into an indigenous form of art."

A brilliant editor once said: "One art is not enough." Dave Williams writes an article, "Towards a Southwestern Architecture," for the *Southwest Review* with much the same solid beauty and good sense with which he designs houses.

The Texas colonists, before the Revolution and after 1836, came seeking freedom of action and freedom of thought. They did not look back. Various as they were in origin, they became quickly one people, citizens of the Republic of Texas, serving the same flag, following the same ideals, fighting the same fight. Since they came ardently desiring freedom, they were not bound down by tradition; and since they were possessed of a common purpose and spirit, their architecture has the feeling of unity which is the basis of a style. They were not founding a new England, a new France, or a new Spain; they were free to build to the glory of themselves, to suit their own needs, to satisfy as best they could the exactions of a new climate and the limitations of the native materials to be found close at hand. They used these materials in the simplest and most logical manner. The houses they built of the stone and wood and clay from their immediate localities were an expression of a people and a cause, structures natural and appropriate to the landscape. These early Texas houses seem to grow out of the ground on which they stand; to be as friendly as the earth out of which they have grown. They are beautiful because they are simple and natural, and because their builders were satisfied with beauty of line resulting from straight-forward structure, simplicity of detail, and ornament which had to serve a purpose. The early colonists wanted no tin cornices painted to imitate stone, no fake half-timber, no tin tile roofs. They wanted honest, comfortable houses; and they got them.

Dave Williams' evocative prose brings to my mind the Alsatian colony at Castroville, twenty-odd miles from San Antonio, where the enduring, soul-satisfying little houses stand nobly against the years. Time can but make them more dear.

The Frenchman's house was a simple Texas house [he continues], as was the German's and the Yankee's, and that of the Spaniard who preceded them and perhaps showed them the way; for having free minds, the early Texans built economically of natural materials to suit the climate, to suit themselves and their own comfort. Fortunately, their own comfort demanded a little beauty and a great deal of good taste. There is not in any one of these houses built in the Southwest before 1850 an instance of imitation of foreign styles, of sham, of striving for effect, of any use of unnatural, unnecessary ornament or of material not structural and fit for its purpose. Yet these houses are pleasing, beautiful, picturesque.

Why are not modern Texas houses equally sincere and satisfying? It is an interesting problem in anthropology to try to answer this question; for it seems almost incredible that architectural practice could have declined from its early level in

Texas to produce some of the monstrosities of the present. Perhaps the answer can be found in the fact that Texas has so recently and so suddenly developed from the frontier stage into the technological phase of civilization. The history of frontiers shows typically two extremes. The early frontier is impatient of the effeminate centers of civilization; Kit Carson's classic "Hell's filled with greenhorns" may stand as a motto. But the moment the frontier ceases being a frontier, there is a violent reaction. Pioneer crudity and simplicity, once virtues, become matter for public shame. And the community whose distinction only a few decades before was its complete unlikeness to anything known in the civilized world, falls into an extravagant admiration for the sophisticated arts of other lands. So headlong is this passion that anything alien is by that very fact thought to be desirable. One has only to remember the pseudo-Oriental craze of fifty years ago in America to realize how uncritically such a lust for the exotic may operate.

My mind raced to one great earthy soul who never exalted the exotic, H. O. Kelly, Texas' primitive painter. I had seen his work and heard of his fine mind. I looked at the Hill Country, rocky and white, dry and austere, but softened by dark green cedars that live, like the natives, on practically nothing; veined and threaded by emerald water purling over white stones, foaming against the reddish trunks of lacy giant cypress trees. I longed to sit in the presence of this artist, to touch the hand that held so sensitive a brush.

Johnson City, Stonewall, Fredericksburg, Kerrville, Leakey . . . the country Kelly loved, and painted with love. I had been over it, had ridden in a jeep to the fabled Prade Ranch, where your daily room rent is not a "down payment" and you are not "nickeled to death," and where I found the only United States post office where you can buy stamps on credit. The post office is a town: Prade Ranch, Texas. The jeep, amphibious critter, floundered its way in a pouring rain over a vast rocky river bed with ruts thirty inches deep grooved by the iron rims of wagon wheels for centuries when the river bed was a county road. The river flowed and the rain poured. But my guardian angel never let a wheel go into one of those devastating ruts. As I looked back, afterward, I felt like Christian in *Pilgrim's Progress*, marveling at the road I had traversed "in the night." Under the cliffs of the Frio Canyon, cliff swallows darted in and out of their mud nests that hung like gourds under the rocks. Through the sheets of rain I saw a simple and beautiful statue of a Madonna, enshrined in the rocks, maidenhair and cardinal flower beneath.

Some sense of urgency made me hurry on to cover the ground for this book and, again, my lucky stars were pushing me ahead. If I had waited to begin my exploration of Texas, four great primary sources would have been lost to me.

"Where will I find Kelly?" I asked. The Gillespie County Fair was sure to bring him to Fredericksburg, I was told. I went to Fredericksburg at Easter. Back of the Nimitz Hotel I looked for "Old Man Kelly." He loved the wagonyard, and I had seen his painting of one just like it.

"No, he ain't here yet, but he'll be here for the Fair . . . horse races and oompah bands! Long's you're here, you won't miss the pageant, will you?"

The Easter Fires were worth the trip.

The resourcefulness of mothers throughout the world is legendary. It seems fitting that one of Texas folklore's most endearing stories should spring from the fertile mind of a German immigrant woman soothing her children against fear of an Indian raid. Fitting that a daughter of Germany, land of fairy tales, Christmas trees, and toys, should let her protective imagination conjure up a quieting and entrancing story for her little ones.

About a century ago, Baron Meusebach relinquished his title and became plain John O. Meusebach, Texan. He chose the most fertile bit of Texas hill country he could find for his colony and named it Fredericksburg. Surely he was influenced in some degree by the sweet sense of familiarity, the remembrance of the German hills of home. The red-bearded baron was a just and industrious man, well trained as a leader with two years of service in the Supreme Court of Justice at Naumburg and Stettin before the Adelsverein appointed him Commissioner-general to succeed Prince Carl of Solms-Braunfels in Texas. He was soon on good terms with the Indians. Or at least, so he and his colonists thought.

Stout cabins housed the first families and the sturdy stone houses that stand stout and snug today were being planned and built in the late spring of the year 1847. On Easter Eve came the warning of a murderous Indian raid on the settlers. The men barricaded the women and children as securely as they could and set off for a conciliatory talk, prepared to appease the savages if necessary.

Late in the evening the men set out, their wives peering anxiously after them into the deepening dusk. Their Easter breads and cakes were baked, for they clung then, as now, to the observance of tradition, regardless of how primitive their resources and facilities for the observance might be.

The children were tucked away in bed, restless as always before any holiday. In the darkened cabin of one of the families, a woman looked out into the night, alert for any sign. Suddenly the hills that form a ring around the settlement were lit with a scarlet crown: the hills blazed with Indian signal fires.

"*Mutter! Mutterchen*," the nervous children whimpered, "we are frightened."

"*Ruhe, ruhe!*" the resourceful one murmured. "Have you forgotten what night this is? Those are the fires built by the Easter Rabbit and his helpers, high in the hills. They blaze under his cauldrons of dye for the Easter eggs."

She must have gained confidence as she went along and her

imagination responded to her need. "He is making the beautiful blue dye from the bluebonnets, the pink from the opal-
cup primrose, the red from the Indian paintbrush, the yellow
from the buttercups, and the purple from the verbena." The
flaxen heads began to droop, heavy with dreams of Easter
joys. "Tomorrow he comes with his little cart with red wheels,
laden with beautiful colored eggs, garlanded with flowers and
ferns from plains and hills."

And so they slept.

Each year the pageant of the Easter Fires is performed in
Fredericksburg by the descendants of these same families.
The entire story is acted out, and from the grandstand in the
fair grounds we watch the rabbits, in semi-darkness, fill the
grass nests that are prepared on the ground that serves as the
outdoor stage. The lights come up and the flowers, beautiful
young girls who have been seated cross-legged on the ground,
with their heads folded down over their crossed arms, slowly
unfold into motion as a flower into bloom. They dance the
flower ballet.

As the legend of the Easter Fires unfolds, the doughty German daughters often have to cope with cantankerous climate, a
factor almost as bothersome as Indian raids.

The Easter Fires must be lit on the far hills at the exact moment the swoosh of the signal rocket is heard at the Fair
Grounds. The synchronization is sometimes thrown off by a
chill, mizzling rain. But the good Fredericksburgers, with their
innate *gemütlichkeit*, their general painstakingness when it
comes to creature comfort, appear in the stadium on the not
infrequently cold evening of the performance armed with
patchwork quilts, many of them very old and extremely beautiful.

The performers, on their guard from one hundred years of
inherited experience in trying to outguess Texas weather, are
prepared to keep healthy and warm with many ingenious con-

trivances under their costumes. Men acting the parts of their
early settler forefathers are warmly clad in black broadcloth
tailcoats, thick woolen trousers, and stovepipe hats rented from
a costumer in San Antonio. The children in flannelette Easter
Bunny costumes and the women in heavy full-skirted pioneer
costumes are fortunate. Like the choristers in cassock and
cotta, they can conceal their winter wrappings. In the hall that
serves as dressing room, the make-up man, a true artist, glues
a curly red beard on Baron Meusebach, while the Alpen Veil-
chen, a band of knobby-kneed, snaggle-toothed, freckle-faced
little boys in early German costume of white shirt, black bow
tie, short straight pants held up by Bavarian suspenders, high
white socks, and peaked Bavarian hats giggle gleefully at their
fathers and uncles busily cleaning ancient muskets or fiddling
with their beavers. The boys make witticisms to each other in
fluent German and look very unlike Alpine violets. They are
quite comfortable as there can be no doubt that they have
warm sweaters under those spotless crackling white shirts.

Frugal and thrifty to the bone, the girls are careful not to put
on their headdresses a minute before it is absolutely necessary.
Many of them take part in the pageant with their hair up in
curlers. It was painstakingly set for Easter Sunday and would
not be taken down until the exact moment of departure
for church. From the grandstand, who can see? A lovely
flaxen-haired girl of twelve spoke to another with great serious-
ness about her German costume of full skirt, black bodice,
white blouse, black silk ribbon headdress, and long black
stockings. "The costume I like. I could wish almost it was in
style. The stockings feel good to me."

"Not with that tacky waist and those awful stockings!" her
friend said.

"Including!" said the gentian-eyed realist.

The music begins and out they go into the night . . . the
pale, Germanic ten-year-old Indian braves, looking very pale

indeed — and not only in the face; long, white, bony feet scarcely touching the cold ground recall the lines:

> Lo, the poor Indian whose untutored mind,
> Clothes him before and leaves him bare behind.

The gelid flowers suffer the most: for Indian braves it is permissible to speed up the tempo of a war dance and scurry through it as best they may. But bluebonnets, wine-cups, and daisies must be stately and unhurried, swaying gracefully to the very last note of the music.

Tasch House

Rain or shine, the Easter Fires are set well in advance of the performance, to be tended by older boys. At the signal rocket, the flames flare rosily on the softly rounded hills behind the open air stage. The cathedral and its spire loom purple-black against the sky. The descendants of the pioneers, with inherited temperamental fortitude, go on with the show in spite of any hardship. Rugged qualities are nurtured and cherished by the people of Fredericksburg. Damp or dry, the Easter Fires burn.

Filled with the Hill Country, I decided that I would not wait until Fair time. I went to Blanket, Texas, to find H. O. Kelly.

It has been said that a cowboy is a man with guts and a horse.

H. O. Kelly is a cowboy who paints.

Kelly gained nation-wide fame as a painter when he was well past sixty. Most of his work was done on a tiny farm at Blanket. Because he was a self-taught artist, he has been compared to Grandma Moses. There the resemblance ceases. Kelly exhibited thirty-three paintings at the Dallas Museum of Fine Arts in 1949. All thirty-three were sold on opening day. His paintings are full of life and animation. "I paint the figures naked, then put clothes on 'em when I'm finishing up the picture." He likes to paint Texas pictures for Texas people. No one is better qualified. *Life* Magazine featured Kelly and his paintings in an article, and he did a colorful cover for the *Lincoln-Mercury Times* in 1950 as well as illustrating a piece by J. Frank Dobie, "The Brush Country of Texas," for the same issue of the magazine.

Kelly signs his letters "H. O." Those fortunate enough to correspond with him treasure his gems of wit and wisdom written on pale pink or aquamarine paper, topped by a "Headlight," a tiny, bejeweled painting like those on old German Christmas tree ornaments.

He is spry, especially getting around the dance floor or the horse lot. His face is seamed and lined; nary a tooth in his head. A gnomish, curved man, legs bent from years in the saddle. His stout back is bent now from years of following the plow as a lad; from the plow and much hard labor. A heart, mind, and soul like his should go on forever — and will, in his paintings and philosophy. I cannot write of him parsimoniously.

He was nearly sixty-four before he began painting in oils.

"Like lots of folks, I was often short around Christmas, so I made a practice of painting watercolors for little gifts. I like to paint the Texas hill country. Every now and then I like to paint

a Pennsylvania Dutch picture with its air of permanent prosperity and simple good living — a few glasses of good keg beer
on Saturday night, a few nice waltzes, church on Sunday
morning, and then watch the quarter horses dust out in the
afternoon!"

Mr. Kelly lives with his wife Jessie near Brownwood. Jessie
is brown, plump, and quick-eyed as a quail. Just ask anybody
where Old Man Kelly lives. His friends come from the ends
of the earth to visit him. He loves Blanket because people don't
"make over" him. H. O. is indignant because some interviewer
stated that he had no electric light in his house because his
landlord wouldn't install it.

"Why, that coulda hurt his feelin's! He's a fine man; give
me anythin' I might ask for. I like the coal-oil lamps for the
soft light they give . . . nice to paint by. Besides, when the
power goes off, I'm not mis-put none."

A man's nationality is not always that of the country of his
birth.

Old Man Kelly's mother came from Mannheim, Germany.
The name Kelly is about all the Irish he inherited.

"Miss Mary, can you play 'Die Wacht am Rhein'? Ain't that
middle part beautiful? Makes you shivery all over. An' them
waltzes! Hardly nobody knows my kind . . . they don't know
what a *Ländler* is. I'll tell you what it is: it's waltzin' on the
grass! I live for the Fredericksburg Fair. State Fair can't hold
a candle to it. Horse races! Hasenpfeffer oompah bands. You
buy tickets for the beer an' the dancin'!"

His slate-colored eyes light up under the brows the same
color as the rich thatch of iron gray hair, well kempt and elegant. Over the door frame of his snug shiplap house hang a
rifle and a pair of maroon sock garters.

"Try some o' my Shiner beer?" It's awful special. I keep it for
company. Eat, drink, and sleep Texas, Miss Mary! Jessie,
where's my anti-smokin' medicine?" He cuts a neat plug of
chewing tobacco and pops it into his mouth. "I quit smokin'

when I had the mumps at sixty-nine. I lay there twenty-one days on my back like a KING! Bring me this! Bring me that! The mumps puts governors on you. Yes sir! I ate every kinda Campbell's soup there is."

"How'd you pass the time?" I asked, imagining he'd said something about a poker party.

"Whoopee John's Polka Party: every mornin' at four o'clock. I got a power pack, so I don't care if the power goes blink."

Kelly, as Jessie calls him, drives a 1935 chevvy. "It's my research car," he says, "but God didn't aim for me to drive one. I am the worst driver in Texas. There's somethin' about the outsides of a horse that's good for the insides of a man! But I get around in it an' see the pretty country." He pointed to the hills. "That there's Spanish oak, where I get all my beautiful colors of the leaves in the fall. Went up in them hills one day an' found, crammed right up under a ledge, the skeleton of a fourteen-year-old child; couldn't tell if it was a girl or a boy, but there was a forty-five caliber bullet in the skull."

He has a cabinet full of fancy beer cans, collects extra pretty ones he sees around the country. He also loves books — and has some good ones. He believes in "Wear the old coat; buy the new book."

"How's Babe's colt?" Babe is the glossy mare he adores.

"Babe's colt was a love-child. I had to destroy it. Sent her to one o' these teasin' stallions: proud-cut. Couldn't get a colt but he did! When a horse is talkin' to a mare, he's the most beautiful animal in the world. The only thing in this life that can take me away from race horses is a hasenpfeffer oompah band.

"They got a feller in Fredericksburg that can play a drum, lead a band, an' drink a case o' beer at the same time. You know they got two Derby trainers from Fredericksburg? With Nimitz thrown in! Texas has somethin' else to crow about." As I looked at the paintings of his beloved hill country, I knew Texas had something else to crow about.

"Ain't them hills pretty, Miss Mary? Where the hell is my
Bible, Jessie? Want to read you that little bit from the Psalms
I like so much. Here it is, belonged to my grandmother, born
before the Revolution. She was 104 years and 8 days old when
she died after the Civil War. She read the Ninety-second
Psalm every day. This is my favorite. 'The little hills shout
with joy. They also sing.' Ain't that hill country, Miss Mary?
'Magine them fellers wantin' to moddenize the Bible! Tamper
with King James, the winner and champ. Made me so mad I
cut out a piece about it! Got it right here: 'Virtually flawless
prose rendition!' Ain't that good? To come from *Collier's?*
Them people that advertise likker an' beer in their magazine."

"When did you start out working for yourself?"

"Back in Pennsylvania my folks was goin' to apprentice me
to a man in a machine shop. A Englishman, he was. 'Boy,' he
says, 'if yer can just keep yer eyes off them bloody 'orses, I'll
make a mester machinist outer yer.' I was sixteen, but I pulled
out an' went to work for a Mennonite farmer. It was hard and
a lot was expected. I purt' near cried to think I wasn't stout
enough to be a man. But by that night I had acquired the art
o' plowin'! He fed me good: sausage, dumplin's, lettuce an'
sour cream an' brown sugar. My dad caught up with me. He
was cold-trailin' me, an' kinda proud because I got out on my
own. I got eight dollars a month: a good man got twelve.
Texas was always in the back o' my mind. Got drouthed-out
in the dust bowl. Worked in thirty states. Jessie an' me come
from sixty miles north o' Little Rock to Texas: we stopped in
wagonyards, had our bed an' skillet an' lid. Right where
Perryton is now. I'm the richest man in the world in friends."

"What about the WPA? Didn't they help?"

"Little ole ragged . . ." he clapped his hand over his mouth,
"schoolteachers out tellin' farmers how to farm? Talkin'
namby-pamby: 'You have to have something green to have
precipitation.' What's a man gonna do when he has to sell for
two bits a bushel? Suckin' on the gov'ment tit, that's what they

were doin'. Back to the Bible: 'I sought him and he was not.' That's them!"

Kelly's painting reflects the man's realism, integrity, and keen vision. He is a primitive in that he is self-taught and paints from memory. His perspective is far better than most primitives. "Kelly gets a lot o' distance into 'em," Jessie said.

The figures are short and stocky, downright dumpy; made to stand up under the rigors of drouth and disillusion. The barnyard animals are there aplenty, frolicking and kicking. The spring houses with butter and milk in them make the mouth to water and the eye to mist. *Hog Killing* is so real that the beholder hears the squeal of the frantic porkers. Depth and detail, humor and earthiness — Breughel in Texas.

Kelly paints lots of rock houses, the real hill-country kind. "I'd like to live in one myself, specially the one with the *Gasthaus* for 'men only' — a retreat from what Solomon called the 'Constant dropping.'"

"Everybody needs a 'Sulking room,'" I agreed.

"I got years o' work ahead. Sell one, an' eat it up. That's a good way to live, ain't it?"

I was thinking how fast some of the self-styled "creative brotherhood" live it up, and leave no lasting signs that they've passed this way.

"You know Lexie Dean Robertson, the poet? She was a lovely woman; lived in Rising Star, Texas. Brought my pictures to the Dallas Museum of Fine Arts. She an' her man had no money to get married on, so they loaded a wagon with peaches an' drove into town an' sold 'em for enough to buy the license an' pay the preacher. They stayed in the wagonyard that night. Ain't that lovely?"

"Let me see Babe," I said.

"If I had my druthers," he slammed the battered hat on, "I'd rather tame little colts one day old than eat. Funny about a horse, proud-cut, how he gets jealous of stallions." We gazed at the beautiful animal a long while. "I'm not jealous of eunuchs," he said, "but let me see one, even across the street, an' the hackles on the back o' my neck come up involuntarily."

I finally had to say goodbye. "We've had so much fun, Mr. Kelly, you and I, slangin' the langwidge! We're horse wranglers and word manglers. Will you let me quote a few lines from the review you wrote of Cunninghame Graham's *The Horses of the Conquest?** I'd like the book world to know how many strings there are to your fiddle."

"Take it. All or any part of it."

As I reread the review, I am sore beset to cut it. Every word is a pearl, by one who knows and loves the subject — but cut I must. H. O. Kelly writes:

> In a style as flowing and beautiful as Spanish, Cunninghame Graham tells the story of the first horses brought to the new world by the Cortez expedition to Mexico. To us who have been fortunate enough to have worked along with the descendants of those first brave men, the Trujillos, Gonzaleses, Morenos, and all the merry, musical, dancing, fighting, drinking *hombres* of the old Southwest, and who have ridden the wiry and often beautiful little horses, this book is a bridge. It is a bridge reaching back to 1519, covered with plodding and prancing horses, mounted by men who were *muy hombre;* men who beat the Indians' ears down so that they could "better hear the word of God," but who gave us fine sounding names for rivers, hills, and valleys, and who stocked the western world with horses, without which the settling would not have been possible.
>
> "For after God, we owed the victory to the horses." Bernal Díaz del Castillo, at the age of eighty-four, battered, worn, not rich, with failing eyes but good heart, wrote in his kind and simple manner: "I wish to put down from memory all the horses and mares that we embarked." Then he described the eleven horses and five mares. These were horses, now, not geldings. Those old boys, like their Moorish invaders, did not have to mutilate a good horse before they dared ride him. Bernal Díaz

* Published in the Christmas Book Supplement of the Dallas *Morning News,* Christmas, 1949.

tells the owners' names and qualifications as riders. "Juan de Escalante; a light chestnut with three white feet. It was no good." That for him!

"Ortiz, the musician, and Bartolomé García, a miner; a very good dark horse we called Arriero, or Muleteer; this was one of the best horses in the fleet." Here is my favorite: "Juan Velásquez de León; a silver-gray mare, we called Rabona, a shorttail, very powerful, very restless, and a good racer." There she is, a little Mae West of a mare, one that takes you places and one to lay your money on! I know she lived a long and fruitful life, for I am sure I have ridden her descendants.

"Those old boys were hard stuff. Spearing Indians, pausing to give thanks to God and His Holy Mother for victory, doctoring the wounds of horses and men alike with dead Indians' fat, rustling corn (and I hope beer), sheltering horses in Indians' houses, spearing the sacred deer for food and sport, and rafting rivers swarming with alligators — never failing to give God and the horses due credit.

Cortez himself, in writing his third report to the king: "That day the people of our camp were in no danger, except as those on horseback came out of ambush a man fell off his mare. At once, she galloped off towards the enemy, who wounded her with arrows. She, when she saw their wickedness, though badly wounded, came back to us. That night, she died; we felt her death, for the horses and mares were our salvation, but our grief was less, as she did not die in the power of the enemy, as we had feared would be the case." Thus speaks the horseman, the man who had done all in his power for his friend and servant. He kneels by, his hand on his friend's neck, sees the four feet beat into a little trot, and the big eyes glaze and the nostrils flutter with a soft nicker. That man knows his horse has a place to go, and sees it, and hopes to be lucky to go there too.

I and many like me owe a great debt to Cunninghame Graham, who with Scottish and Spanish grandparents, was well educated to see, remember, and describe what the world can offer to a real soldier of fortune, a debt for his fine book; and another debt to the tough, venturesome Spaniards of whom he writes. For if it were not for them, I would not have a fine

horse standing in my yard, "a good chestnut mare, very powerful, and a good racer." Brother, bring your horse and we will
have sport and racing.

So wrote Old Man Kelly, horseman, painter, and humanist.
He wrote as he lived and painted: out of the richness of his
great heart and soul.

On December 13, 1955, H. O. and Jessie were eating chicken-
fried steak in a café in Brownwood.

"'I ain't had white beans in the longest time,' he said. I
looked up and he was gone," Jessie told me as she stood bereft
at the grave on a hill in Blanket, near his beloved hill country.
A lone, bent cedar tree stood guard. "This is where Kelly'd
want to be." I thought of his lines describing the feeling of the
conquistador whose mare died of Indian arrow wounds. "That
man knows his horse has a place to go, and sees it, and hopes
to be lucky to go there too."

In the Pastures of Heaven, or where the thoroughbreds go,
that's where Old Man Kelly will be.

These are a few of the present day pioneers in Texas arts.
They share one great attribute: a total lack of artiness.

The trail was blazed for them and the scores of other dedicated men and women who are creating beauty in Texas by
three great, sky-scraper individuals. In the intellectual darkness that threatened to becloud Texas for a period from the end
of the First World War up to the late Thirties, three men illu-
minated the path like beacon lights for all who were to follow.
Certainly every student of Texas and the Southwest, present
and to come, owes a debt to the triumvirate: Bedichek, Dobie,
and Webb.

Dobie, Bedichek, Webb

6. THE UNWHOLLY INTELLECTUALS

RECENTLY a writer, new to Texas, seemed to be making a water haul so far as material was concerned, dragging his net in empty. He went to a man who had been described as possessing great knowledge of the state.

"I want to talk to the men who made Texas," the visitor said.

"In that case," Bob Pool replied, "you'll have to go to the cemeteries."

It is extremely fitting that Austin, the undisputed and very senior cultural center of Texas, should be able to claim as citizens beloved by Town and Gown alike three men who have "made Texas" in an intellectual and cultural sense: Roy Bedichek, J. Frank Dobie, and Walter Prescott Webb. The order stands on two counts: alphabetically and chronologically. Each is an internationally known writer of unquestioned ability,

large productivity, and unsurpassed authority in his particular
field.

I call them the Unwholly Intellectuals because they share a
rich, earthy humor and a passionate interest in the humanities,
never losing sight of Pope's statement that "the proper study
of mankind is man." As I observe the three men busy with
their production, but never too busy to help others secretly —
without thought of recompense or even appreciation, manag-
ing their business affairs, taking part in civic and regional activities, enjoying the outdoors with well-selected friends, doing
missionary work in the vital field of water and wild life
conservation, I think of something Schiller said about man being the measure of all things. "If our standard measure prove
false, all our measurements are vitiated."

These three men are as Texan as the *caliche* dust on their
boots. They live within a mile or so of each other and are lifetime friends. Wherever they might have been born and raised,
they would have risen head and shoulders above their fellows.
Their three separate yet similar gifts are truly Texan in their
scope, concept, and expression. Each has mined his material
from the rock whence he was hewn. They embody regionalism
in its finest and fullest sense.

Roy Bedichek achieved international fame as a naturalist
with his *Adventures with a Texas Naturalist* written when he
was almost seventy.

Frank Dobie has recorded in imperishable form the tales of
Texas, the lure of the Brush Country, and the lore of the Mexicans, all saturated with his own individual and rugged philosophy. In years to come, those wanting to know "what it was
like on the open range" will have to refer to Dobie's work to get
the full flavor of that vivid life.

Walter Prescott Webb's *The Great Plains* is ranked as the top
book by any living historian by John Caughey of the University
of California, writing in the *Pacific Historical Review*, present-

ing the results of a general questionnaire. Dr. Webb spent ten
years writing the book and has made one of the few original
contributions to historical knowledge of universal interest in
the last generation.

"When did you begin writing *The Great Plains?*" I asked.

"When I was four," he said.

In his characteristically dour manner, Dr. Webb told me that
he lacked imagination and drama. I smiled, and reminded him
of a quiz section he conducted in Medieval History back in
1924 when I was a sophomore. To our consternation, he told us
to draw a picture of the Middle Ages.

"I don't care whether you can draw or not . . . just show
me graphically what the Middle Ages means to you," he
drawled.

My crude pictographs tickled him and he held them up to
the class, saying that they showed imagination, audacity, and
perhaps a touch of genius. Though neither he nor I knew it at
the time, he may have started me, unconsciously, on my life
of literary crime.

"Aw, I never did that, did I, Mary?" asked the man who a
week ago gave as one question in the final exam on his course,
The Great Plains, instructions to his students to write a letter
to a friend who never saw the Great Plains. "Make him see the
country as it was when the white men came, and tell how it affected the lives and institutions of those who came to live
there."

Such tactics are part of his gift: he makes history live and
makes people live history.

Dr. Webb started the Junior Historians movement in the
schools of Texas to stimulate interest among teen-agers in Texas
history. They do truly astonishing work, and are to my mind,
a rebuttal to the current outbreak of juvenile delinquency.

The Handbook of Texas, Holy Writ in two volumes, was his
brainchild, wet-nursed to final sturdy form by his devoted

students and disciples. The man possesses the power of inspiring deep loyalties, possibly because it is done by example rather than by precept.

No doubt Dr. Webb's most popular achievement was making the Texas Rangers live in dramatic and imperishable form. His wry sense of humor is frequently in evidence, as when he says that in Texas a man's life depended more often on a fast horse than on a just cause. Like Thornton Wilder and his scholarly Spanish studies, Walter Prescott Webb, too, has a *violon d'Ingres* . . . in his case, real estate investments. Ingres, recognized as a leader among the classicists, best known for his nudes, but in reality a historical painter, could play the violin a little bit. He was more proud of this achievement than of all his paintings put together, so goes the legend.

I have a sneaking suspicion that Dr. Webb is more proud of his canny, long-headed real estate deals than he is of being the first man from West of the Mississippi to be President of the American Historical Association. Hence, he qualifies one hundred per cent as an unwholly intellectual.

These three men have lived practically every word they have written. The valid, firsthand quality in their art is one of its prime virtues. They are nothing if not authentic. Each has made immortal at least one phase of Texas life.

Indirectly, Roy Bedichek, the nature writer, is the product of Frank Dobie and Walter Prescott Webb. Entranced by Bedi's conversation, erudite, fanciful, and enchantingly humorous, his two cronies decided he should be writing. Bedichek had fathered and tended the Interscholastic League Program of Texas for nearly fifty years. Such a widespread venture requires, as any Texas school child can attest, the patience of Job, the strength of Samson, and the faith of Elijah. Bedi had the necessary qualifications. After all, he was the man who undertook the job of changing the name of the state of New Mexico to the unlikely one of Lincoln. Any Texan could see why that enterprise was doomed to be stillborn. Part of the task of the League Director was to put out a publication, *The Interscholastic Leaguer*. Into what could have been a stodgy paper, Roy Bedichek injected a certain liveliness and wisdom. Notes sent back and forth to his two close friends convinced them that he had an unusually attractive natural writing style. He had something to say and knew how to say it.

"You ought to be writing." Dr. Webb made an opening, and sneaked up on his friend's blind side trying to slip the bridle on.

"You must write." Frank Dobie said.

"I think writing would be a fine thing," Bedichek replied in his mild manner, "but I do a full time job at the Bureau of Public School Service. What I should care to write from my copious notes could not be tossed off in odd moments . . . it wouldn't be fair to my job or to my writing. I am getting along toward retirement in a year or two. We'll see what happens then."

His two confrères cannily dropped the subject for the time being. They were busy doing what is known in Texas as "puttin' your money where your mouth is." Dr. Webb is not a loquacious man. His voice has a somewhat anguished tone even when he is happy. It can best be described as saying he sounds like Ned Sparks, the dead-pan comedian, wired for sound. But the merest grudging word of assent or syllable of approval from him has more "valiance" to it than most people's statements signed and sealed before a notary public. When Walter Webb sets his hand to the plow, he seldom looks back. One thing is certain: what he starts, he will finish. Frank Dobie is kind, and Bedi is the beloved friend of both men. When the two *compadres* next approached Bedi about writing, they had, in a manner of speaking, a year's leave of absence for him in one hand and sufficient money, the equivalent of a year's salary, handsomely gift-wrapped in the other.

I can just hear Mr. Bedichek saying, "I couldn't start before tomorrow morning! It is never too late to change your life," he told me with conviction. "I changed mine radically at seventy."

Adventures with a Texas Naturalist and *Karankaway Country* may very well have changed lots of people's lives, by making them aware of the vibrant, vital processes taking place in nature all around them.

His two friends gave him three great gifts of life: time, money, and solitude. Bedichek went to Dr. Webb's Friday Mountain Ranch and holed in. He cooked and cleaned — after a fashion — but he had peace and privacy. There in that great rugged room he labored and brought forth his first-born, a beautiful and moving book. The man's vast knowledge of life and how it is lived, his rich classical background, and immensely poetic feeling for the humblest, earthiest details concerning all God's creatures, his love for the most insignificant life forms all add up, in my mind, to "he prayeth best who loveth best all things both great and small." I think his two friends had something to do with the coincidental appearance of Lee Barker, of Doubleday, who entered the picture just when a publisher should.

"Whom do you consider the best American nature writer?"

I asked Bedichek as we sat and toasted our hides on the Philosopher's Stone at Barton Springs.

"Thoreau and Joseph Wood Krutch," he replied. Then with an impish hand over his mouth he whispered: "Krutch thinks highly of me! He put Thoreau first and me last in an anthology!"

Austin women with an intellectual streak hover around "The Dowager's Delight" eager to get a word with him. A sprightly woman tanned to a rich *café au lait* came and sat beside us. The dragonflies, sometimes called darning needles, were plentiful, skimming over the water, darting after insects and lighting on the legs and arms of the bathers.

"Never kill one of those insects," Bedi said. "They destroy mosquitoes and other harmful insects."

My mind raced back to my childhood.

"We called them mosquito hawks in Brownsville," I said, "and used to tie a long thread to the end of their tails, and tie the other end of the thread to the head of the bed. They were supposed to eat up the mosquitoes that would have bitten us."

"I never heard of that," Bedichek said.

"Look, Mr. Bedi, look at this one," the lady cried. "It has four wings! Lots of them have! Some of them seem to be double! Why are they like that?"

Mr. Bedichek lowered his voice discreetly: "I hate to go into the physiology of this, Mrs. C., but those dragonflies are mating!"

Frank Dobie arrived in the nick of time. Don Panchito, as I call him, is in fine physical condition. At least, I judge so on the basis that the skin is the largest organ of the human body and its condition, smoothness, color, and suppleness is said to be an index to the health of an individual. Richly tan, Don Panchito has not a single visible "defect in the hide." His gleaming white hair and vivid blue eyes twinkle in the sunlight, especially when he gets off a choice bit and glances up at his listeners like a child that knows he is naughty and says in his look: What are you going to do about it?

Much copy has been written about Dobie's writing. I am concerned with the man. He is, to me, half of the team of Frank and Bertha Dobie, warm, wise, and generous people, thinking and acting independently of the world and each other, and demanding personal liberty for everyone else.

Bertha Dobie's garden is famous in Texas — it would be outstanding anywhere for its deceptive simplicity, simple only to those who do not know that art is to conceal art.

"I like a garden that says 'Linger here,'" Don Panchito says to guests in the comfortable lawn chairs, near the creek bank where high shade from live oaks and elms provides perfect conditions for the pale mauve Japanese anemones that take the place. As the toddies got lower in the glasses, I noticed a large clump of white ginger, the blooms perched like hordes of white butterflies above the green canna-like plant. "The fragrance of white ginger is evocative," I said, "it carries me back to Tutuila, Samoa."

Bertha Dobie's quizzical eyebrows went up over her dark eyes, the color of water in woodland pools. "Evocative!" she said. "That's why Frank doesn't care much for any flowers except the old-fashioned kind they used to have at the ranch: the others don't evoke anything."

I knew how much Don Panchito valued her opinion on any writing he happened to be doing. Once he went into the kitchen with a sheaf of manuscript in his hand while Bertha was cooking supper: "I wouldn't give you a dime for your cooking time, but I'll give you a hundred dollars for your critical time!"

A neighbor once saw Mrs. Dobie hurrying more than is usual with her, carrying large bags of groceries, a rather preoccupied look on her usually serene face.

"The little brown men are coming!" she almost whispered. Her friend began to wonder if Mrs. Dobie had not been working too hard lately. It was not until the next day that he learned from the newspaper that the Little, Brown men were Don Panchito's publishers from Boston.

Someone commented on Mr. Dobie's excellent bourbon and I thought of the time he won the Carr P. Collins Award for literary excellence. The prize is one thousand dollars, bestowed by a notorious "dry." Asked how he planned to spend the money, Frank Dobie announced, accepting the check, that he would buy Jack Daniels sour mash whiskey with it.

Freedom. Freedom of thought, freedom of speech, and above all — freedom of action. Throughout all of Dobie's works runs this outstanding characteristic of the man. In his *Guide to Life and Literature of the Southwest* these words are printed opposite the Table of Contents:

NOT COPYRIGHTED
Anybody is welcome to help himself to
any of it in any way

He has put into imperishable form three other lovers of freedom: the longhorn, the mustang, and the coyote. He has made them a symbol of his own philosophy. In a sense he is a little like those three rebels himself: sturdy as the longhorn, untamable as the mustang, and smart as the coyote. Nobody, except gentle Bertha, ever put a brand on J. Frank Dobie.

When I think of these three men, cast in the heroic mold of Texas herself, my heart is lifted up. Then hard reality closes her fist around my heart as I realize that only a part of each of them can live forever. But I can never be downcast for long . . . to do that would be, in a sense, to reject the works of my three friends. If their work is as valid as I think it is, somewhere under the blue Texas dome, from her arid plains, from her teeming pastures, and her throbbing seashores, there will emerge three young men, strong and fearless thinkers, spiritually sired and inspired by Texas' Unwholly Intellectuals.

7. THE PLAINS FROM THE SKY

AFTER TALKING to the Number One authority on the Plains, I became very discouraged. I had spent considerable time in that area but what could I say that would not sound like a piping treble after Walter Prescott Webb?

"I'll fly through what Stanley Vestal calls the 'sky-gardens,'" I decided. "By day and by night, high and low. It's the only way I can ever get an all-at-once, overall picture and know what the Cap Rock looks like all of a piece."

There was little I could add to the vast amount that has been written about the Plains and the life of that "country." The cowboy and plainsman were better known than any other kind of Texan. All I could do was to hold my compass in my hand and hope the pilot would fly low. I wanted to know what it was like going north, and west. When I got tired and wanted to visit friends, or see an out-of-the-way place, I could always do so — and hop another plane later. None of my acquaintances owned a DC-6, so I would travel on commercial planes.

While there is no aerial viewpoint high enough to bring the whole relief map into focus, at least I would not be "looking through a knothole." If I could only remain stationary at a vantage point, say, over Brady, the geographical center of the state, I could look at parts of the four great regions of the North American continent. Millions of years ago they met in Texas. And I would still be looking at Texas, for there are one hundred and seventy-two million miles of it. It is two hundred and fifty times the size of Rhode Island. Big country, even for Texas!

If the plane would just stand still, I thought, I could be looking into the southern extension of the Great Plains which run east to the Rocky Mountains. Looking due north, I would see the Red River Country and the last of the North Central Plains which sweep upward through the United States. Looking east, I could see the Coastal Plains, which flank the Gulf of Mexico all the way to Florida. Still facing north, but veering around to the left, I could look right into the rugged country known as the Trans-Pecos, an extension of the Rocky Mountains. What I needed was a helicopter, but a plane would have to do. I boarded one at Austin for San Angelo, Midland, Odessa, Lubbock, and Amarillo on a sparkling-crisp October afternoon. The pulsing motors of the airplane carried me over gray and black soil of limestone origin. I knew this was the great sheep, cattle, and mohair region, below me.

At the north edge of the Edwards Plateau I saw two towns, Veribest and Sanitorium, Texas. Why don't they incorporate and have Veribest Sanitorium? I wondered. I'm over Tom Green County now, the mother county of the Concho Country. Here in San Angelo is Fort Concho, one of the most typical of the frontier forts.

The land seemed to be part prairie, part mesquite woodland.

Much of the terrain was rolling plain broken by flanking hills and a few isolated peaks.

I was surprised as we got ready to take off from San Angelo to see some cedar. There is little farming although the growing season is 227 days. I saw a load of stupid, sullen sheep in a truck, but no cattle.

I could see the land getting higher going west; northwest to northeast, it's downhill all the way. Texas is like a tilted platter. From an elevation of 4000 feet in the west, with the exception of peaks in the Chisos, and Guadalupe Peak that rises over 8000 feet, the land slopes to sea level in the southeast. The geologists say that Texas used to be low and flat where it is now high; that mountains existed where plains now roll away to infinity. The upheaval of the land and the mountains must have had a lot to do with Texas soils. Wind blowing dirt and rain on the rocks with great force, beating down on the rocks, boulders crashing about at a great rate knocking plant life loose all combined to produce the soil.

Grass began to grow, and vast herds of buffalo and other animals fed on it. Then the Spaniards came! They understood the value of the land for range and grazing and encouraged the early colonists by granting them large parcels of land. When Mexico became independent of Spain, she honored the agreements of impresario Austin and his later followers in all that applied to Texas. After Texas revolted in 1836, her government sold, granted, and traded large tracts of land to ranchers and cattlemen.

Charlie Goodnight and his partner Loving, the X.I.T., the Matador, all pioneered in the ranching enterprises that flourished in spite of every obstacle man could possibly have to contend with: weather, lack of water, poisoned water holes, hostile Indians and Mexicans, and crafty frontiersmen who decided to increase their own stock by branding other people's calves. I wondered how any of them had ever survived. The cattlemen hated the farmers who came to the Plains. The booted ranchers called them "shoe and stocking men." But they sure came to stay! More than half of the surface land of Texas today is still grazing land, but the cattle industry can no longer claim first place.

We were safely on our course over Midland and it was getting late.

"This is a country of vast distance." I asked my seat mate if he didn't think I could get top money with that in the Colossal Cliché Contest. He didn't say anything but went on looking out the window at the flat gray earth broken by occasional white sand dunes. In the gathering dusk I could see the oil derricks below gleaming with red and green lights like jeweled pagodas against the cobalt blue sky.

There wasn't a thing here to break the sweep of the northers as they roar down from the High Plains.

"Nothing between them and the North Pole but a barbed wire fence and that's down most of the time," my companion said. "Oldest joke in Texas."

I was glad to get out of the plane and feel good old "terra cotta" under my feet again, as Helen Hokinson's ladies used to call it.

As I looked about, I remembered the Odessa woman, twenty miles away, who complained about the lack of trees when she first moved there. Two years later she went to visit in the Piney Woods of East Texas. "The trees made me nervous," she said. "They kept getting in the way of the scenery."

"Look at the Taj Mahals!" my friends said as they drove me around Midland. One rambling brick structure reminded me more of a suburban railway station in Connecticut than anything else. A large, white, curved object served as a hitching post in front of a sprawly house. "He shot it in Africa," a woman in the car said. I thought the man was a dentist preserving his first Texas-size extraction.

In a less populous section, the wind was kicking up dried,

round tumbleweeds that executed a mad dance rolling across the plains.

"They spray them with white glisten-y stuff and make Santa Clauses out of them: big round tumbleweed for his belly, smaller one for his head," one of the women said. "Texans will decorate anything."

We stopped at another house for refreshment. Two youths of fifteen were coming out of the garage. The lads looked back wistfully. "Shore purty," the redhead said. He looked lovingly at the Cadillac convertible. "Poppa gave it to me for my birthday, but it'll be ten months till I'm old enough to drive it alone!"

"It's all true what they say about Midland!" I said. "Easy come, easy go, I guess," my friend replied. "But they raised $500,000 in one afternoon in Midland for a church. Got sixty of them now, and more on the way. Symphony orchestra, too. Somebody asked a native lady how they supported it, and she said 'By conscription.' That's the truth! 'Specially those husbands who don't know their Shostakovich from a gin whistle!"

When we drove back to town, I saw a round aluminum dome about twelve feet high in one of the back yards. Too little for a silo, I thought, and it's not an air conditioner. Nor a lighthouse. "They were so pleased when Junior got interested in astronomy," my friend explained, "he's only thirteen you know . . . they just went to work and bought him his own little observatory for the planets. What else could you expect in a town that has the highest per capita long-distance telephone bills in the United States?"

The oil fields toward Odessa were an entrancing sight, dollar signs on the landscape. The Permian Basin was getting a big play — all the way from Permian Drilling Company to Permian Basin Hamburgers. I saw a huge signboard with a pair of human lips drawn on it.

"I don't get it," I said. " 'Welcome Home! We Spent Many Happy Hours With Your Wife!' "

"It's an advertisement for a radio station in Odessa," was the reply.

Midland's not high, but it's wide and handsome.

As I took off next day I thought of how tired everyone must be of hearing about what Texas HAS all the time. That's why the town of Gail, in Borden County, is so interesting: because of what it *hasn't* got.

First of all it is the only town in the county. It has no bank, no theater, no railroad, no hotel, no doctor, no preacher, and no lawyer in the county. Visitors are welcome to sleep in the jailhouse. The owner of the only café has the key.

I thought how pleasant it would be to live in Gail, away from the screech of automobile tires peeling rubber night and day. "Only time you see cars is when court is in session," I had heard. Back in the days of the school land rushes in 1902, the claim filers tried to maintain a position at the door of the county clerk's office until the day designated for the sale of the school lands. The cattlemen of the country put up stiff resistance to the farmers or nesters who tried to file their claims by having their cowboys fight it out with the farmers standing in line. But in true western tradition, everything was "fa'r an' squar'." Only fist fights were allowed inside. The sheriff collected all six-shooters at the door. Borden County is still cow country.

Gail Borden, for whom the town and county are named, and the inventor of condensed milk, was a gifted man. He came to Texas in 1829 — and began raising cattle. In 1835 he established a very famous newspaper at San Felipe: *The Telegraph and Texas Register*. In March 1836 he had to move the press to Harrisburg on Buffalo Bayou on account of the approach of Santa Anna's army. The Mexican army smashed the type and threw the press into the bayou. Borden bought more type and went right on publishing.

President Sam Houston appointed him Collector of Customs at Galveston in 1837, and he had plenty of free time to indulge his genius for invention.

His first achievement was the meat biscuit, which won a prize for him at the World's Fair in London in 1852. The pemmican he invented was used by Dr. Kane on his Arctic expedition.

Gail Borden thought he would have a great thing for the armed forces with this compact, concentrated ration and sank all his resources into its manufacture. The army contractors crossed him up and he went bankrupt. Penniless, over fifty years old, he turned his attention to condensing milk. It took three years and many difficulties before he got his patent in 1856, after he had to sacrifice almost two thirds of his interest in it.

I almost laughed aloud when I thought how little business methods have changed over the years. The fee-splitters are still at it. Everybody gets a cut. But when the Civil War came along Borden's product was much in demand, and developed into a great American success. Everyone knows Elsie, the Borden cow.

He condensed tea, coffee, and cocoa, also fruit juices down to one seventh of their bulk. Borden product plants are all over the United States. It is unlikely that many people know Gail Borden was a real Texican, here before the Revolution.

On up to the foot of the Cap Rock we soared. Cap Rock says just what it means, I thought, a cap of rocklike formation neatly turned down over the edges of the plains.

Going into the western plains from central Texas is an odd experience. Flying along fairly level country, you will see an area of high hills and mountains ahead. When you reach them, you find they twist and wind around a great deal and suddenly they are gone. You look back but you can't see them. Actually, a traveler climbs a series of steep rocky stair steps, gaining altitude as he goes westward. The cycle is repeated several times in the Panhandle plains country and the sheer cliffs and rocks are thrilling, especially when the structure is such that the great rocky fault, or escarpment, that raises the plains country above the level of the rest of the state can be seen clearly, as it can be seen from a car at Crosbyton, Lamesa, Matador, or Post.

The Cap Rock itself is a layer of highly mineral material. It is really nothing but *caliche*, which underlies the Llano Estacado, the Staked Plains, and overlies the other rocks of the plateau. It appears at the top of its high eastern escarpment and literally caps the area and protects the sediments beneath from erosion. The slope from the high plains down to the lower plains to the east is known as the Cap Rock.

Rising from one hundred to nearly one thousand feet within a few miles, the Cap Rock is so designated because it is the point at which there is an end of the erosion that has, through the ages, lowered the earth's surface to the level of West Texas' rolling plains. The whole Llano Estacado is divided into the North or Panhandle Plains, and the South Plains. From the airplane I saw the division clearly.

Right at the foot of the Cap Rock is the town of Post. C. W. Post, the inventor of Postum and Post Toasties, didn't live to see his dreams for this part of the country come true.

The land was nothing but a vast wasteland of sand, shinnery, and cactus, plus a few prairie dog towns until Post traveled over the area as a drummer in a horsedrawn rig. He decided that farming would be profitable in the area and that cotton would be the principal product.

I thought of the fate that befalls all farsighted individuals. Everybody calls them crazy visionaries, as they did Mr. Cobolini in Brownsville when he talked about deep water. Fortunately Post was a wealthy man, and carried his projects through. He suffered from indigestion and went to Dr. Kellogg's Battle Creek Sanitarium to study health foods. Although he made millions out of Grapenuts and stuff like that, he wouldn't eat any of it himself.

Cotton did come in as a big crop. Post died, but his enterprises live and prosper. Garza County produces many sheets

and pillowcases from cotton grown nearby. They are marketed under various famous trade names throughout the
United States. It is said that no matter what fancy brand you
pay for, you are getting the same sheet that J. C. Penney sells.

I wanted to see John Lott's place, the old Slaughter Ranch.
I had heard he was rounding up cows by plane.

The Slaughter Ranch takes in two hundred and fifty square
miles. Mr. Lott was just driving off in his station wagon with
a man and a woman.

"Headed for the ranch now. I'll take you out there," he said.

"I have found," he explained, "that the cows hiding out behind clumps of brush can be easily choused out if someone in
the plane spots them and tells the cowhands where they are."

"How do you manage that?" I asked.

"I use a kind of walkie-talkie radio. The cowboys have numbers on the backs of their jumpers, just as football players do.
Those old cows are wily and sly when it comes to hiding. I call
out over the radiophone and say to Number Eleven, 'Jack,
there's a cow and calf behind that clump of mesquite to your
right,' and he rides over and pokes 'em out."

Since seeing calves running after a pick-up truck for cake
made of cottonseed meal or cubes with mineral content, I could
believe anything.

"Planes are a big help on a ranch this size," Lott said. "When
I go away for any length of time and return after dark, I have a
system rigged to turn on the lights on the landing strip. A radio

beam from the plane turns the lights of the field on for me." He stopped the car in front of a big rock ranch house and we got out.

"See how comfortable the bunkhouse is," he said. It wasn't a bunkhouse at all. It was part of the main residence. "Hands are so hard to get these days we have to treat them very specially."

"So I see," I said. "Air conditioning. TV. Deep freeze. Where's the chuck wagon?"

Mr. Lott shook his head sadly.

"No chuck wagon and hardly any horses. The pick-up truck has just about replaced horses. We have a woman to cook and her husband to help her. Lunch, if you please, is served any time between eleven and three. It's got to be ready and it's got to be hot. The cattle are so far from the house that we find it more economical to have the hands drive in and eat than to take the chuck wagon out to them. They don't want beans and sour-dough biscuits these days."

"Plain old dinner at noon was what cowhands had. Now they demand three kinds of quick-frozen vegetables and icebox pie: lemon chiffon, probably. For a bunch of waddies!" someone said.

"Here's where the unmarried cowboys sleep," Mr. Lott opened a door. I saw through the window that the quarters were pretty fancy. Expensive leather boots were strewn every which way over the floor, some sticking out from under the beds.

"Yay Texas!" I laughed. "Every one of 'em has his best hat wrapped up in tissue paper and put away in a fancy hatbox flossier than a chorus girl's. They really live up to their name of 'Single Buttons,' those bachelors. Airplanes, numbers on their shirts, frozen vegetables! Hollywood is responsible for all this."

As I flew off for Lubbock I thought the present-day cowhands had kind of taken advantage of the Slaughter Ranch brand — U Lazy S. In a private plane I took a quick look at Buffalo Point, a ledge over which hunters once drove herds of buffalo, killing hundreds of them. Down below I saw a queer beast that had me stumped for a moment until I remembered what it was: a cattleoe, the result of a cross between cattle and buffaloes. The scenery over the entire ranch was enthralling. It is so full of gorges and canyons, ledges and varicolored rock that no one could ever complain of monotony. The South Plains Area Council of the Boy Scouts of America really have a field day here. Mr. Lott encourages their interest and gives much time to the youngsters. "But," I thought, "it's a hell of a place to get lost in!"

"Visibility unlimited," the pilot said. "On a clear day you can see thirty miles from the top of a windmill tower. But there is such a thing as the air being too clear: it does things to human vision."

He flew on into Lubbock, the cleanest city in Texas, and right over the bookstore where I had walked in one day and said: "I thought I had all of Marcel Proust. I never knew he wrote a book called *Cuties of the Plains*." He meant cowboys, no doubt. I had actually read the title that way, and it is easier to credit the heady air of the plains than to say I need glasses.

With other friends, I went over to Texas Tech and saw a fine building with various desirable qualities and virtues carved all around the eaves. A paunchy man in a bow tie and expensive loud tweed jacket was reading them aloud: "Patriotism." "Enterprise." "Wealth," a nice, frank approach.

"If the irrigation people don't stop lowering the water table at an alarming rate, there won't be any wealth in this part of the country," I was told.

Funny how much cotton grows here. A man planted half a bushel of cottonseed as an experiment. He had bought the cottonseed to feed his old raunchy cows, and planted a little of it just to see if it would sprout, and look what happened! The Coastal Plains and the South Plains swapped: once they raised little here but cattle. Now cotton is king.

I watched the greedy, agile steel fingers of a mechanical cotton-picking machine stripping the rows of their snowy crop. Kind of depressing, all those machines. But it's an up-and-coming region! Lubbock is one of the few towns where it rains mud-balls when at times the wind blows like fury and the sand sifts into everything. Nevertheless, there is an energetic, thriving quality to it that is stimulating. The high, thin air crackles in people's lungs like wine. Nobody that comes here ever seems to want to leave. The department stores in Lubbock have the finest values in merchandise of any store I have seen in the United States. Stunning Italian leather handbags and glamorous shoes, devastating lingerie, all for a little over half what they would cost on Fifth Avenue. Finding them in a newish city, an ex-cowtown out on the high plains, is exciting and proof of the fact that Texans have always demanded the best in clothing. Cattlemen and their families have always bought the most advanced and costly things available. They had to, because nobody could predict now long they might have to wear them, so they better be good! Fat years in cattle are few and far between. Maybe the fact that Lubbock has a woman bank president has something to do with the quality of the merchandise!

I know big Eastern bankers who are loading up on Lubbock's municipal bonds. They better pray that the water supply holds out! But the future of Lubbock is making itself felt in the present. The rate of growth, in building and industry, is tremendous. There is little sign or symbol of the past. I think the newness of the city makes for a great feeling of pride in its citizens, a feeling of having had a hand in all this opulent progress. It was with a sigh for the zippy ozone of Lubbock, that I took a plane to Canyon for a look at the Pan Handle Plains Museum and the Palo Duro Canyon.

The Panhandle Plains Museum is a gem. All the specimens
in the Museum are tastefully and naturally arranged in dio-
ramas, even the brands and spurs, and all other remnants of
frontier life are displayed in a striking way. The figure of the
old cowboy near the entrance is so lifelike that it fools most
people. He even has natural-looking dirt ingrained in the
cracks of his hands!

And the miniature camp scene, all done to scale, around the
chuck wagon would send a child into ecstasies. The little
quarter of beef sewed up in a muslin bag and hung up in a tree
was enchanting. Everything was perfect down to the last detail, including a tiny sack of Arbuckle coffee. It is the most
complete and interesting museum so far as a region is concerned that I have seen. They have a lifelike restoration of a
shovel-jawed mastodon, the fossil skeleton of a prehistoric
horse, and all kinds of archeological and paleontological col-
lections — life and artifacts, with trained paleontologists putting them together right side to, not backwards like some I
have seen. The bronze doors are magnificent with highly dec-
orative and significant Texas brands on them. I am going to
go back when I can stay longer. Maybe I can mooch them out
of that ancient windmill with the wooden blades held together
with leather thongs. I'm windmill-happy and always was.

I drove twelve miles to the Palo Duro Canyon in the Palo
Duro State Park. It is a great gash eroded by a branch of the
Red River coursing toward the sheer drop of the Cap Rock es-
carpment.

"The colors are like those of the Grand Canyon," I thought.
Quite incredible, really, like one of those super technicolor
movies where the color film runs amuck. I looked down from
the rim of the mighty chasm and marveled at the fantastic
formations of rainbow hues: purple, brown, yellow, blue, and
red, all blended into beauty by a soft purple haze. Those formations didn't pop up overnight. The rock boys at the University say they are of the Pliocene epoch and the Triassic age.

Another good look at the striations of the rocks showed me that they spread out in seemingly ruffled layers.

Spanish skirts! I thought. That's what they are like. The ruffled, flounced skirts of a Flamenco dancer. Coronado and his men felt right at home. Why doesn't somebody write a symphonic tone poem about them? I peered over the ledge and thought of Charlie Goodnight, the fabled pioneer rancher, founding the ranch in the basin at the bottom of the canyon, safe and snug if man or beast made it down alive! It is said he took the wagons apart, piece by piece, and lowered them to the floor of the canyon where he put them together again. It's the only possible way he could have got them down there. A roadrunner cocked his head at me inquiringly, and I began to notice the other birds.

Roadrunner

The Wild Life Preservation had just flown in three hundred Red Legs from Spain. I noticed the Red Legs had some odd-looking companions.

"What are they?" I asked my guide.

"See-see birds from Pakistan!" he said. "Seems like the experts say there's parts of Spain and Pakistan like the Palo Duro and they're supposed to feel right at home because this is like their native habitat."

We went down to the ticket office at Sad Monkey, Texas, and watched the sightseers load up on the little toy train. I loved the whistle and the baby engine, but when I saw a spieler pick up a megaphone, I decided to forego the pleasure. "I'll go to Amarillo instead."

Amarillo was sired by buffalo hunters and bone gatherers, nurtured by cowboys, freighters, gamblers, land speculators, and pioneer cattlemen. Ask anybody today, "What's the difference between Lubbock and Amarillo?" and the answer will be, "In Amarillo the Joneses haven't taken over yet." Quite a lot of rivalry between the two cities. Amarillo is still the metropolis of that prairie empire unofficially designated the Panhandle. The struggle to settle this country of interminable dry, cold prairies has been an epic of the Great Plains.

I took a quick look at costly and tasteful homes, vast towering buildings and the well-kept, beautifully landscaped parks. The State of Texas certainly sold the Panhandle short. They exchanged ten Panhandle counties, 3,050,000 acres, to a ranch syndicate for the cash to pay for the state capitol. They didn't think the land was worth anything or could ever be settled. Now there's scarcely an element of Texas natural wealth and endowment that is missing in Amarillo. A large percentage of the world's helium supply is processed here. They've got everything in Amarillo, beginning with agriculture and ending with zinc! They've even got Kaiser Wilhelm's granddaughter!

I had seen the Plains! A picture that would never leave me had been completed in my mind. Having seen the shape of the land, I could appreciate the lines of Stanley Vestal, master craftsman, in his book *Short Grass Country:*

> The buffalo grass clothes the earth as with a sheer garment, and every contour, plane, and curve of the land appears fresh from the hand of those oldest of sculptors, the Wind and the Rain. A man is in despair because his hands are too small to caress those carven hillsides, tilted planes, arc, hollows, and gracious undulations. The High Plains are not easily painted, only a sculptor could hope to render them adequately — but there is no stone large enough to carve them on.

As usual, I had overextended myself, but having gone this far I went to the Red River Country, for a look at a totally different kind of Texas from any I had known. It has a feeling of the plains country, broken into valleys.

It's red country, red water rolling over red clay. The blood shed in the past was plentiful, angry and turgid like the river. Indians and outlaws left a bloody creek across the fertile Valley.

> I must say as to what I have seen of Texas it is the garden spot of the world, the best land and the best prospects for health I ever saw is here . . . I expect in all probability to settle on Bodark or Choctaw Bayou of Red River, that I have no doubt is the richest country in the world, good land and plenty of timber, and the best springs and good mill streams, good range, clear water and every appearance of health. Game aplenty. It is in the pass where the buffalo passes from north to south and back twice a year, and bees and honey plenty.

So wrote David Crockett to his children in Tennessee, in early January of 1836, taking in roughly the hundred and fifty miles between Denison and Texarkana.

It is still rich country, though the buffalo come no more.

From Wichita Falls to Texarkana, I was impressed by the feeling of prosperity and thrift all around me. There is still much hard-sinewed pioneer stock here. The sense of being in the Bible Belt, in a solid, down-to-earth religious atmosphere, was strongly pervasive. The feeling is stronger than all the legends of desperadoes put together, Belle Starr among them. Once Judge Lynch held open court in the Valley, but formal law and order reigns now.

What struck me most forcibly about the region were the farms: clean, modern, and well-tilled. Tight, snug barns. Fruit trees with white-painted trunks. Farms that looked like farms, not ranches — Texas style. I have seen such productive well-kept farms in Iowa and Illinois. While distinctively

Texan in most respects, the "Sherman Valley," as the Red River Valley was sometimes called, is another example of the contrasts in externals found so frequently in Texas. The same principles prevail inside those stout dwellings that prevail in parts of the Piney Woods, but the exteriors show a different kind of energy and bustling efficiency on the part of the landowners. I knew this was a land where they still play dominoes and Forty-two, where families make fudge and pop corn in the evenings. It was conceivable to me that many of these hardworking people tithed to the church. Prayer meetings, revivals, and all kinds of church activity are still a controlling factor in the way of life of the Valley.

And yet so far removed are these people from the people of my own personal "country" that I felt it would take me many months to learn to know them. The assorted humanity that makes up Texas is a big part of the fascination it holds for me. These were the hair-splitting, argumentative, almost-too-honest people of the old school. Blunt. Unswerving even a hair from any principle in which they believe: a people who see black or white. No gray. Their code is rigid, but they will still die for what they happen to believe in.

There is oil and mineral money too, but it is cannily tucked away out of sight. The Red River Country is not a land of ostentation.

To me, one of the most vivid descriptions of how red the river really is, was written by a survivor of Hood's Brigade, Valerius Cincinnatus Andrew Jackson Giles, of the Land Office force in Austin.

Just after the close of the Civil War [Val C. wrote to an old comrade in arms], thousands of cattle were driven from Texas to Kansas and Nebraska. There was not a foot of barbed wire fence between the Rio Grande and the Missouri River. The boundless prairies were green in waving sagegrass, and herd after herd of fat cattle moved northward through the open country like a great army. There were no restrictions then, and they passed through towns and villages unmolested by citizens or inspectors.

In June of 1867 there were more than 50,000 cattle held on the Red River between Preston and Colbert's Ferry. Owing to the heavy rains in the northwest, the river was booming full and half a mile wide. On account of the reddish tint of the water the cattle could not be induced to take to the river, either by persuasion or by force. They openly rebelled and stampeded every time they were forced to the river bank. New herds were arriving every day, the grass was getting short and the cattlemen were gloomy.

While we lay there waterbound on the Texas side of the roaring river, an old fellow named Shapley came along with a herd of a thousand Texas-raised goats. He was on his way to Springfield, Missouri, and time, with him, was money. He had a jack, a cart, a small boy and two dogs. The boy drove the jack in the cart, and the old Colonel looked after the goats with the two dogs to assist him. He said he could not afford to wait for the river to go down and appeared to have fine control over his herd, but when he tried to force them into the blood-red water, they rebelled and positively refused to go in. He appealed to the cattlemen to give him a "lift."

A hundred cowboys and half-breed Indians agreed to help

him and see the fun. They formed a circle around the herd by
holding each other by the hand and gradually closing in on the
Billies and Nannies.

An old cottonwood tree stood at the edge of the water, leaning out over the river at an angle of about 45 degrees. The top
had been broken off and it was about fifteen feet from the
jagged end down to the water. Slowly and quietly the cowboys
closed in on the unsuspecting bunch. Finally a venerable old
Billy walked out on the log, closely followed by others. He
was the Grand Mogul of the herd and wore a little silver bell.
Gradually they pressed the old patriarch forward until he stood
on the pinnacle, high above the muddy torrent. In attempting
to turn back, the dead bark on the old snag slipped from under
his feet and down he plunged into the water below. Two half-
breed Indians who were in a canoe watching for that very thing
to happen, grabbed the old fellow as he rose from the water,
threw a rope around his horns and lit out for the other side of
the river, towing Billy behind them. The goat who stood next
to the leader, hearing the familiar tinkle of the bell as the old
hero went down, followed with a loud bleat. The balance of the
herd, taking it for granted that their leader knew his business,
began to plunge in after him.

Chug, chug, chug they went: each one leaping from the end
of the old cottonwood tree, jumping as high in the air as possible, and giving a plaintive bleat — a kind of farewell wail.

When they hit the water they went out of sight in the muddy
flood, but rose snorting and following in single file their leader
who had become very much attached to the Indians and their
canoe. Every one of the thousand goats took the water from
the jagged end of the old tree like boys from a springboard.

Old Colonel Shapley stood on the bank waving his hat, shouting: "Go it, yer damned grass-raised rascals! I learned every
mother's son of yer to swim like ducks when yer was kids!"

The current was rapid, but the Indians in the canoe paddled
fast and snaked old Billy after them, the whole flock following
in a long curved line. They drifted down the river more than
half a mile before they reached the Indian Territory side, but
not a goat was lost. They were white, genteel looking goats

when they struck the water, but they were red when they landed.

Old Colonel Shapley expressed his thanks to the cowboys in a small speech, then crossed the river with his jack, cart, small boy, and dogs. He went over in the ferry boat, inviting the crowd to go over and return at his expense. When the Colonel reached his herd, he found a pitched battle raging. The Billies and Nannies didn't know each other in their painted suits and took each other for strangers and interlopers.

I met Colonel Shapley in St. Louis six months after that, and he told me that the goats fought for two days and two nights. When they reached Springfield the red stain was still on them.

If you should ever have occasion to bet on the swimming capacity of a four-legged animal, put your money on the common, Texas-raised goat.

Mr. Giles was right: there is nothing like a goat for hardiness and self-sufficiency. A cedar-cutter friend says "a goat is a onruly animal," but he is a mighty handy thing to have around during a drouth! As I looked at the river, I could see that scarlet herd bleating its way to Missouri, and wondered again at the Texan's ingenuity in getting out of a tight spot.

The late "Judge" Neville, of Paris, still editor of the *Paris News* when over ninety years of age and authority on the Red River Country, told me a yarn I thought rather typical of the "country" about a bunch of card sharps who got hold of a country jake who was not exactly a stranger to the cards on the bottom of the deck himself. The crooks dealt and showed four kings. The farmer turned up with four aces. "How'd you get them four aces?" the slickers challenged. "Come by 'em honest, like you got your four kings," was the answer. They paid.

At Telephone, Texas, near Bonham, the Speaker of the House, Mr. Sam Rayburn, has a ranch of nine hundred acres. It is solid and modest, nothing with any reek of the pork barrel about it. It is probable that in a few years "Mr. Democrat" will retire there to look after his herd of registered Herefords.

He is interested in Brangus cattle, too — that sturdy breed produced by crossing Brahma with Black Angus. He is building his herd, selling most of the bulls, and keeping the hundred best cows for breeding to the fine bulls.

After watching "Mr. Democrat's" expeditious and conclusive wielding of the gavel when he puts a motion through, I expected Mr. Sam's cattle to be "all ayes and no noes."

In the town of Bonham on Powder Creek, Fannin County, up near the Red River, there was a Saturday morning bustle and hustle around the courthouse square. People were doing their trading. I saw a man selling seed corn from the back of his automobile. Some attractive corn hung from the lock of the turtle shell of the car. A few of the ears were rosy red, and others creamy white. The shucks were turned back gracefully, and the person who arranged them had picked the old, mystical number seven.

A tall, slender man with clear blue eyes and a shining ruddy-bronze face was leaning against the car. His overalls were worn, faded, and spotless.

"Did you fix that corn?" I asked.

When he smiled, I saw his clean, white teeth — an unusual thing with country people.

"That's jus' some I picked out by flashlight las' night so's people'd know what I was sellin'."

There was a homemade sign on the pavement: SEED CORN. ONE DOLLAR A POUND. FIFTY-SIX POUNDS TO THE BUSHEL.

"It's beautiful grain," I said.

"Sure thank ye, ma'am. The field where I rose that corn was wore-out blackland. I know the secrets o' raisin' corn. Ain't tellin' 'em to ary livin' soul but my two boys. I know how to make the ears grow long an' full, how to make a lot or a few to a stalk. I ain't tellin' nobody but them!"

"Nobody can say you don't know how! And you keep the corn so well."

"I got a certain weed I pull . . . kinda mint outa the fields

to put in the crib to keep the weevils out. 'Fore that, I used
Hi-life."

"Where do you live?" I asked.

"Out on the highway. I rented for eleven years, but that's
no good. I was a little short o' money, but I went to the bank
an' borried the rest. Bought me a hundred an' fifty-three acres.
Ninety's planted, an' the rest is pasture. I paid it out in jig-
time. It's mine. Free an' clear. Built me a house, too. I borried the money on my life insurance, my cattle, my tractor, an'
my tools. I'd never soak my land! That ain't my way o' doin'.
Keep your land clear."

I said that was right.

"My house is most paid out," the man continued. "Drove
down a well, hit water at eighty-two feet that pumps fourteen
gallon a minute. Hit won't never run dry tell the end o' the
world."

"Seed corn your money crop?"

"Cotton. An' I sell six hundred dollars o' milk a year to the
cheese factory. They pick it up for sixty cents a hundred."

He was so agreeable that I decided to ask a very personal
question. In his middle thirties, at the very latest, he seemed
to "have it made."

"You live off the land?" I asked.

"Purt' near. I raise my own meat, plus forty chickens for
eggs, oats, an' . . . ," his eye strayed back to his beloved seed-
corn. "Hit woulda disappeared but for me. Wouldn't one in ten
thousand a done what I done for that corn. When the old people come from the Old Country they didn't bring but two
kinds o' corn: Tennessee Red Cob an' Chisum White. I kep'
it pure, an' 'cep for me raisin' it, they ain't no tellin' where
you'd have to go TO FIND IT!" He loved that corn and knew I
was not a prospective buyer; loved it the way the early settlers loved it when they brought it as all they had to live on in
the move from the Old Country: Tennessee and Mississippi.

"Get a good catch from it?"

He reached into a worn leather wallet:

"Good catch, lady? Look at this!" He unfolded a much creased piece of paper that bore the letterhead of the State Department of Agriculture, Seed Laboratory Division, Austin.

CORN TEST

Germination	96 per cent
Purity	99.90
Inert	10
Other crops	none
Weeds	none
Noxious weeds	none

"Man, you beat Ivory Soap! Farm all your life?"

"Yes, ma'am . . . an' accordin' to my own ideas! Never done but thirteen days' public work in my life. I thought one time I wanted to quit farmin' an' went to work on the highway. I knowed right then I'd been doin' what I wanted to do all along."

"You said you had some pasture?"

"I build it by soddin' . . . made me some moody grass terraces."

"Bermuda grass is good to hold dirt," I agreed.

"Sure is. When I lose me some dirt, I go right down to them terraces an' haul it back! The highway department tore up the moody grass front o' my house. The road cultivator dug it right up an' thrown it over my fence. I hated to see it wasted, so I run some furrows, dumped them sods in, an' covered it over. Coulda had five more loads if somebody'd a holp me."

I ran my hands through the glistening grain: "I saw some of the gruesome, deformed grains of corn that were grown on Bikini for an experiment after the A-bomb test. Gave me nightmares for months. I won't have to feel bad about that twisted corn any more."

He put out his clean, callused hand.

"I'm sure proud to know ye," he said.

Texas can be proud of her seed-corn man. There are lots more like him, filled with an enviable singleness of purpose and passionate love of the land. She can be proud that her land will, when spoken to with secret coaxings, produce the pearly pink grains of life such as the seed-corn man "rose" on his "wore-out blackland" up near the Red River.

The difference between the lonely immensity of the Plains, where the wind draws the water and the cows provide the wood, and the opulent, teeming growth of East Texas that I had read about, convinced me more than ever that Walter Prescott Webb was right when he said: "When one makes a comparative study of the sections, the dominant truth which emerges is expressed in the word contrast."

In less than a week I was to see for myself the truth of his observation.

8. THE BIG THICKET

PRIMED AND READY for the Green East, wanting to see the section where "a common cow pasture is as velvety green as a manicured City Park," I made a preliminary foray along the Dogwood Trail between Woodville and Livingston. Jasper and Lufkin, Marshall and Jefferson, where even the jokes are colored by a Louisiana border flavor, gave me the chance to soak up the flavor of East Texas. It became increasingly apparent to me that climate creates custom; the Eastern way of life is gentle, slow and lazy.

Hound dogs and blowing horns. Blackeyed peas and hog jowl. Sausage, with a flavor unrivaled, red-pepper-hot, solid pork — meat with some substance to it. Grits floating in fresh butter or red-eye gravy. Hot biscuits and mayhaw jelly. Kids selling buckets of haws by the road spell it "may halls." A poky mule turning a syrup mill. The land where *The King and I* means nothing but an old-time gospel hymn. Gray silvered shacks with bitter oranges and chinaberry trees near them . . . the yard a bleached sweep of hard-packed earth, an iron washpot turned over near a round white spot on the ground where the suds from strong yellow lye-soap wash water had been emptied for years. The broomstick used to punch the clothes down, boiled to the color and smoothness of old ivory. Grove's Chill Tonic and Slaughterine for Pains. Crisper's Hot Shot Nerve Sedative.

The country where a midwife is a "granny woe-man"; one a 92-year-old mulatto woman with slender steely fingers who was said to have delivered a live baby from a dead mother. "White doctor say she daid, so I cain't say she ain't." Signs saying "Wheels Spoked." Negro help leaping the fence to "git away fum de cunjerin' powder on de gate posts," placed there by some "cunjer" man or woman in the hire of an ill-wisher. East Texas, where they do things *right*, not cloddish. Negro children shouting "Santy Claw comin'? Santy Claw comin'?" when you want to take their pictures: "How he gon' know me on paper?" The stompin' ground of a blind, toothless guitar player: "Play me some blues." "I don' play no sinful songs, lady!" His gigantic wife, Billie, emerging from out back hollerin' "An' me lookin' like Who'd-a-Thunk-It!" Razor-back hogs and hickory nuts. Light-bread and sweet milk. English walnuts and Irish potatoes, and firecrackers at Christmas. The smell of fresh-made lye hominy, and the lacquered cypress beams of the smokehouse. A hint of frost in the air, and the sweet mouth of a coon dog when he trees.

I burrowed into the heart-land of the Deep East, even though I had been warned that the Thicket would not be easy territory. I meant to stay until I had seen what I came to see.

What is the Big Thicket? Where is it? The very name is

magic. It conjures up images of an impenetrable wilderness; a solid, choked mass of thorny, spiny brush.

I expected an entirely junglelike growth, where passageway would have to be hacked with a machete. There are still many such spots in the Thicket, but in its opened up, road-riddled state today, it resembles most of all a giant wild gar-

den that is being looted and despoiled. Tram roads leading from the highways to oil wells and what is left of the virgin forests have cut the Thicket up into patchwork to haul out the costly lumber and greasy black fluid that are a major part of the wealth of Texas. These same roads are destroying forever what has been until recently the one relatively unimpaired treasure of Texas, a biological island of rare plant and animal life, the refuge of that fast-disappearing animal, the natural man.

The Big Thicket is not, as the guidebooks would suggest, one certain clearly defined, fenced-off spot. It is a state of mind: an eerie place in the minds of those few Texans who have heard of it, where the Bogey Man goes at night after a hard day of frightening little children.

In Liberty, a government surveyor with years of experience and knowledge of the Thicket and its people said: "Watch out

for those people, Mary. I just come outa there today! They
don't like furriners. And furriners are somebody from the next
county. Even if you do go, and I reckon you will, don't go off
the roads and into the Thicket itself. You'd get lost sure. The
forest is impenetrable, full of swamps and baygalls."

"How will I get to know the people?" I said.

"They don't want to know anybody! They don't like to be
asked questions."

That last statement cheered me, for at least we would have
one thing in common.

Over in Anderson, near Navasota, a wise old colored stockman had said: "Miss Mary, don't GO in the Big Thicket! Don't
go IN it!" I began to feel like Br'er Rabbit: once my curiosity
is aroused, "Goodbye, John!"

Near Kountze we stopped a big colored truck driver to ask
the way to Saratoga.

"Sa-a-a-a-togy? Thass in the Thicket, ain't it?"

"You ever been in it?"

"Nossuh. I ain't."

"I heard there's varmints in there."

"Yassuh. Tell me dey is."

"You ever been in the Thicket?"

"Nossuh. I ain't been in an' I ain't studdin' 'bout goin' in!
Sa-a-togy, it's dataway!" He pointed a thumb as thick as
a chocolate éclair and gunned the truck off at sixty miles an
hour.

I went in and almost didn't come out. Not because I was
lost, but because I didn't want to leave. It was my great good
fortune to see the Thicket with two outstanding hunters of the
region, two men as different in interests and personality as it
is possible for two men to be. Lance Rosier, the naturalist from
Saratoga, hunts flowers, plants, and trees. John Knight, over
at Segno, is the Mighty Hunter of the Thicket. With guns and
traps he has won government citations and awards as Federal

Predatory Animal Exterminator. I asked him if he knew Lance Rosier.

"I've heerd of 'im," John Knight said and shifted his quid of tobacco to the other cheek. "That there's *one* end o' the Thicket. This here's a-NUN-urn!" I was to learn before the year was out that John was right: it was indeed another one.

At Saratoga, toward the southeastern corner of the four counties that make up the Thicket, Liberty, Polk, Tyler, and Hardin, I learned that the area comprising the Big Thicket, even in its now reduced state, is a forest jungle of approximately two thousand square miles, the home of more than two thousand classified trees, plants, shrubs, and hundreds of animals.

There are hundreds of varieties of birds and of snakes, many alligators, turtles and frogs, lichens of infinite and startling variety, fungi that are unknown and unnamed, much less classified, within its fastnesses. Here is a veritable gold mine for someone wishing to make a contribution to science.

Mosses, algae, slime molds, and diatoms abound in the Thicket, all fascinating life forms. There are two hundred and seventy-five varieties of mosses to be found there, two hundred and fifty-two of them within a three-mile radius of the town of Liberty. Dr. Eula Whitehouse of Southern Methodist University, a noted authority on plant life, says that in a short while we will be cooking algae, green mold from the tops of ponds, vitamin loaded and — now comes the unbelievable part — incredibly delicious. Jo Ruth Graham, a young scientist at the University of Texas, is working on a concentrated high-protein food made from algae to be used by fliers of space ships, to eat on their trips to the moon! I have sampled it, and it is fresh, nutlike in flavor, and pure clear green in color.

The simple, unromantic forms of plant life such as pond slimes and algae do not get the attention they deserve because of their inconspicuous, almost invisible nature. It is interesting to know that a distinguished botanist like Dr. Whitehouse has written a book on slime molds and algae. She is also preparing a book on mosses, many of them native to the Big Thicket. I was told there were sixty-three varieties of mosses in Liberty County.

This botanical paradise once stretched in pristine glory from Nacogdoches to Beaumont, from the Sabine River to the Trinity. It now covers the larger portion of the aforementioned counties instead of twelve. There are those who will debate the inclusion of Liberty County, but there is no disputing the fact that, like parts of Polk County, it is on the fringe of the Thicket proper.

The Big Thicket resembles the Big Bend in one respect at least: the region's boundaries always lie just a little farther on from the person you are talking to.

"Hit's over hyonder," they will tell you while they are standing right in the big middle of it. Many of the settlers dislike being known as Thicketers. They look down on it. But this I learned firsthand: some of the old-timers, the real McCoy, are proud of their land and identity. Many of them are not above adding on a few years to their age, stretching a yarn for the sake of a good story, or throwing in an extra larding of Elizabethan English for the benefit of the listener.

For years they have lived off the bodies and pelts of animals in the woods, and the fish in the streams, catfish generally being called "meat." There are still fish in the streams, ponds, and bayous of the Thicket, but the poisoning of the waters by the oil wells and the pernicious practice of "telephoning," killing by electric shock, has decimated the fish.

The Big Thicket soil is largely sandy humus. There are some low-lying hills with many crawfish flats among them. The rainfall is between forty-five and fifty inches annually and the region is traversed by numerous creeks and rivers. Marshes, swamps, bogs, and baygalls are common to the region.

Long-leaf pine formerly dominated the area, but most of the virgin timber has been cut. Today through many parts of the Thicket, stretches of grass and flowering plants can be seen thickly studded with blackened stumps, remains of the former forest. Occasionally a wispy, spindly pine tree stands as a mournful relic of the grove that once lifted its head in pride. The culls, rejected by the lumbermen, are pitiful and dejected as they struggle somehow to survive, but they do furnish the seed that reforests the cut-over area.

If the cut-over lands are protected from grass fires and nurtured by the lumber people, it may yet be possible to restore the splendor of the original virgin forest. Pines grow quickly and make a fine comeback if given half a chance. The Forestry Service of Texas is conducting an intensive and widespread campaign to educate the public in preservation of the natural resources of the state. Cigarettes carelessly thrown are responsible for much loss. Lookout towers and effective fire-fighting systems are helping to reduce the damage caused by an ignorant and careless public.

The lumber companies are gradually coming to see the light: they realize they are killing the goose that lays the golden egg. The millions of acres of cut-over land in the Thicket and the Piney Woods region in general could be restored to their pristine beauty — and value — by planting and reforesting under government supervision. The lumbering operations on reforested regions would have to be conducted by processes so controlled as to keep the stands virtually intact. Selective cutting is already in practice with some of the less greedy and more enlightened lumbermen. The lack of the long view is what holds up the show. The potential return is great, but it is not immediate. Private owners are reluctant to replant a forest for others to harvest.

Regardless of what private enterprise does about the forests, the government should aid in making possible the preservation of at least a fragmentary example of the glory that once was the Big Thicket.

Along stream bottoms of silty texture, rich with humus, many hardwoods are found. Evergreen smilax canopies the loftiest treetops. Swamps of tupelo and bald cypress, once so plentiful, have been almost totally destroyed by lumbering operations.

My brief look at the Thicket showed me the necessity of securing a guide.

I, too, had "heerd" of Lance Rosier. Just drove up in front of his enchanting dwelling, the old Vines Hotel, actually concealed by ancient ivy, at Saratoga. I told him "Howdy."

"Wait till I get my hat," he said. That's all there was to it. Just say "prowl the thicket" and he's gone away! While I waited for him, I studied a magnificent evergreen lacy-cut climbing fern rambling up a tree trunk in the yard. The scarlet blossoms had me running a high fever until I got out to examine them more closely. They were bunches of the red pleated wax-paper cups that come in fancy boxes of cookies, wired onto the fern at intervals.

That Monday in January, Lance took me for a short prowl

into the Thicket near Kountze. No one would be rash enough
to walk even a few feet off the highway alone, for fear of getting lost, except a native hunter or surveyor's guide. Tourists
are carefully warned about straying into the woods and most
natives of surrounding towns would not dream of going into
the Thicket without a competent guide — and they are few,
indeed.

I literally could not see the forest for the trees. The great
pines, magnolias, and sweetgums I was prepared for, but not
the huge beeches that reached up and rubbed shoulders with
giant *Magnolia glauca.* How had they landed here, of all
places? The ice floes must have swept them down with the
rest of the rare vegetation. One explanation for the biological
island of plant life is that the vegetation found a perfect home
in the Thicket. In the northern part of the United States it was
too cold, and the tropical section to the south of us was too hot.
The Thicket was the perfect breeding and growing ground for
these treasures.

Less than six feet from the highway, Lance pointed out to
me five varieties of fern I had never seen before. He showed
me native rhododendrons and *Azalea viscosa.* The magnolias
and bays towered above the terrestrial orchids, wintergreen,
bearberry, and scented myrtle that trailed underfoot.

"I wisht you'da come in the spring," he said shyly. "This
orchid is getting ready to bloom in July." He turned the two-
bladed plant so that I could see the magenta underside of the
eggplant-colored leaves. "There is a white kind called Ladies'
Tresses. It thrives in the Thicket."

I was soon drunk with the bizarre beauty all around me in
what passed for the dead of winter.

I sat down on a stump and studied my new friend and guide.
Instinctive as an animal about people I like or do not like, it
had taken me exactly forty seconds to lay my heart down.
Here was great knowledge and philosophy, a Big Thicket

Thoreau. No striving to impress, no reaching for the world's goods, a Roman contempt for superfluity. I thought of Gustav Belfrage, the great collector of insects on the frontier, who lay for years in an unmarked grave in the Norse Cemetery at Clifton, Texas. His titled ancestors lie in their vaults in Sweden, but Belfrage's insects repose in museums over the world. Poor Belfrage's estate, including his cabin, amounted to four hundred dollars, I believe, when he died. And in 1882, whiskey was only twenty-five cents a gallon in Bosque County. Instead of putting his insects in the alcohol, Belfrage put the alcohol into himself.

That won't happen to Lance. He doesn't drink or smoke or "dip" and eats very little. He has never owned a car. He walks wherever he wants to go, but seldom has to complete the trip on foot.

The naturalists of the frontier were an illustrious company, and one day Lance Rosier will take his place beside them. A slight man, small-boned, weighing perhaps a hundred and twenty pounds soaking wet, he has the ageless quality of a faun, and the same pointed ears. I reckon he is around fifty-six. His eyes are gentian blue, rubbed in with a sooty finger. They squinch up at the corners exactly the way his battered felt hat rolls up in front. Like Cyrano de Bergerac, he'll put it on crosswise if he feels like it. His mouth is sensitive and wryly humorous, like his speech.

One Sunday in Liberty he was dressed up like a natty leprechaun. A Nile-green turtle-necked sweater stood out in contrast to the rich rust color of the long-sleeved gabardine sport shirt that he wore open in a deep V against the green pullover. His slacks matched the shirt and were sharply creased. We prowled the woods just the same — Lance all dressed up and my navy blue Claire McCardell dress not too happy with the hiking boots I always carry in the back of the car "just in case."

"Mary, it's a man over in Newton County found a wild ca-

mellia in the woods. Wanted me to tell him what it was. I got
out my Corey and Parks and when I studied the leaves, I knew
it couldn't be nothing but a camellia." His eyes blinked in excitement.

"A true camellia?"

"Plenty of 'em right here in the Thicket. White as dogwood.
Bloom from October to spring." He knew that a wild camellia
hunt would interest me even more than the "tame" camellia
show where I was to make the awards at the Liberty Camellia
Society, one of the most exclusive in the world. It has only
three members: President, Vice-President, and Secretary.

"I couldn't start before tomorrow morning," I said. "I really
came to see the insectivorous plants. How long can you stay
in Liberty?"

"From now on, if you say."

"Can we go to the Thicket again tomorrow or have you something planned?" I asked.

"Me?" Lance shrugged. "I'm just like an old goose: wake up
in a new world every morning."

Lance may wake up in a new world every morning, but
there the resemblance to a goose ceases. He never misses the
stirring of a leaf or the flutter of an eyelid. His own eyes bat
continuously with humor or excitement. I suspect they can
bat with anger on occasion — and the blue sparks will be
flinty. His observations are complete and penetrating. His
speech reflects a keen, hard-hitting perception that is not deceived by man or his motives. He lives too close to nature for
that. Lance Rosier is realistic beyond the point of realism.

"How did you ever learn such a tremendous amount about
trees and plants?" I asked.

"Just prowling the Thicket. Walking around finding things
out," Lance said with his enchanting inflection, so peculiarly
his own. It consists of a rising note at the end of a sentence,
not questioning, exactly, but more in the nature of a grace

note, a "don't you think so too?" that is part and parcel of his personality.

One summer he taught flowers and plants at a Methodist Encampment.

"I didn't want to do it. 'Fraid they'd ask me something I didn't know." Lance waved his tiny hands with the spatulate fingers. He never commits himself on a question unless he is on sure ground. "There's three kinds of people that ask you questions, Mary: the earnest, sincere people; the people that ask out of curiosity only, and when you tell 'em, don't even listen; and then there's what I call The Trapper. He gets to you in a sly manner hoping to catch you in a mistake."

I was thinking they'd have to get up early to catch Lance.

"I was walking around in the woods this day," he went on, "and it was just about time to start the nature study class. I come up on something I didn't know, and I ran for my Corey and Parks text to look it up. It turned out to be a real common clematis. I just hadn't seen it before. It wasn't twenty minutes till here come a knotheaded boy, shoved one of 'em in front o' me and says: 'What's this?' "

"What do you do in the woods besides finding out things?"

"My work is always in the woods. Acting as a surveyor's guide. Timber. Buying and selling. Estimating quantity and quality."

"They take much out?"

"More timber goes out of the Thicket than anywhere else in Texas. Smell this." He reached down and pulled up a tiny plant and held it under my nose. The root was delicate in structure, a beautiful pale pink. It smelled like the purest extract of wintergreen.

"Candy root," Lance said.

"What do you do in your spare time?"

"When I'm not in the woods I go to church. Over here. Brother Ramby, the Assembly of God preacher, is just fine. We go into the woods. He takes colored pictures of flowers. I show him where they are and he photographs them. Then he develops and prints them."

"Does his own color film processing?"

"Oh, yes! Definitely so! Brother Ramby's a fine man. Not like all these preachers preaching about hell fire and Christ coming and He ain't got here yet!"

Lance's occasional worldly phrases combined with his homespun woods talk always charm me. There is never any telling what he will say.

Brother Ramby showed me a series of colored slides of flowers of the Big Thicket in the darkened little Assembly of God Church in Saratoga. My note pad gave out at six hundred names. The list reads like the perennial section of the finest garden catalogue ever printed. Many of our American tame flowers, hardy perennials and annuals, are native to the Big Thicket, including a rare iris that "keeps union hours, opens at daylight and closes at two." The names of the flowers are poetry to stir the heart of every gardener.

I sat there in complete disbelief at what I saw: *Lobelia cardinalis* five feet high; bergamot, cream and gold. Bluebells, the heavenly cups studded with black centers. *Lilium canadense*, wild petunia, Drummond phlox, winecups; coral bean; giant trumpet vine; wild wisteria; pentstemon, a climbing form rare in most other parts of the world. Wild honeysuckle and verbena. Great blankets of gaillardia and blazing star, spider lily, yellow fringed orchid, the tway-blade, and white fragrant orchid. These are but a scant handful of the beauty native to the Thicket.

A love of flowers, more or less passionate, seems to be one of the better traits common to most human beings. Nearly everyone loves plants and trees. Brother Ramby says they are lovely to photograph because they don't run and hide, or try to pose.

I saw the mauve of the Judas tree that blooms before the

leaves appear: Texas redbud. Drifts of dogwood and buckeye. Witch hazel, wax myrtle, sweet bay, and yaupon, the Texas holly that the early settlers loved. They made tea from the leaves that was comparable to a fine Bohea. Lance discovered a yaupon with canary yellow berries instead of the usual scarlet. The three magnolias: *glauca, florida,* and *acuminata.*

Hollies reach a perfection of growth in the Thicket that is rarely seen elsewhere. They are beautifully shaped enormously tall trees, heavily berried. A diameter of three feet is not uncommon for holly trees. At Liberty, I saw one holly tree with a trunk thirteen feet in diameter. In the Thicket, hollies are often cut for Christmas trees. The leathery, broad-leafed evergreens contrast markedly with the McCarthy Rose and French mulberry, callicarpa, that grow into shrubby plants and face down the taller trees. They love the shade and grow in abundance to dazzle the flower lover.

"Now you take perilla," Lance said. Fortunately I knew perilla. I had grown it in pots as "beefsteak plant."

"Perilla grows wild in the Thicket. Loads of it. It's rare other places, and valuable. The seed brings up to ten dollars a pound, for use in the manufacture of fine varnishes and lacquers. The doctors come from faraway places and collect the seed to grow it commercially. Same way with stillingia, the Chinese tallow tree." Lance reached down and pulled up a dry grayish, mealy looking weed from the roadside.

"*Scopera adulcis,* sweet broom," he said. "Dr. Blau of the Humble Oil Research is experimenting with it as a cure for sugar diabetes. We've known about it forever in the Thicket. I loaned a woman several hundred Indian remedies I'd wrote down. She said she was working on a thesis and needed the material. Some college of pharmacy. She never did send 'em back."

"Get them! Write to her."

"Do you know, I don't have her name or address? Just seemed like a nice sincere woman."

I thought of some of the tight-fisted, vault-locking, suspicious personalities I had known, and decided that if Lance had to go to one extreme or the other, prodigality was better than parsimony.

I looked with great happiness at a person who had never known the stultifying effect of city life. It seemed fitting to me that one of the great self-taught naturalists of our time should take his surname from a rose tree. It accounts for the faintly French accent that a keen ear will detect in his speech.

"Your people were French."

"Doke on right!" Lance smiled. "My father had an inferiority complex about being French, so we never spoke it at home."

"You know so much botany, and you use the Latin names correctly. Where did you get all that? You didn't pick that up prowling the Thicket."

"I took it up in 1936. Got me some books and started studying them. Corey and Parks came here and did the biological survey of the Thicket, and they taught me a lot."

Lance Rosier would never say it, but that "teaching" was an even-Stephen deal. Naturalists and botanists from many sections of the globe come to hunt up the gentle, obliging nature lover in Saratoga. When it comes down to bedrock, they have to get Lance to take them where the plants are to be found. And after they find them, he has to tell them what they are.

"The Doctors!" Lance makes a tolerant little grimace as he thinks of the Ph.D's.

"Louis Kronenberger," I told him, "dramatic critic on *Time* Magazine, says the colleges have started a new religion: Ph. Deism."

"He's so right!" Lance chuckled as he named some of the "Doctors" who had visited him from Venezuela, Norway, and Japan. They come seeking his expert, practical aid. It is never withheld.

One of the shameful situations in Texas publishing is the fact that Lance Rosier is not mentioned in the sole printed gospel available on the Big Thicket today, Corey and Parks, *Biological Survey of the East Texas Big Thicket.* Except for Lance's guidance and selflessness in co-operation, this valuable piece of work could not have been accomplished. But it's a low bush, indeed, that the sun never shines on, and Lance Rosier is coming into his own in Texas not only as a sound, reliable naturalist, but as a rare personality.

"Let's go back into the Thicket to the first place you showed me," I said to Lance four days after our first excursion. "That spot where the ferns were so thick and the *Azalea viscosa* was budded out."

"Take you right to it," he said. We went. It wasn't there. In less than five days the bulldozers had flattened the forest and rough planks had been laid down over which dripping oil trucks rattled and stank.

"Can't anybody stop the Juggernaut twins? Oil and lumber . . ."

"In ten years it will be gone," Lance said.

All I could think of was something out of the Bible I had probably garbled: "I sought it and it was not."

"The Big Thicket Association, it's just a handful. The few that cares. They haven't been able to get the land set aside; the 435,000 acres is just a little dab, but it could be saved for seed! Something to show how it once was, though there's scarcely any virgin forest left. Mr. Jackson has a small plant preserve the Santa Fe let him have. He's a retired train conductor."

"Bess Reid, the bird woman. A few interested people in Beaumont?"

"That's about the size of it. They've almost give up. Paid their own way to Austin time after time . . . even as far as Washington, D.C. The lumber and oil companies block it."

The handful of people in Texas and in the United States who know anything at all about the region are sick at heart, indignant, and impotent to stop destruction of one of the world's treasure houses. The depredations of the oil people and the lumber companies become greater every day. They made sure when they bought the land that they got all the rights: "clear down to China and right up to the sky." A few intelligent and interested people stand by stricken to watch the last rites: the boy in Holland with his finger in the dyke had a sinecure compared to what these men and women are trying to accomplish. They have fought valiantly for over twenty years against cruel odds to save the plant life of the region they love from inevitable extinction.

If anyone wants to see what is left of the Big Thicket, he had better hurry. Texans, like most Americans, are losing their legs by atrophy. They refuse to walk. In a few more generations, legs will be nothing more than flippers, little vestigial appendages. It is possible to drive into the Thicket now, worse luck. But it is better to see it by car than to miss the Crown Jewel that is being hacked up daily by crisscrossed, ugly little roads. Its beauty is going. Like Humpty Dumpty's shell, it can never be put together again. The many rare natural phenomena need this special habitat for their survival and development. Students of nature are losing a storehouse of rarities in spite of everything they can do. Lance and I walked away silently, greatly downcast.

"Lichens need two to make a living," Lance said, and showed me an interesting specimen. "It's a fungus living symbiotically with an alga. One breathes in the air while the other one eats. Sort of living in sym." He smiled and I knew he was trying to cheer me, but his efforts were of no avail. I had seen with my own eyes in less than a week the galloping progress of a man-made disease that was ravishing an absolutely irreplaceable wonder of the world. The world will soon be able only to "review the remains," as the Southern colored people say.

As I thought about Lance's personality, I wondered about the traits of the Thicketers in general. Who were these last remnants of a hardy breed that dug their heels in and defied the world to try to take over and run their lives for them? What last stand of courage might be left there that would encourage free men and women everywhere to defend their personal liberties from the onslaughts of presumptuous, self-appointed buttinskis? What kind of reception did the semi-official Meddlesome Matties of our day get from the Big Thicketers? It was a tonic to talk to people who would not be harangued into sheeplike submission.

The original settlers of the Thicket came largely from the "old states": Tennessee, Kentucky, the Carolinas. Some came from Alabama and Georgia. There was a large helping of Scotch-Irish among them. They left a wooded, watered country and stopped at the first similar place they hit as they came west in search of fortune, or merely in search of richer trees and fatter game: East Texas. I know there is a lot of Scots blood there, because to this day the natives have a strong dash of the Scots' ruling passion: hatred for the Tax Man. Most mountain folk have it. They don't like revenuers.

Two amusing stories were told me, both true, for one happened while I was in the area. A man on the fringe of the Thicket had a tiny country store: coal oil, snuff, jawbreakers, smoked jowl, canned tomatoes, chewing tobacco, a few patent medicines, rat cheese, and the ubiquitous sody-pop.

One day a tidy young man drove up and showed him credentials from Mister Whiskers.

"You have never reported any income tax," he said.

"What's that?"

"That's the money you take in from your store. You have to show how much profit you make and pay tax on it. That's the law."

"I don't make no money."

"Where are your invoices?"

"What's that?"

"The bills for your goods; what you owe."

"Don't owe nothin'."

"Well, how much did you pay for your stock on the shelves?"

"I don't know."

"Where did you get the money you paid?"

"Takened it out'n the till."

The T Man began to realize what the phrase "lives of quiet desperation" meant. He looked in the till and saw one dirty dollar bill, two quarters, three dimes, and a penny.

"You'll just have to start keeping books. From now on, keep all the bills for everything you buy. Get receipts for everything. Keep track of every cent you take in. You've got to account for the difference between gross and net. You've *got* to know what you spent and what you made. It's the way to do business. Besides, it's the law. I'll talk to them again over at headquarters."

The storekeeper spat resoundingly on the stove as the T Man drove off. He'd heard tell that morning that the fish were biting so good at the forks of the creek that a man had to hide behind a tree to bait his hook. He opened a fresh box of Garrett's snuff and went off to see if it was true.

About a year later the postmaster brought him a letter and read it to him because it was important: no stamp, so it musta come from the guvver-ment. The storekeeper was ordered to report to the headquarters of the Director of Internal Revenue some twenty-odd miles away, and to bring with him his books, ledgers, bank statements, invoices, and all "pertinent data" by 10 A.M. of a certain day.

The storekeeper cut himself a fresh snuff switch, started chewing on it, and lit a shuck for town in his Model T. The gentlemen of the treasury were waiting for him when he came in. They looked surprised when he dragged a large burlap grass sack behind him and placed it carefully between his knees as he sat down.

"Did you bring the receipts and papers?"

"Shore did," the storekeeper said and upended the sack, covering the floor with myriad bits of paper, receipts, bills, even chain-store cash-register tape tickets for his own personal purchases. "I done what you tole me. They're all yourn."

Not since I heard about the Irish tearing up their ration coupons during World War II and throwing "thim little bits o' paper" into the sea have I known such pure bliss as that story gave me.

During my stay in the Big Thicket the second significant incident took place involving the so-called gentler sex. In the heavily wooded area an old family living on a stoutly fenced large tract of land, plainly posted, had trouble with deer hunters. The season was tempting and deer were plentiful in their lush timber.

A trespassing hunter shot one of the dogs belonging to the family, and logically enough, one of the family shot one of the hunters. It is said on ungallant but reliable authority that a lady fired the shots.

No information seemed to be forthcoming as to the identity of the Avenging Angel, so the poor losers sent the sheriff out for a parley.

When he went out to interview the owner of the property, who is also head of the clan, he was met by an elderly spinster of somewhat uncompromising cast of countenance. She is known locally as "Ol' Trap Mouth."

"Now you don't have to worry about a thing, ma'am," he began, "I just came out to ask you a few questions . . ."

"On my land, Sheriff," she cut his water off, "if there's any questions asked, I'll ask 'em." This temperament flourishing in so lush and fertile a region struck my funny bone. No Rousseau philosophy here.

The increasing interest in nature study in the United States over the last few years has cheered me greatly.

Most of Texas is an earthly paradise for the nature lovers, especially for plant lovers. Even dour Drummond, the discoverer of the sassy annual phlox, that gayest of native Texans, known and planted around the world, was intrigued with the region of the Big Thicket. He wrote home dreadful things about Texas, which fact in itself was sufficient to tip off anyone who understands Scottish reasoning. His real feelings were something different. The Scots have a proverb: "Those who slight my mare would buy her." When Thomas Drummond died in Cuba about 1836 on his way back to Scotland, his effects contained papers and documents showing that he was in the process of trying to buy a substantial parcel of Texas land.

I have always been blest, or cursed, with a lively curiosity as to what went on in the world and why. Here was my chance to indulge my passion for knowledge to the fullest. Lance Rosier didn't help the situation by bringing up new and exciting natural features of the Thicket for my delight. I have read enough to have a fair background of knowledge for plant study. Nurtured on the nature study works of my distant kinsman, Sir John Lubbock, whose study of the ants and work on the Piltdown man are internationally known, I was still totally unprepared to find the magic of these rare phenomena operating in Texas, a state strongly influenced and well marked by other Lubbocks. Kent and Surrey are a long way from the Big Thicket. How many times I wished for Sir John on these explorations! His knowledge as a naturalist and skill as a nature writer were needed to convey even a sketchy idea of this wild wonderland.

There are five carnivorous plants known in the world: bog violet, sundew, bladderwort, pitcher plant, and Venus's-flytrap. The first four of them are native to the Big Thicket. I have seen them at work and marveled anew at the logic and ingenuity of whoever planned their cycles. If anyone is in doubt as to the existence of a Master Plan, let him study the plant world.

As a child I read in a set of books called *Chambers' Miscellany* the story of the bladderwort and bog violet. Never did I think to see them. Especially not in Texas. Siberia could not have been farther from Brownsville than the Big Thicket. Not nearly so far, in fact, for I had read quite a lot about Siberia but had never even heard of the Big Thicket.

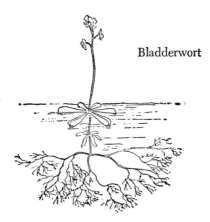

Bladderwort

Lance and I went into the Thicket one afternoon in late April and found the bladderwort at work. To him they are as common as dandelions in Newport. I found them beautiful and mysterious. The plant is made up of five floats which lie directly on top of the water in stagnant baygalls or other boggy places. The floats are about the size of a match stem, beautifully beveled and miraculously full of air. The yellow bloom is in the middle of the float, rather violet-shaped. The bloom and floats are attached to the top of the roots which hang down a considerable depth in the water.

"The little miniature traps on the roots is what catches the bugs," Lance said. "They spread out like a seine for about a foot or two. These traps are all over the roots, so when an insect of any kind swims near and stops on the traps, they open up and catch the insect and hold it up till it's digested. Then the trap opens up, and the parts that are not wanted are thrown out. Then the trap is ready for business again. There may be a hundred or more traps on the roots of one plant. There's another bladderwort that grows in the mud, and it works the same way, except that it catches the insects in the mud. There are eight different species of bladderwort. Some bloom in the spring, and some in the fall."

I picked up one of the plants and squeezed the floats, feeling the air resist inside.

"Those flowers will stay open about a month," Lance said. "When the seed gets ripe, it turns dark brown and falls into the water to come up next year. Then all the air goes out of the floats and the plant itself becomes dormant, and sinks to the bottom of the water. Next spring the whole thing starts over again."

The plant I was holding appeared to be several years old, judging by the floats of former years that clung to the roots.

Again I felt like the Mexican on the porch of the store at Castalon in the Big Bend studying the mountain peak before him: "I wonder who made it?" The Sierra Del Carmen, the forest, the bladderwort, and a tiny sundew. There were many specimens of the sundew around the boggy places.

A red rosette of rounded leaves with fragile flowers of bright scarlet tipped with diamonds. It seems to have little connection with earth. Sunbeams and water, fire and dew, these are the things on which it seems to feed. Those shining dewdrops which give the plant its Greek name, *drosera*, are not hung upon the leaves for ornament. The sundew, like any human creature, lays traps to catch its prey, and the traps are the dewdrops on the hairy fingers of the leaves. Every coveted morsel

Sundew

is caught and held by them — then enjoyed. It is human in
its movements.

> You call it sundew; how it grows,
> If with its color it have breath,
> If life taste sweet to it, if death
> Pain its soft petal, no man knows:
> Man has no sight or sense that saith.

We walked deeper into the woods to the heart of a magnificent group of beech trees. Lance leaned down and plucked a
wedge-shaped growth that I thought was a seedling.

"Beech drops," he said. "See how it looks like a tiny wedge?
On the point it's a bearded hook. When the seed ripens, it falls
on the dead leaves below, dropped usually from a distance of
about eighteen inches above the roots. The wind blows the
seed-laden leaves around. Those that light on beech tree
roots germinate. All the rest die."

The infinite planning and cunning that went into their design fascinated me. "What makes them choose beech trees?"

"Beech drops is a parasite," Lance said, "and they only
fasten on the right host."

"People again!" I laughed.

Lance nodded. "Parasites are all coral colored. No chlorophyll. All but mistletoes. Mistletoe is the only green one. In
the parasite family, anything that's green is like a princess is
to the common people."

"What about the devil's-stinkpot, that fungous growth you showed me? It looked like a crown made out of boiled lobster claws all yellow and red and smelled like the Cloaca Maxima. How common is it in the Thicket?"

"It is considered rare in Texas. It loves the saprophytic, decayed matter and soil. I think it looks more like a snotty-nosed baby."

"Do you think there is any of the Thicket at all, even a little, left in a pristine state?" I asked.

"A little bit around Saratoga, the heart, and a few spots near Kountze and Segno," he said. "In less than ten years it will be gone. All gone. The plants are already nearly gone. The magnolia, that reproduces so slowly, due to grazing cattle, is being looted by nurserymen. French mulberry, myrtle, azalea are hauled out in loads. The birds're going. The ivory-billed woodpecker is supposed to be gone, like the wild pigeon, but they're NOT. I know where two pair are. I showed 'em to Bess Reid."

"The Audubon Society will want to know about that," I said.

"We want 'em to know. Maybe they'll help us do something to stop the destruction. Woodpeckers are just too good a target for BB guns and twenty-twos. Do you know," his manner of emphasizing the words always precedes a bit of lore that he senses is new to me, "that wood ducks nest in holes in the trunks of trees? They carry the ducklings down by the scruff of the neck the way a cat carries kittens. They take them down to the water and teach 'em to swim while they're riding on their parents' backs! As soon as they think the ducklings are getting the hang of it, they swim out from under 'em and leave them to it."

I asked if he thought Texans would allow themselves and the nation to be defrauded of an area so rich in natural lore.

"I hope they won't, but it doesn't look too promising." He blinked his eyes very fast. "Do you know there is something in bloom in the Thicket every month of the year? If it's a warm March, the yellow jessamine is in bloom."

I shall always remember the arrowhead shape of the evergreen leaf and the vanilla scent of the lemon yellow trumpets of the climbing jasmine.

We drove on down a smooth sandy road into the heart of the forest going toward what was once the town of Bragg. The mixture of pines, huge and towering, the spiky hollies and broad-leaved magnolias, with scented myrtle beneath them made an unforgettable picture. The stretch of sandy road runs through a large pine forest and is edged on each side by a low natural hedge of smaller leaved palmettos. Sweet gum, black gum, hickory on the ridges, white oak, ash, maple, tupelo, linden, and a few pale green sycamores shoot high up into the sky after sunlight. Occasionally a crape myrtle reaches up and sends out a spike or so of fringed pink bloom, proving that once a home-seat or a sawmill stood among those woods.

"There goes the wealth of Texas," Lance said as a truck

loaded with great felled trees went down the road. We stared after the truck, helpless and depressed. Quick to sense a mood, Lance gave out his two-note chuckle that signified he had remembered something I would enjoy.

"You would have loved Larry Fisher, Mary."

From the many things I have heard, I am sure I would have enjoyed knowing Larry. He was a musician, photographer, student of nature, newspaper feature writer, dramatist — the Renaissance Man of East Texas. He wrote a play dramatizing the Keyser Burn-Out, produced and directed it; took the entire cast by bus on a barnstorming tour over a considerable portion of Texas. I had been cold-trailing information on the Burn-Out for many months and got what little information I have about it in the Thicket. Fisher dropped dead while making a speech at a banquet and the world lost probably the best source of information on the Civil War "strike." Everywhere I went, people in Texas deplored the untimely death of Fisher.

"Do you know . . ." Lance stopped to point out a clump of exceptionally good palmettos, "Larry got the idea of making Venetian blinds out of palmetto hearts. They can be boiled and dyed like a piece of cloth. They make wonderful rope too, except it's too expensive to process it."

"What did you use for dye?"

"Oak, cherry laurel, that's brown. Pokeberries for scarlet and sumac for light brown. Used some mulberry. Then we got to experimenting with a loom. Had all the kids in Saratoga holding thread for us. Trying to make palmetto mats."

"You had an interesting time with Fisher?"

"I was his first and best-loved friend," Lance said. "He loved music and had a wonderful record collection. Symphonies, Strauss waltzes. You know, he lived here for quite a while. Set up his picture-taking studio, and when he was making all the shots, group and individual, for the High School graduating class he had to work awfully hard. Larry hated country music with a passion. These oil people round here, you know, they get up real early: four o'clock in the morning. They generally been lousing around with the hooch all night, and the minute they wake up, they turn on the all-night stations and get this hillbilly music. The windows and doors're all wide open, and they turn the radio up as loud as it'll go. Larry simply couldn't stand it. He might have been writing all night and was just getting to sleep good, when here would come that racket!

"But he finally got the best of 'em. When he worked in the darkroom, afternoons, the oil people would just be getting home, ready for bed. So Larry would load up his record player with a Beethoven symphony and turn the volume up as far as it would go. He was happy with the music in the dark room, but that classical stuff almost drove the oil people out of their minds."

"Saratoga was a health resort once, wasn't it?" The sulphurous water I was trying to drink put me in mind of it.

"Yes," he said. "Around 1865 to 1904. And it was one of the very early oil fields. See that old-fashioned pump out there? That's what they call a dead-man. The bootleggers used to sneak out at night and hang a keg of whiskey on that cross beam that goes up and down all night. It was to age the whiskey."

"I've seen a keg strapped to the back of a rocking chair."

"Saratoga's the capital of the Big Thicket. Thirty-five years ago three or four thousand people lived here. Now only a few. The cows sleep on the wooden porches of the stores at night." Lance looked out the window at a few people over at the filling station: "Most people bore me to death. They act crazy: going nowhere, but all running."

"Did you ever see any whooping cranes in the Thicket?"

"Oh, yes, definitely so. They always get together in the spring, just like a bunch of people, around by the hills. I crawled up on top of a low sandy hill one time, about twenty years ago, right over here a little ways, and they was eight in a group. They make this funny whooping noise and jump up and down in a queer dance. They look like they're doing a clumsy minuet, all the time giving this hoarse whooping cry. Just like people on their way north." I had seen some odd demonstrations by tourists in my life but never had noticed anything outstandingly odd about "people on their way north." Better pay attention, since I'd obviously missed something choice.

"Any roseate spoonbills?"

"Used to be. You hardly ever see one any more. Even the plain woodpeckers are being killed off! Whole stands of pine have been destroyed by the pine beetle because the woodpeckers are gone. They are the only ones equipped to really dig those grubs out. Over in Votaw they used to call an ivory-bill a cake."

"They have different names for the big woodpeckers, haven't they?"

"Indian Hen. Wet Hen. Good God. Lord God, and By God."

"How come?"

"Two fellers came out from Beaumont to run down the reference and they found out that two hunters, new to the Thicket, were in there an' the big birds came at 'em and scared 'em: 'Good God, what a woodpecker! Size of a brown leghorn hen,' they said. And if you're lost in the woods you're lost as a By God." I could understand the appropriateness of that, for you'd be really lost!

"You're supposed to know more about this region than anybody else," I said.

"I'll bound you a dollar I know one woman didn't tell you that!" He smiled. "Religious folks don't 'bet.' They 'bound.'" I laughed, because she *had* called him a "kinda Nature Boy."

The juke boxes and cheap pix magazines have penetrated to the Thicket bringing their banalities with them. "Anybody says anything good about me is denied about it by that ol' hen. Pure dee hard-down meanness! Do you know: one time I really didn't know much, an' got told about it. I was looking for Indian pipes. Knew a place that was ideal for them. They just had to be there."

"You mean those leafless saprophytics? They are snow white and turn black later?"

"Yes. The flower looks like the bell, or bowl, of a pipe. They grow on dead matter, stumps and rotted logs. I knew they'd have to be in that place, and started out to find them. Two boys came out of an old road, and kinda tagged along. They lived way back there with their folks who made a living burning charcoal. They wanted to know where I was going and I told them to look for Indian pipes. 'You ain't got much to do, have you? Whyn't you get something worthwhile to do?' the other one says.

"I kept right along and they followed me. Pretty soon we passed a house and I happened to notice a piece of a myrtle bush hanging on the gate. The boys saw it too. 'Well,' says one, 'the baby's been sick, but it's better now.'

" 'How'd you know?' I said.

" 'Piece of myrtle bush hanging on the gate, bottom side up. Anybody'd know the baby was sick an' needed attention. You don't know much, do you, Slim?' "

"They've got lots of lore left," I said. "I wish I could be here at night sometime. These deserted places fascinate me."

"Some still have coal-oil lamps," Lance said. "They give a soft, mellow, ghostly-like light that's real nice. Maybe we could show you the white-crested herons and the green-crested. The whippoorwills fly low."

"Lance," I begged, "the Thicket is just one part of Texas. At least, in this book."

"What you need is you a place down here," Lance said. "You could help us fight for the Thicket."

"Don't tempt me. I've taken a solemn oath that when I build a house in Texas I'm going to stand blindfolded in front of a map of Texas with a bow and arrow in my hands and let fly! Wherever the arrow lands, that's where I'll settle. It's the only way I can possibly choose The One Place."

I have had only one nemesis in all the bushwhacking on this book: chiggers. They are the only thing in Texas I have not been able to circumvent. They seem to be able to jump from thirty feet distant to land, ravenously hungry, in a jeweled belt of ruby-red welts around my itching middle. They are impervious to Campho-Phenique and seem immune to the classic remedy of sulphur and lard. But there is a compensation, a kind of by-product, that makes worthwhile every bruise, sprain, and scratch; all the sunburn, raw nerves, and backache from driving too long at a time. Even worth braving the chiggers for are the friends I have made all over Texas, very specially in the Big Thicket.

Shared enthusiasms are binding. Sensitive, perceptive companions with vast knowledge, willing to impart and to share, are strong ties to this enchanted land. As a three-year-old, the pockets of my pinafores were filled with roots, seeds, and cuttings. The laundress used to complain all the time. I cannot remember when I did not grow plants. Every empty olive bottle was treasured to turn upside down over some plant I was rooting. They must have sensed it, for in the space of a day or so these people accepted me as one of their own and opened new vistas of experience to me.

"Mary," Brother Ramby said, "we'd be glad to have you here. We have too many people with knowledge in the head. Too few with it in the heart."

I looked at Lance and thought how his love of all living things, plants, birds, snakes, insects, and even a few lucky peo-

ple, had enriched his life. Just to watch the way he handled
a leaf shows what true affection is like. Roy Bedichek told me
that Lance took him into the woods once and they saw a copperhead. "Catch him, Lance, I want to examine the wonderful
color under the jaws."

Lance raised and lowered his arm, with his hand pointing
straight out, over the reptile several times, as though charming
it to stillness. Bedichek studied the venomous snake and
looked at the rosy copper of the scales all he wanted to.

"Anyone else would have killed a copperhead. Lance just
touched it sort of lovingly when I had looked enough, and let
it go."

One of my many privileges is to have Lance Rosier for my
friend and to share him, even so sketchily, with the readers of
this book. For he has an ancient wisdom, from another world.
He would be at home in any age, in any place. There are no
"little Saint Francis" affectations about him, although he, too,
is the Little Brother of the Poor. He is rich because his wants
are few. He cares little or nothing for material gain. And why
should he? He lives in the middle of one of the great treasures
of the world. He is its curator, the custodian of its secret life.
He owns the key to the woods.

Thumping the Thicket stimulated my mind in many respects. Who would leave even a passable record of the won-
drous region for the world to come? It would have to be someone who knew every facet of the place, and they could be
counted on my thumbs. It would also take a gifted writer to
breathe the spell of the region onto the paper. Would Roy
Bedichek's heavy writing schedule permit him to do such a
work? Had he the time to assimilate the amount of material
spread out over four counties, and to transmute it into his own
singing prose? Must the Big Thicket pass into legend as have
the Llano Estacado — the Staked Plains — and Mustang Desert, a region whose location can no longer even be found?

I met a woman of whom I had heard it said: "Roy Bedichek talks to her like an equal." Recognition from an internationally known naturalist must mean that Bess Reid of Silsbee, near Beaumont, was an authority in her own right. She is all of that. She knows every phase of the Big Thicket. Birds and snakes are her specialties. She says you can't love birds without getting interested in their enemies and what they live on. She knows plants and flowers too. A rare violet, something like the bird's-foot violet, *Viola reidi,* has been named for her by Southern Methodist University at Dallas.

Unfortunately, I was not able to see the Thicket under Mrs. Reid's guidance. In my case, it was "duck or no dinner," as another famous Thicketer says. It seemed preferable to share the handful of crumbs I had picked up from the groaning table than to forego writing about the region until I knew it better. No one will ever see all of the Thicket. Now the primary sources have all but disappeared, along with the characteristics of the region itself.

I had to ignore the advice Bess Reid gave me:

Don't publish anything about the Thicket until you have been piloted around by me. Unless you have been to McGee's Hill and the great stretch of woodland valley below it that will go under when the projected Angelina River Dam is built; the old graveyard, also to be drowned; the ghost gardens that come up briefly every year, where completely vanished sawmills once operated; the mysterious rock-wall (natural or crudely man built?) not far from Zavala; the "silver bullet mine"; the first petroleum derivatives or instituents found in Texas (the old tar pits), Blue Hole; Potato Hill; Boykin Springs; Bowden's Lake; McMahon's Chapel; the former site of the Texas Villages, Atoya and Ayish (commonly called Irish); bayous and their swamps (location of some wonderful plants); as much as possible of the whole watershed of the Neches and the Angelina rivers and their affluents. *All* part of the original Big Thicket, and most of it known to just a few of the *real* old-timers that have not died off.

Roy Bedichek is right about Lance Rosier being a great naturalist. He knows the present Big Thicket, centering in Hardin
Country, lapping over into Polk and Liberty counties, as does
no one else alive. Only Lance has studied its *wildlife* — he is
the nearest to a fully self-taught man on the subject I know.

I've been privileged to see more of both the original and
present limits of the area than any other woman. Because it
has so fascinated me all my life we bought land thirty years
ago on the edge of it. Again, I have the closest of friends living
in and around it. I am a good pedestrian and I have gathered
more tales of the Thicket's actual and traditional history than
I can ever live to reduce to permanent form.

I am planning, God willing, to spend at least one week each
of February, March, and April in the district soon to be sub-
merged. I feel certain we can extend the known growth limits
of Reid's Violet.

Everyone who has written about the Thicket has penetrated
only into small sections of its now so awfully restricted boundaries (the boundaries are rather nebulous at that).

I was ill when Bedichek was here and had to let him go to
what I think is the least interesting and most abused part of
today's Thicket.

The Reids live on their large woodland acreage near Silsbee
the year round. It is a refuge for animals, birds, and plants. I
understand that the property is to go to the Audubon Society
eventually.

The Reids' house is built primarily as a shelter that will be
adequate but steal no time from the precious business of nature study. There are cages for sick and crippled birds on the
comfortable porch.

"Birds are scared of hats," Mrs. Reid said.

Not without reason, I thought, having in mind some of "Mr.
John's" finer flights of fancy. I could see nothing startling in
Mrs. Reid's knitted watch cap. She handles the birds with
ease and confidence and is said to be the only person known to
hatch and raise hummingbirds in captivity.

Mr. Reid was frying fish to take to an Episcopal covered-dish supper. He is a mild, even-tempered man: he sits in the car and reads while Bess prowls the Thicket for hours on end, hunting birds, plants or snakes. But he gets his innings: every Friday they spend the entire day at the Beaumont Club. Mr. Reid has his day.

They have both worked hard and intelligently all their lives and have earned the right to live for their pleasures. "Simplify, Mary, simplify!" she said. "Throw all that household ballast overboard."

I thought of the silver and china and glass, the exquisite formal gardens that had taken so much time and money to care for. Each year I have tried to work toward just such a rivered life.

It is an uncommon joy to see people dedicated to doing what they want to do, especially in a constructive, creative fashion. Commonly, such singleness of purpose is seen only in those bent on going to the dogs. In Texas I have seen many individuals living in this same quiet, well-organized fashion: building their lives around their interests, living for what they love, and counting what little they lose well lost.

At the edge of the Big Thicket, in Camden, Lumbertown, I saw a company-owned project in operation. The Carter Lumber Company owns and runs a settlement that looks like the toy wooden villages we used to play with as children. It is the oldest sawmill in continuous operation in Polk County.

The town is in a low, sweet valley studded with old Texas houses, white with red or green tin roofs, spread over the gentle slope much as a sick child would spread his wooden houses over the mounds made by his knees under the counterpane. The owner's "mansion" is there, too. There are railways, American Express, postoffice, beauty parlor, barber shop, and commissary. The drugstore is complete with pharmacist. You can buy anything from a canoe paddle to a coffin. There is even a made lake, principally for industrial use. The road leading to the main office is made of boards. The place has a self-contained fairy-tale quality about it.

The mill is devoted entirely to the processing of hardwoods, with the exception of pine.

I wanted to see the oxen at work. Carter is the last lumber company that uses oxen in Texas. They are kept for tradition's sake. Now tractors are used for logging in the woods. At one time oxen were employed in the actual lumbering operations in the woods. They are steadier than mules and do not panic so readily. Now they are used to unload the great stacks of fine lumber logs off the trucks. The logs are cut in the forests, brought to the lumber mill by railway, and loaded onto trucks from which they are pulled by the eight oxen: four yoke, who unload the entire load at once by the use of heavy chains and steel cable.

Some of the woods are: sweetgum, red oak, black gum (made up into furniture and sold as cherry), white oak, hickory, elm, ash (for baseball bats and axe handles), magnolia (wood that does not shrink or warp much), and cypress, which lasts forever.

A red oak thirty inches in diameter is generally about one

hundred years old. The average log, even fifty years ago, was from cut-over timber. Even then, there was little virgin timber left. Saw-logs are very usable: twenty-four to twenty-seven inches in diameter, sixteen feet long. The truckload that the oxen pull to the ground is usually made up of forty to fifty sixteen to twenty foot logs.

Ox driving is a lost art. Willie Redman, the middle-aged colored driver, has been handling oxen since he was fourteen years old. He is also a millwright, and was born on the place. The command the oxen like to hear the most is "On the spot!" To oxen that means rest. Willie has a whip, but I didn't see him use it. He drives the eight beasts with skill and intelligence.

I had heard no names so suitable since Saint Nicholas' reindeer: Blue, Rowdy, Dude, Dick, Brandy, Beery, Lamb, and Jolly. One extra ox stays in the pen to take over for a disabled ox. They work nine hours. They eat three sacks of chops and two bales of hay every other day.

Blue, a Brahma, fetched the ox behind him a sharp kick in the muzzle. The yokes creaked as the oxen turned and wheeled. Willie always drives them from the left.

"Where you point the whip, that's where they go," the driver said.

I looked up, startled, as a colored woman drove by in a new red Mercury. It seemed curiously out of place.

Small pigs, some chickens, and geese were in danger of being trampled underfoot, but nothing could keep them very far away from the well-fed oxen.

The association of ideas is strong in most human beings. Seeing the oxen work brought to mind an incident I filed in my mental cabinet under "Operation Stalled Ox." Oddly enough, that unique stunt was also the result of the association of ideas.

The Chamber of Commerce of Corpus Christi, Texas, learned in 1952 that the 600th anniversary celebration of the

founding of Corpus Christi College of Cambridge University
was going to be held — minus the traditional roast ox because
of the stringency of British meat rationing.

What did the City by the Sea do? She sent an ambassador of
good will, Buster Shely, and a thousand-pound steer — from
the city of Corpus Christi to the College of Corpus Christi.
Shely barbecued the steer at Cambridge, England, leaving the
United States fully cleared by the State Department, on one
day's notice.

"Where did you get the steer?" I asked, thinking it would
cost too much to fly it over.

"Swift and Company got it for us in Northern Island,
butchered it, and flew it to Cambridge. Cost over six dollars a
pound by the time we got it served. The Britons loved it — and
the gesture."

The London *Times*' leading columnist named Shely "Man of
the Month" over Churchill and Eisenhower. I thought of the
Book of Proverbs: "Better is a dinner of herbs where love is,
than a stalled ox and hatred therewith." The Britons got their
stalled ox and love therewith because one of Cambridge's
Colleges shared the name of a town in Texas.

I watched the complex operations of the lumber mill and
learned of many new jobs: graders, worm-hole detectors, bug
hunters: all hardwood inspectors. They were loading Number
One lumber, green; grading it to be sent to the drying kiln for
RCA Victor radio and TV cabinets. No SMOKING signs were
everywhere — and plenty of evidence that chewing tobacco
was used.

Number One is judged by the absence of worm holes, warps,
twists, bark, knotholes, splits, bird pecks, and knots. The
graders are skilled at turning over the boards, measuring width
and thickness with a board rule, a long stick with a hook in the
end of it. As always when watching any craftsman, I was fascinated by the sureness and dexterity of their movements.

The hardwood sawdust from the mill is very coarse, called hog fuel and is used in the furnaces. They never have enough of it.

"Come in where the electric saws are, lady," the foreman invited.

Not to appear sissy, I went.

When the huge power saw snarled into the bleeding, four-foot heart of a giant magnolia tree and ripped it apart with an angry shriek, I stumbled down the stairs of the saw loft of the lumber mill deep in the heart of the Piney Woods of East Texas and out into the open air. For the first time in my life, I felt that I was going to faint. It was like being under the cruel machinery myself.

"Dizzy spell, lady?" The plant manager was kind.

"I can't stand to hear the trees crying." He looked at me out of the corner of his eye, but he knew what I meant. He was an East Texan. He would rather be sitting under that magnolia fishing than to have to supervise its calculated murder. He was a nice, mild-mannered man doing his job.

"I'm all right," I sat down on a stump. "I can't watch the result of centuries of slow growth being ripped apart to make cabinets to house Howdy Doody. I could as soon watch an electrocution over at the penitentiary at Huntsville."

The subject of the trees of the Big Thicket is very close to my heart. The inordinate, perhaps abnormal love of trees that dominates my life can only be accounted for by a set of genes — inherited from Scots forebears who performed Druidic rites and believed that spirits lived in their trees.

Tin, glass, or the new plastics. Let the wood butchers experiment with them, and stop destroying the health-giving trees, man's comfort and joy.

At the company store I saw Ladies' Suits, $13.89. All kinds of dry goods and furniture. Air conditioners. Salad dressing with sauterne in it. Celeste figs. Gumbo filé powder. Anchovies in tins. They run a grocery sale on Friday. As a special, they reduce the price of staples and the women stock up for the weekend.

"Sawmill people are the happiest people on earth," a man told me. "When some people die and leave their loved ones, everybody helps. We got so much here money can't buy! Rent's cheap. No lights or water. He realizes he's gotta have *us Labor*. Seventeen dollars a month for a five- or six-room house!"

I watched the clean, attractive children running from the store to their storybook Texas houses after school and began to understand why sawmill people might be very happy indeed.

A huge colored man got down from the truck he was driving and stretched his mouth into an enormous grin: one of his front teeth stood out among the cubes of ivory that filled his mouth. It was covered with gold, but not in the usual way. The gold covering had a five-pointed Texas star cut out of it allowing the white porcelain of his tooth to shine through. Prosperity was not around the corner: it was in Camden, Texas.

The variety of persons and places I had seen within the Thicket fascinated me. John Knight's reputation had preceded him and I was eager to talk to him, if he would talk.

As the sandy road twisted through the forest toward the Knight place at Segno, redbirds flashed across the roads and mockingbirds sang with an almost unbearable sweetness. Martens darted into their "apartment" houses on gateposts or into their gourds. Occasionally I saw a bluebird. I was thrilled, for I had never seen a real bluebird; only a little blue enamel one on a brooch I wore as a child. Dwarf palmetto edged the sides of the road with graceful fans facing down the yaupon and holly. Behind them the pines bent and sang in the January wind. Majestic magnolias shone in the sunlight. For some reason sunk deep in my childhood my mind went back to *The*

Girl of the Limberlost. Never in Texas had I expected to see a forest so beautiful and vernal as this. Ferns, mosses, flowers, birds, moths: all the life that had enraptured a whole generation of adolescents was incarnate before me.

A little moss, not enough to be sinister looking, but just enough to soften the rough edges of the forest, hung from the trees. Mistletoe fed itself on whatever host it could find, seeming to prefer the oak family.

A log house of classic proportions had two gigantic live oak trees in front of it: I would guess they are two hundred years old, draped with moss and covered with English ivy. The chimneys in most of the old houses in the Thicket are of mud and stick. Few have native rock fireplaces and still fewer have brick chimneys. The mud chimneys are functional and have the added virtue of costing nothing. The pines and hickories, beeches, sweet gums, hawthorns, and mayhaws creep up on the old houses and shroud them in mystery. Most of them are still occupied. There is little chance of buying one of them. Most of them were "heired" and the natives are not "studyin' about" selling them. A few stand empty and blind. Oil comes, and with it the inevitable human erosion: the exodus to the city.

The pastoral tone of the ride was rudely shattered by the sight of a bulldozer in the middle of the road, pushing down a sixty-foot magnolia tree. I had the car door open and was half way out into the road before Bob Pool grabbed the tail of my skirt and hauled me back: "Mary! Now Mary, don't you jump that man! He's just doing his job. Don't you say anything to him."

What I was saying to myself was anything but complimentary to the man's ancestors and I was imploring the saints in charge of the Tortures of the Inquisition to put on their thinking caps and come up with something really worthy of the inventor of the bulldozer.

"Long as he's killed it and got it on the ground, I might as well save a few branches for the leaves," I said. The fresh green fragrance of the sap smote me where I live. I didn't say a word to him, but the man wore a puzzled frown, as though saying, "Honest, lady. I ain't done nothin'." It saddened me to see the giant specimen uprooted, leaving its lovely companions, to make wider roads for trucks and cars to stink up the air and fill it with dust. Not in this last surviving beauty spot, the teeming, lush backwoods! Back, and on back the car ate into the deep woods. I felt as though time had been telescoped a hundred years.

Occasionally through the state, I felt that flashback in time, where I could see life going on in these identical surroundings, exactly as it had a hundred or more years ago: people looking much as they do now, without so much aid of artifice, dressed in simple homespun clothing, their demeanor dignified and gentle, the speech the same as it had been three hundred years ago. "He holp me right good." "Come riddle me how to make the soap." "He's a rare one: talks long and droll." "They used me good; wouldn't suffer me to be alone a minute." "Dull as a frow, it were." A frow, I learned, is a "double-bitched" axe used for splitting cypress shakes and shingles. The trees were just as green, maybe greener, then, and the flowers just as bright. The snake fences and split shakes were weathered even then. "Postes" were cut and yards fenced off. Cows gave off the same sweet comforting smell, and pigs . . . pigs is pigs. Goats ranged perkily and gaily and horses were treasured. Hounds lounged and loafed in the dusty yards, scratching abstractedly, one eye out for pot-licker or a scrap of cornbread.

These people have had their homes and living here always, loving the land and the Thicket, making a living from the bodies and pelts of the animals, from the streams and the forests while in their pristine state, which endured for many a long year.

Until the depression of 1929 and the subsequent Government Rescue Missions, most of the Thicketers lived in conditions very little different from those the first American colonists knew. They had been the sovereign lords and owners of this virtually impenetrable wooded region from "who laid the chunk."

Now they are making a last stand along with the only tribe of Texas Indians, the Alabama-Cushatta, who live on a reservation at the edge of the Big Thicket, the whole of which once belonged to them and the other tribes long ago dispossessed. They would not have had even this meager remnant of land if Sam Houston had not befriended them.

The Thicketers are using the same native intelligence that enabled them to outwit hostile nature, warring men, feuds, runaways, hide-outs, "revenooers," illness, and poverty. They are sturdy, independent, and self-contained men and women, making, in many cases, a good life for themselves in the most ideal of ways: by combining the best of the new with the best of the old.

The Alabama-Cushatta are doing the same. In their burying ground at the reservation they still keep up their custom of placing on top of their graves the artifacts of this life that they found most useful. Safety razors are going to be needed in the Happy Hunting Ground, along with flashlights, if observations are worth anything. An occasional baby's grave will have a toy on top: a celluloid pinwheel or a red tin automobile. You often see mirrors, and sometimes a fancy glass sugar bowl. I was cheered to see on several tombs a shiny beer can opener.

At Huntsville I saw the Alabama-Cushatta team from Big Sandy play basketball in the auditorium of the Sam Houston State College. They won the tournament five years hand running and went to State for the finals each year. The players were fine-looking boys, extremely clean and neat. Some spectacular basket shots were made, and their speed was unusual. Teamwork and instant co-ordination made the game engrossing.

The stands were filled with Indians: grandfathers and grandmothers, mamas and papas, big and little sisters and brothers, and babies, babies, babies. Unblinking as dolls.

"If they win," a Houston sports writer told me, "they will all pile into buses and go to Austin for the finals. Everybody in the tribe, the grannies riding herd on the bunch. They have gone every year."

The faces were interesting: absolutely expressionless. Many of them moved only their eyes as they watched the rapid plays and movements.

As the goals piled up and the game got real hot, a few Indians chewed their gum faster. That was all.

Their clothes were quiet, neat and decent. The teenage girls wore the gaudy rayon blouses and circle skirts — magenta, yellow, green, and purple — that the teenagers wear throughout America. A few pony tails were in evidence, infinitely preferable to the frizzy heads of some of the girls. The home permanent is Big Medicine on the Reservation.

I felt bad when they lost the game. No trip to Austin. I should have liked to follow the grannies over the campus just one day. For after thirty years' absence from the campus of the University of Texas I should welcome an Indian guide to help me find my way around the Forty Acres.

There seems to be good spirit between the youngsters in the contests. It is all part of the civilizing process that is taking place throughout the Western world. Fear is based on a lack of knowledge, and I often think of the man who feared the snake lying in the road until he came up to it close enough to see that it was only a rope. There is a certain caution among the old settlers. It is not a bad thing and is a hangover from the days when it was a matter of life or death to find out whether the stranger was friend or foe. Speaking of John Sylesteen, the head man at the reservation, one of the Thicketers told me voluntarily: "When they had the Christmas tree at the Reservation, the Indians wouldn't come up and get their presents. Sylesteen made the teacher bring 'em to 'em! But he seems like a fine feller, FUR AS WE KNOW, that is." I wish I had a dollar for every time I've heard it in New England. Fur as we know!

When I saw the country around Honey Island and Segno, I began to understand why the Thicket had always been a hide-out for people who did not conform to what was considered proper at the time. The impossibility of tracking anyone who chose to hide in that jungle, the closed-mouth natives, and the plentiful supply of game, water, and whiskey made hiding out a pleasure. Fish in the streams, wild turkey, deer, squirrels in abundance; haws of many varieties, persimmons, pecans, hickory nuts, black walnuts, and an occasional bee tree to rob of its golden honey. Small patches of rich silt in the creek bottoms were planted to corn, sorghum, and sweet potatoes to furnish the mainstays of life; they were relished along with the meat of the wild razor-back hogs that roam through the woods, eating acorns and anything else they can find. They are known by the graphic name of "rakestraws" and furnish an inferior grade of meat. In hard times, the Thicketers have been known to eat armadillo, smoked good and brown. It is a greasy meat something like possum. With "shinny," the real East Texas name for corn likker, and terbacker, a man could have it mighty good, even if he was layin' out fum the law.

During the Civil War, groups of conscientious objectors hid in the Thicket. They tilled their little patches and tended their "distills." When the essentials were provided, they robbed the bee trees of their pounds of honey. Then the women, always giving aid and comfort to the enemy, in this case, their men, would come into the Thicket, carry off the honey and take it to the nearest trading post and swap it for tobacco for their hide-out husbands or sweethearts. That's how Honey Island got its name.

Before the Civil War, various groups of people came to the

Big Thicket from the "old states" because they had no slaves, and did not relish the prospect of fighting for other people's "livestock." Many of the settlers were well established by 1840 and were ardent followers and admirers of Sam Houston. They believed in him teeth and toenails. Old Sam was against secession. That was good enough for the Thicketers. "We won't fight neither," they said.

Then Sam went with the tide, and accepted the inevitable. Not so his constituents in the Thicket! Having come out "agin," how could he possibly be "fur"? Once committed, they never changed an opinion and how could he, their White Hope?

The Confederate Army had to send forces to the Thicket trying to force the recalcitrant natives to bear arms against the North. Some families hid in the depths of the Thicket and when the guvver-ment men arrived, first trying bribes, according to some, and then resorting to arson, the families stayed stubbornly in the area and whatever became of some of them is still a mystery.

There is little known and almost nothing written about the famous or infamous Keyser Burn-Out.

I went into the heart of the Thicket to look at the place twice . . . it is eerie. Death and desolation to the soil — a scorched-earth policy that was lasting! What did they do to stop the growth of the trees in that ever encroaching jungle for nearly a hundred years? The blackened, burnt-over grass roots are still visible, but no tree or shrub has grown back. I could picture the refugees and the game fleeing before the blaze. What kind of heat must it have been to scorch forever so fertile an earth?

I talked to two men whose families remember the Keyser Burn-Out. They are just about the last primary sources available. When I asked why the men went in there to escape military service, taking their families with them, the answer was identical both times: "They didn't want to fight for the niggers."

During World War I the Thicket was a sanctuary for conscientious objectors. I am told that it served the same purpose in World War II, and gave shelter to descendants of the very same families who holed up there in 1917.

Escaped convicts from Huntsville sometimes make it to the Thicket and if they do, their chances of capture are lessened considerably unless bloodhounds are used in pursuit. But the roads the lumber and oil people are opening up like ugly little wrinkles all over the face of the Thicket make a hide-out pretty much of a lost cause these days.

The fact that schools and government programs have reached the old inhabitants through their children has in a great measure changed their way of thinking. Rural electrification programs have changed the mode of life and the ideas of many of the people. Radio and television have penetrated the forest fastness. My guess is that the families whose sons fought in World War II and Korea, and will fight in the next rumpus, will be less likely to give aid and shelter to dodgers when they stop to ask themselves: "What's these fellers got that my boy ain't?"

We were back into the truly deep Piney Woods now: Segno, the tiny settlement where John Knight lived. The smell of cordwood, ranked evenly, took me back to my childhood. There was the gray relic of a store by the roadside, and a well-fenced cow lot. A tidy garage stood open, and behind it the forest rose straight and high. To the right, beside one of the largest holly trees I have ever seen, was a neat inconspicuous frame house.

"I'll go see if I can jump anybody up," Bob Pool said.

I was watching the hogs chomping acorns under the trees. Bob came back with a tiny woman. Her face was pure Scots formation. Her eyes had the shiny look that comes from spending most of the time outdoors. Her hair was the color that used to be known as "sunny brown."

"Paw's tendin' his traps," she said. "Orta be back any time.

Git down an' come in the house." She led the way and welcomed us in. "Hunters messin' up the house all the time," she said, pulling up two comfortable chairs in front of a cozy gas heater. I looked at the immaculate floors, the general cleanliness and polish over the house.

"Doesn't look like hunters or kids have been messing this up," I said.

"We ain't even got a young un' to go to school, but we gotta pay school taxes just the same."

The house was sealed with sheet rock, and tastefully wallpapered. The furniture was sturdily comfortable, the atmosphere homelike and warm. "You have butane?"

"For the heaters and the stove. Paw gits up at one in the mornin' an' sets till daylight. Got the electricity, too, for the pump and the lights."

Radio and television, I observed. In the immaculate kitchen I saw an electric icebox and deep freeze.

Mrs. Knight showed me the entire three-bedroom house, her shining, modern kitchen-dining room with a large white sink and counters, cabinets above and below, linoleum on the floor, and crisp curtains at the windows. There was a back entry or service porch, a gleaming bathroom and water heater.

I don't know what I had expected: probably an iron crane and pothook in a stick and mud "chimbly," and a bucket with a gourd dipper in it. Shuck mattresses and pallets, maybe. I was totally unprepared for the high standard of excellence in the house furnishing and housekeeping. I might have known what to expect when I looked at the neat, stocky figure of the lady of the house.

John Knight came in and I studied him with interest amounting to usury.

"You'll be wantin' a cup of coffee," Mrs. Knight said. I was busy looking at the souvenirs of World War II pinned up on the living-room wall. She went into one of the bedrooms and came back with her hair neatly combed. She had just taken a fresh calico apron out of a drawer, for the air was filled with the clean scent of dried lavender.

Everything seemed so right about the place that the people who lived there had to be right, too. These people knew how to live: here was one family that "had it made."

On the wall hung framed certificates of award from the National Fur Show, a rattlesnake skin from the "King's Ranch," over near "Sant Antonio." Right at the start, I decided Mrs. Knight and I had *one* thing in common: our geography was a mite shaky. We were taking each other's measure, slowly and surely.

"Those fawn hides are beautiful" — the little spotted rugs were satiny and supple.

"Ol' Uncle Lige Cain dressed them fawn hides. These here badges is all takened off'n dead Nazis. My boy got 'em in Germany." Knives, bayonets, and a Nazi rayon undershirt hanging on a coat hanger adorned the wall, alongside impressive antlers, well mounted, and a rosary from the Vatican.

John Knight is in his late sixties, an agile, limber man close to six feet tall. His eyes are bright frontier blue set in a ruddy face, with a sensitive mouth and extremely intelligent forehead. The bones of his forehead are of most interesting shape, with a somewhat U-shaped depression plainly visible in the bones beneath the skin just above the wrinkled brow. I noticed the same characteristic mark on the brow of his brother Buster.

John's clothes were the cleanest khakis I had seen in a long time. He wore black rubber boots and a Stetson hat that would have passed unnoticed in New York.

"Bin tendin' my traps," he said.

"This time of year?" I asked.

"Now's the time. Mink twenty-two dollars a skin, twenty-six dollars for the big un's. Beavers and beaver castors, them little sacks . . ."

I could see it embarrassed John to talk to me about that part of the beaver's anatomy, the musk sack that male beavers have between the anus and the external genitals.

"What do they want with beaver castors?" I asked.

"Well, hit don't never fade out . . ."

"You mean the smell? For trapping lure and scent?"

"That's hit."

"Someone told me they use the musk from the castors for the base of expensive perfume and to make medicines against the spasms."

"The Indians knowed that," John said. I wondered what size book it would take to hold all the Indian remedies and healing lore of the old-timers in this region. Would one measly lifetime suffice to dig out the knowledge of these people?

"You don't mind if I ask you a lot of questions about the Thicket, do you?" I asked. "You're one of the few people who really knows anything about it."

"Tell you anythin' I know. But I'm kind of a iggerunt man. My boy, now . . . he's gettin' a real ejjication."

Pride in the new generation was everywhere I went, including the Big Thicket. I could only hope the youngsters would not pass up the yarns of the old folks, only to regret it later.

"I think you have ignorant mixed up with unschooled, Mr. Knight. You might be a little short on book learning, but no man that knows as much as you do can be ignorant."

"Reckon that's right," he agreed. "I had two o' these here schoolteacher fellers workin' for me in the WPA . . . an' you know, I couldn't learn 'em a thing."

"Too many educated fools."

"That's them. Half the time he'd talk an' I didn't know what it were! I cain't talk fine nor nothin' . . ."

John Knight's speech intrigued me and has, in some degree, rubbed off on me and those around me. His expressions just seem to fill the bill in a way that modern speech never can.

"You talk the way people talked when Elizabeth was Queen of England and Sir Walter Raleigh wasn't just a name on a tobacco can. I hope you won't be offended if I put down the exact way you talk. I don't want you to think I'm mocking you, or anything like that."

John grinned good-naturedly.

"You know," I continued, "how today people are saving all they can of the past? Like putting old-timy things in museums for the future generations to study and learn how people used to do? That's why I am putting your talk down exactly the way you say it. Not trying to 'flower it up.' It won't be long before the old manner of speech has disappeared from the country, and I would like to leave a sample, like a relic of how folks really talked in the early days of the frontier."

"Some makes records," John said. I showed him a tape recorder in the car and told him how it worked.

"I don't like it," I said, "first of all, it scares folks off and then when you've got your tape made, only a few people can get the benefit of it. This way, everybody that can read will learn what real Thicket talk is like."

"My daddy was sixteen in the Civil War. Come here from Alabama and Mississippi . . . when he was a baby. I'll tell you anythin' I know."

"Show her your old scrapbook, John," Mrs. Knight said.

John Knight has a scrapbook, same as any Hollywood star, the only difference being that his exploits are not trumped up. Most of the pieces came from the Houston, Dallas, and Beaumont papers. The more I sat in the house and visited with the Knights the better I liked them. My respect and affection grew at every meeting.

"I hate to ask you questions because I can't stand people who ask them myself, but there isn't any other way to find out what really happened. You must have heard, firsthand, what happened in the Keyser Burn-Out."

"My daddy an' the ol' folks told me differents and differents o' times. Keyser takened his fambly an' went in there an' hid out in the switch-cane."

"Where?"

"Above Union Wells Pond. Keyser an' his fambly was in there alone, layin' out the Civil War. Up to the Wells was twenty-five to fifty men."

"Why?"

"Did it to keep from fightin'. Didn't want to be shot. They didn't want to go to war; didn't know what it were." I had read this theory in the few sources on the subject and it seemed logical enough.

"They didn't want to fight for the South?"

"No, ma'am. They was for Sam Houston. Teeth an' toenails.

He was agin Secession. Then he changed over. An' they sent the Confederates up into the swamps and thickets after 'em. Was nigh on to a hundred men in there, but they never did locate 'em."

"How come they set fire to the place over there that they call the Keyser Burn-Out?"

"First the Confederates went up there an' offered 'em money. I heerd Keyser takened it, an' lit out back to the Thicket where his folks was. The man that showed 'em the way was named Lilly. You'll hear a lotta differents o' stories, but all agrees Lilly was the man, 'cause he was shot in the fork of his galluses."

I liked the way the proof of Lilly's treachery showed up, and told John Knight an ancedote I'd heard about some little boys who were "playing soldiers," re-enacting the Civil War.

One boy, Nat, was the grandson of the surgeon to Hood's Brigade. One day his playmate came and told him that he was not allowed to play with Nat any more.

"Why?" the boy asked.

"Because my father says your grandfather went off and left him on the battlefield with his wounds untended," the boy said.

Nat told his grandfather about the slander.

"Go ask him where his father was shot," the surgeon said. "*I* was treating those shot in the CHEST!"

"Them folks hidin' out: Jayhawkers they was called," John said. "Them Jayhawkers worked little fields o' corn an' 'taters while the Confeds were lookin' for 'em. They killed them Confeds quicker'n rain. They'd catch one at the house, where they'd be a-settin' fur 'im. They ran ten-twelve cows on the range, trapped, fished, an' had plenty o' deer an' turkey an' squirrel."

"Reminds me of when the United States sent troops into Mexico looking for Pancho Villa. The Mexicans were on home ground in those mountains."

John grinned.

"Some o' that Keyser bunch raised terbakker, pressed it in a tree notch with a lever an' block, put molasses on it an' pressed it good for chewin' terbaccker. They dressed hides to git money for ammunition an' store vittles. Had powerful good ranges for longhorns in them woods."

"What happened to the Jayhawkers when they couldn't catch them? Not even after that awful fire. No trees grow there to this day."

"They went free after the war, 'cause the North whipped. Did the South a-winned, they'da bin court-martialed."

So it happened — if the South had won, these people would have been worse than mere draft dodgers. All of this within one hundred miles of Texas' largest city — the remembrance was strong, handed down from father to son.

"It's a chilling sound, the death rattle of the Big Thicket," I said.

John Knight moved his quid of tobacco to the other side of his mouth:

"Hit's makin' noises like hit's a-gonna die."

John Knight ought to know. He has lived in the Thicket — and off of it — from way before the time the bear ate the feet off Old Man Reisinger until the present day of butane, deep freeze, and TV.

"Did the bear really eat Mr. Reisinger's feet?" I asked.

"I reckon he did! He clume a tree an' the b'ar right atter him."

"Where was it?" I could not believe that I was actually hearing a man say "b'ar" as simply and naturally as he would breathe.

"In a baygall . . . one o' them low, swampy places in the Thicket, full o' black gum, gall-berry an' possum haws, wh'ar the b'ars always stays. Biggest baygall I seen was two or three miles long. Hear some of 'em was five mile long, outside-a Saratoga, kinda on a dreen. Cows bog down in it. You have to put up some forks, put up a windlass an' hooks to git 'em out. The

cows gits paralyzed, an' you gotta haul 'em out over timber an'
brush you put down. Daddy come by a baygall one day when
I'se a purty good size boy . . . he seen the buzzards hoverin'
an' when he went in the baygall, he seen the hogs dead.
Takened the cholera. There set the ned b'ar . . . his paws on
the hog . . ."

"What do you mean: ned bear?"

"The grandaddy of 'em; the biggest. Like you'd say, 'That's
the ned buck I ever shot.'"

"Please don't stop." His stories and language were a link
with the vanished frontier.

"Daddy, he put the dogs on the b'ar. The b'ar clume the
tree an' waited till three deer come by to scrape up agin the
tree. B'ar was eight or ten years old. Killed all three deer . . .
you could hear him beatin' on 'em for a quarter of a mile. So
the next day I started out walkin' with Old Man Reisinger an'
he was aimin' to show me some baby buzzards, white down on
'em like a goose. I warn't goin' inter no thicketty place to see
no buzzards. I'd figgered to kill me a deer with squirrel shot.
All at oncet the five dogs bayed: it was a b'ar. Mr. Reisinger
went up the tree an' the b'ar atter him. He couldn't go up no
further. He had 'is shoes on. He's afraid to git down, 'cause
'twarn't far from his house an' he's afraid the b'ar would kill his
wife. My shot wasn't no use. I eased out just like I went in. Et
the old man's toes plumb off. He warn't wuth a mashed bullet
after that."

John Knight has told me this story three times since that first
day, over widely spaced intervals of time and he has, in the
manner of all great primitive raconteurs, never altered so much
as one syllable of it.

"How many wolves have you trapped for the government?"
I asked. "Tell me you saved the farmers and stockmen over
one hundred thousand dollars trapping timber wolves."

"I caught better'n two thousand," he said. "A wolf kills
about a thousand dollars worth o' hogs, sheep, goats, calves,

colts, poultry, besides game, in its lifetime. A pack, anywhere from two to ten may be follerin' the lone wolf. A vicious wolf will kill fifteen to twenty head o' small livestock in one night. He's cunnin'. Gotta take every precaution when you're huntin' them. Cover the ground with canvas, use gloves, special animal scent, for lure. Only two per cent gotten away fum me. Biggest un' I ever caught weighed eighty-seven pounds — he was coal black with a white tail."

"You had to keep your wits about you."

"Lady, hit's duck or no dinner."

John Knight spat into a bucket of sand and looked out the window at his impressive woodpile.

Brother J. B. Carroll sat in the next room, apparently dozing upright on the deep red sofa of the back parlor. J.B. was Mrs. Knight's brother, a gentle, slow-spoken man with a soft fuzz of gray whiskers and a halo of gray hair. He had a faraway look in his eyes, almost trancelike. You wouldn't think he was paying any attention to what went on in the other room but he would fool you teetotally. He wore navy blue and white striped overalls and stroked his whiskers. The unobservant might have thought he was asleep. He was merely conserving his strength and his voice.

"I've cut a million cords in my life," John Knight said, still gazing at the woodpile.

"Oh, Lord!" Brother J.B. intoned from the next room.

"Do you suppose I could get a horse around here cheap, Mr. Knight?" I hoped to see the woods for myself on some gentle old carcass.

"Cheap? Buy one for a song," he said.

"An' sing it yerself," drifted in from the next room in Brother J.B.'s trancelike tones. "Ain't a day they don't carry one off to the soap factory."

"You work for the surveyors sometimes, don't you?" I wondered if he would talk about the vacancy outfit.

"I show the corners. I know where the landmarks is. When the vacancy outfit come . . ."

"Who are they?"

"Bunch from town wantin' to change the fence lines so's they could take our homes, now that oil was found."

I had to smile. Of all the poor prospects for help in that direction, it was John Knight.

"They picked the wrong guy for that kind of stuff."

"Squatters' rights; best title in Texas," John Knight's blue eyes twinkled. "They couldn'ta knowed my daddy named Segno hisself. He just drawed that idee. He was b-a-a-a-d to read, an' had a fair amount o' ejjication on him."

"Wonder if he knew that Segno means sign in Italian? Maybe Latin, too, for all I know."

"He might could," John said. "He had him a lotta books an' could work the telegraph. Grampaw was a faith doctor."

"How come?"

"He was a seventh son of a seventh son in the family. If one o' your kids was sick, all he had to know was hit's name an' when hit was borned . . ."

"Doctors in Houston has got machines that tells ye what's wrong wi' ye," Brother J.B. volunteered drowsily from his throne on the red sofa.

"Today when they take the toe-ache," John said, "they hunt the doctor."

"Calomel and quinine. That's all she wrote." Brother J.B. rose slowly and scratched his whiskers. "An' they'll pop it to you. Time to pen them goats."

"When our kids was cuttin' teeth, Pretty Bird was havin' a bad time. We cut willow roots an' swamp lily roots. Take 'em apart at the joints an' string 'em round the kid's neck. Had her sweatin' in no time."

"The television calls them there Fogey Ism ideas." Brother J.B. delivered his slow opinion as he went out the front door.

"How many deer dogs you ever train, Mr. Knight?" His dogs were well known through East Texas.

"Trained fifty anyhow. Take 'em out, find a track, pop your finger, an' he'll folly it. Half cur, an' half houn': vicious. I picked out a b'ar track for one of 'em, half of the dog took to it, an' the other half ran — so I shot him down." No schizophrenic dogs for John!

"Paw was a government trapper for the state. He got a salary," Mrs. Knight said.

"I worked some for the state an' federal," John said. "Official Predatory Animal Exterminator. Killed about two thousand timber wolves, an' kept me a pet wolf for seven years. Made him mind better'n ary dog I ever owned. Never tied him tell he was a year old. Best deer dog I ever had."

"Was he any use to you in trapping?"

John hesitated a minute: "Well . . . we collected his . . . urine."

"How?"

"In a pan. To put on the traps to make the other wolves think it was all right."

"Did you ever get lost in the woods?"

"Hit ain't no way to get lost by the stars. On a cloudy day a feller might. One time, come a little harrycane, an' things blackened up, but I'd figgered up the moss was on the north side of the trees. You can make a course no matter where you go. I was turned around on a prairie oncet, but I had a compass in my pocket. My boy putt up four years in the war. He's a good un': never got lost or turned around on a prairie. Plenty got lost this winter, stayed lost day an' night. Easy to do . . . ain't ary house 'tween here an' the Santa Fe Railroad."

"You do much hunting now?" All this "city life" might have softened him; push-button paradise might have changed things.

"Hit's a huntin' buddy! Yes, he air! An' Willis, too." Brother J.B. spoke in oracular tones from the next room.

"I hain't popped a cap or wet a hook this year, but I allus

buy my license. Lotsa times I fergit 'em an' leave 'em home."

"He's bin workin' too hard," Mrs. Knight said. "Buildin' that last pasture. Split postes an' split 'em; so heavy a horse couldn't hardly pull 'em. Dead people don't need pastures."

"Is there much deer left?"

"Bout all gone. I carried the mail six year, an' trapped for fifteen, twenty-one all told, an' I ain't never failed killin' a wild turkey spring o' the year. Got to go in anurr county now to kill one. Hyeerd any?" I only wished I had, for there is no sport I know of more exciting than shooting a wild turkey.

"No, but I heard somebody with a turkey yelper," I said.

John Knight reached behind him and produced an instrument that looked like a narrow cedar box about an inch and a half deep and seven inches long, with a lid on it and a long handle on the narrow end of the lid. He held the box in the palm of his left hand and took the handle in his right. He moved the handle sideways, delicately lifting the lid and scraping with it ever so lightly along the edge of the box. The sound of a wild turkey yelping made me jump.

"Bridges makes 'em out o' cedar. Sells 'em in Sant Antonio. Gets two-fifty apiece. This is the best callin' 'un he had, made out o' seasoned mulberry."

"Bet that brings the turkeys on the run."

"I was out one day, an' hyeered a bunch gobblin'. Went in a house an' borried me a gun an' fo-five shells. Single-barrel shotgun with half a pound o' haywire wropped around the barrel. Didn't have no sight, but hit was a deadener! I called to 'em. Then I hyeerd 'em strut. They come up to my back. They wheeled around and kinda flourished, then one of um went off to hisself, and stuck his old white head up behind a myrtle bush. I'd done tole the women to go pick some flowers; I'se aimin' to git me a gobbler . . . on'y thing the game wardens could do was make me pay a fine. They couldn't eat me."

"Much excitement left in the trapping?" I asked.

"Tied up a big wolf one time, an' he broke the chain while he was still in the trap. I tied up his mouth, but the chain an' collar broke. He made for me, but I roped him, an' wropped his mouth with haywire. All that saved me was the trap hook hung on a root. He'da fought like a tiger, in the trap, specially. I carried a six-shooter, colt's thirty-two, but I always takened a rifle with me to the traps. Hardly ever lost one. One time I seen I had one, he had pulled his toes off. I shot his tail off, an' caught him later over close to Carmona."

"Mrs. Knight likes to fish, doesn't she?" She had told me how much fish she had in the deep freeze, all of which she had caught herself.

"Got the Dam Fever," John smiled. "Caught her a foot tub full of trout the other day."

"We used to camp out for fun two or three times a week," Mrs. Knight said. "We'd camp out on quilts on the ground. Twist an' turn, turn an' twist. 'There's a root in my back.' Sometimes we neared about freeze to death. But with straw under the quilts, it was warmer than a tent. I love to fish. Over at Dam B some folks uses two hooks at a time, fishin' with a reel. They'll run you off if they catch you."

"Sounds like fun to me." I thought of how relaxing it would be to sit and fish and just listen to the Knights talk.

"One time a feller lived off huntin' in the Thicket, name Dobbs, went out deer huntin' at night with Peter Wiggins. They had 'em a firepan — you ever seen one of those?"

I had seen a colored slide of two men hunting with a firepan. They sling the pan from a pole and carry the pole across their shoulders, I suppose to keep their hands free for the gun.

"They shine the deer's eyes with the light," John said, "an' the feller with the gun shoots him. They'd put coals in the firepan an' had cut pine splinters to make a light on the coals. Wiggins was in front an' Dobbs carried the gun. They walked an' walked an' didn't see no deer. The splinters was all burned out so they stopped by a rich pine stump to fire up agin. The splinters fired up good, an' fust thing you know Wiggins, up front, seen two pair eyes: 'Hand me the gun!' he whispered.

" 'I lef' it back whar I cut them splinters!' Dobbs whispered.

" 'By God, you nee'n't to whisper,' Wiggins shouted, 'hit won't do no good now!' "

The humor of the past was not dead. To John Knight sitting by his television set, the firepan light for hunting was as close as yesterday.

"You all certainly had fun," I sighed.

" 'Specially them Wigginses," John said. "Come a real col' night an' we was huntin' turkeys; gone out a-horseback an' was layin' on the ground on saddle blankets. Peter Wiggins' wife let him have a quilt, an' he takened some straw with him an' spread it on the ground not to git the quilt nasty. For fun, the boys set the straw afire, an' burnt the quilt.

"Peter Wiggins had him on a see-sucker coat, split up the back. Wouldn't take a hundred dollars for it. It were burnt about half off when he woke up fightin' fire. He was mad about to die, saddled his horse with his coat burnt off 'tween his shoulders. 'Where you a-goin', Bobby?' they hollered, laughin' at his bobtail coat. Them Wigginses played rough." It was apparent that lots of things were rough, both work and play, on the frontier. I had heard they still play rough even in some of the towns at the edge of the Thicket.

"Ever go to dances in the Thicket?" I wondered if religion had interfered with their pleasure.

"I was ba-a-a-ad to dance! Square or round. Them Wigginses was at a dance with me one time. Had us a ol' fiddler, he didn't exac'ly play by note or nothin', just picked it up. Played 'Cotton Eyed Joe,' 'Gal on the Log,' 'Eight of January,' " John said. "We'd have a log-rollin', work all day, then have a big supper and dance all night. They git adapted to it, you know. Hits like a damn fever. Peter Wiggins an' me seen a feller squashin' a girl up agin a ol' plank house. We got us a maul, sneaked in thu the back side o' the house, counted the planks till we come to the one he was standing up against, and hit was the eight plank. We hit the plank with the maul hard as we could and hit knocked him crazy, right out into the middle o' the yard. He got his hat an' lef' fum there. Knocked her plumb loose from her seat. He thought he was sure cuttin' his okra." The twinkle in John's blue eyes gave me the idea that such shenanigans would still appeal to him.

"Are you more or less retired now?" I asked.

"Part o' the homeplace is leased for oil," he said. "Last year I caught twenty-six mink: $544.44. You know them wimmen pays up to six thousand dollars for coats out of 'em? I do good with my traps, muskrats aplenty an' they's a beaver dam on Menard Creek. Worlds of surveyin' and guide work with geologists an' oil-lease men. Carter and Kirby and the oil people beat the vacancy outfit. Them lines been here hundred and seven years. They tried to change 'em, but they couldn't do hit when I showed them corners. I know where they belong."

"Kind of wasted their money when they hired you," I said, "but I'll bet you enjoyed the job. What's the biggest change you notice in the Thicket?"

"No more oxen," John said.

"They all got these here Farmalls." Brother J.B. was heard from. "They done quit this here walkin'."

"What about the soil? What's it good for?" I said.

"Good to keep these here creeks pushed apart." Brother J.B. was going strong. "Things is changed since my daddy's day. I bought me a forty-dollar suit o' broadcloth clothes on the credit, an' my daddy found out about it at church. 'Don't never do nothin' like that nummore. If you haven't got the money to pay for anything, leave it alone.' When he spoke one word, the next word was a whuppin'."

John smiled and said:

"Hit's all different now!"

Of all the places I had been in Texas, nowhere had I seen the very old ways so harmoniously combined with the new. And they purely loved it, as the Knights would say!

The color of the Thicket extends even to its fringes. Over at Livingston a while back, they caught a small black bear, one of the very last in the Thicket. He got away and they roped him. Bruin "clume" a tree, rope and all. The crowd must have shattered his aplomb, for he slipped and hanged himself neatly and undeniably dead. The citizenry barbecued him and "et" him at once.

On a cold January day, I sat with several of the Livingston pranksters in the White Kitchen looking out at the display window of the florists, Flowers and Potts. "God is my Judge!" as Alex Woollcott would say.

In these men there is a strong strain of the adolescent: an odd mixture with the pioneer. A well-known criminal lawyer was bellying up to the counter for more peppermint stick candy to stir his ice-tea with.

There was to be a hog auction at three that afternoon and the place was full of country people getting their "dunner." The menu set forth the following:

Our Noon Day Lunch, White Kitchen, Livingston
Red Kidney Bean Salad   Southern Style Blackeyed Peas
Buttered Fresh Cut Corn   Mashed Creamed Potatoes
Hot Rolls   Cornbread   Oleo Margarine
(All vegetables included in lunch)

CHOICE OF MEATS

Dessert: Apple Cobbler
Chicken-Fried Steak with Cream Gravy   .75
Baby Beef Stew with Fresh Mixed Vegetables   .75
Baked Stuffed Green Pepper and Candied Yam   .60
All Vegetable Plate with Boiled Egg   .60
CHOICE OF DRINKS: EXTRA

No wonder they were full of spizzerinktum! Six starches in the so-called "vegetables." I took chicken-fried steak, not because I like it, but because common sense tells me to choose what the natives like wherever I happen to be. It is certain to be less bad than their conception, say, of "ros bif."

I looked at the lean, beaky noses and buttoned-up mouths. Over at the Fair Grounds that morning I had seen signs: "White Exhibits" and several doors down: "Colored Exhibits." And they meant it!

The day before I had found artificial bedbugs in my bed and almost stepped on a stuffed snake on the floor. A man in the same hostelry found his shower stall crawling with baby alligators, hatched from eggs in the night.

I was prepared for most anything but the sound I heard: a blood-chilling roar that shook the walls of the café. Not round, but square goose bumps stood out all over my body. I am no coward but when a bad "li-ron" or a mad Brahma bull is coming through the door roaring and rumbling, I am no Osa Johnson: I stand not upon the order of my going.

"Get back down, Mary." Some giant but gentle paw dented my right clavicale permanently. "It's just Peeto and the dumbull."

"What kind of bull?"

"Just a dumbull — all in fun."

I looked up and saw about three hundred pounds of leaf lard

bearing down on me, grinning like a "chessy-cat." Brown eyes
were hidden by the chuckles. Enormous dimples appeared and
disappeared in his shaking cheeks. His handsome, intelligent
face was reminiscent of a pleasant Charles Laughton.

"Had you goin', didn't I?" He brandished the small nail keg
he held in his hand. One end of the keg was open. The other
was covered with a tightly stretched circle of rawhide, tacked
down and held fast by an iron hoop. In the middle of the rawhide "head," I saw a large knot. It was the end of a rawhide
thong about thirty inches long and one-half inch wide. The
thong hung down about twelve inches below the open end of
the keg. The knot fastened it securely on the outside and kept
it from slipping through the small hole in the "head" of the
dumbull.

"How?" I said.

"Rozzum." He grinned and tucked the keg under his left
am. In his right hand he held a piece of rosin which he pulled,
in his closed fist, down the entire length of the cord, producing
a paralyzing kind of bellow sufficient to shake the faith
of any Daniel braving the lion's den. The greatest bull fighters
of all time would have blenched at the sound.

"Why?" I said.

"Scare folks!" he laughed. "That'll make 'em really tear up
the pen, won't it?"

I agreed it would do all of that.

Outside a gaunt, bearded old man and his angular raunchy
old wife strode by the café. The old man had a long flowing
beard, dirty with yellow tobacco spit. He had rheumy, clotted
eyes and his wife's long white hair hung down unkempt between her shapeless black hat and rusty black coat. They
both carried tall heavy staffs with knobs on the end — big
chunks of root left on stout saplings. They whined and pan-
handled up and down in front of the café, looking like a couple
of the more unsavory characters from the Old Testament. They

hirpled and hobbled, held their hands on their backs where they imagined their kidneys were and put on a show of being pretty well stove-up.

"I hid under a culvert with this when they were goin' home late one dark night." Peeto patted the dumbull.

"I couldn't imagine you doing that," I said, for he is a kindly man and gentle of heart.

"Listen! They'll thumb a ride and if you don't stop for 'em, they swing at your car with the knot on the end of those sticks! I can show you deep dents they knocked in brand-new cars!"

"What happened?"

Peeto smiled like a cherub: "They're a whole lot more limber than they let on! You oughta seen 'em cover that ground! Pretty soon they quit runnin'! Clear up in the air, just driftin'! Do good in the Olympics!"

I looked at the weird instrument of torture and wondered how many people had ever heard of one, much less seen one. They are virtually unknown in Texas, and outside of Livingston, I was not able to find a person in the heart of deep East Texas who had heard of the dumbull. It must be an invention of the purely local devils.

"One time Dr. Flowers was holdin' classes in First Aid for the Fire Department out at his place in the country. We had a camp out in the woods there, and there were about twenty fellows all learnin' artificial respiration, splints, how to fix a broken leg or a wrenched back. We'd simulate people in accident condition. Doc Flowers kept tellin' us he had a new, bad Brahma bull — fierce business and to keep out of his way.

"We had this feller, he was supposed to have a fractured spine and a broken leg. We really trussed him up: bandages and splints till he couldn't move. We transported him on a stretcher made out of two saplin's with two coats buttoned over it. While they were bindin' him up, the signal came, a bobwhite call and a man came tearin' through the brush yellin':

'The bull's loose! Comin' this way! Run for your lives!' Everybody ran. They dropped the stretcher, patient and all, and
taken out! The dumbull was roarin', louder and louder, nearer
and nearer. 'Co'se my weight, crashin' through the thicket like
a mad bull, didn't lessen the impression any. That was really
a noise. I mean!"

"He could have died of fright, unable to move. What happened?"

"You know," Peeto said gravely, "he never *did* take the Written Exam!"

And because Texas is a land of caviar and clabber, that
same afternoon, less than fifty miles away, in sleepy Liberty,
old in the time of the Republic, I was the guest of a polished
cosmopolitan, a woman as well known in Back Bay, Boston, as
she is in the Big Thicket: Geraldine Humphreys, granddaughter of A. B. Hardin, for whom Hardin County was
named.

Our meeting took place in a purely Texan fashion: I was
taken to call on her by the son of a family I had never even
heard of an hour earlier in the day. They didn't know me from
Adam's off-ox, but it didn't make a bit of difference.

I noticed a truly spectacular vegetable garden for January
when Bob Pool stopped to ask directions. It was large, well
fenced, and in full sun. It grew in a way that makes gardeners
green with envy, not chlorophyll. Not a leaf had been nipped.
Turnip greens, seven-top, lettuce, beets, cabbage, onions, col-
lards, and peas. Peppers, strawberry plants, figs, camellias,
roses, a lemon tree with some bloom and a few lemons on it, a
row of pecan trees, and a row of sugar cane. Sweet peas in
heavy bloom covered the fence at one end.

The people who belong to the garden live on seventy-five
acres of land in the heart of town.

"The front yard is in the city, and the back yard is in the

country." Mr. Gerald Partlow, the owner, turned out to be the uncle of Governor Price Daniel. "Mr. Gerald" told me he planted the garden forty years ago and the clumps of okra have never been replaced. He put two horseshoes around the trunks of a pair of cedar trees the day he brought his bride home, and they are now grown over, completely hidden from sight.

In back there was a great barn of cypress, an almost ever-lasting timber. Cattle, hogs, dogs, chickens, peacocks, ducks, quail, and fawn roamed there. There was a smokehouse of cypress too, stained a deep chrome yellow from the years of smoking meat and sausage over hickory chips. I saw an electric fan on the floor of the smokehouse, used for blowing the smoke on the sausage, freshly made and incredibly aromatic.

Sam Partlow, a prematurely gray young man, carried pans loaded with sausage into the house to place in the deep freeze. The old and the new again!

We had stopped only to ask directions, but were invited to come in the house and have something to eat, even though it was long past "dinner time." There were huge baskets of eggs and crocks of butter on the kitchen table, cream that was ladled out and practically cut with a knife before being slathered over home-canned peaches. A wood stove and a parrot in the kitchen, where an electric range gleamed. An electric churn and a desk were out in the "breakfast nook" that seats twenty-eight people at one table when there is a family gathering. Something told me "Miss Voe's" kitchen was no place for calorie counters. Here was real security, in the smokehouse.

Mealtime is any time a car happens to drive up at the Partlows'. It is one of the fast-disappearing kind of houses where the sound of the gate opening always elicits the order: "Put another plate on the table."

During my first Sunday dinner in that house, a "plain Methodist Sunday dinner," according to Sam, a whole lifetime seemed to flash before my eyes. "Mr. Gerald's" sweet voice in the bless-

ing gave me such a lump in my throat that I could scarcely
swallow the succulent roast and nine or ten vegetables that
accompanied it. In the next breath he told me a rather robust
story about Pierre and Boudreaux, the two characters who in
East Texas correspond roughly to Pat and Mike.

Three times during the meal, Mr. Gerald cried out: "Sam,
get the book!" And Sam "fotch" the dictionary to settle whatever word we were splitting hairs over. Bludgeoned, I tried to
push away from the table, still licking my chops over the homemade lemon ice cream, and thinking how pleasant it was to
turn the clock back a few years.

Mr. Gerald came up to show me his fine handmade Sunday
boots. They were impressive. Fine black vici kid, trimmed
with green leather appliqué, too fine, apparently, to wear even
on ordinary Sundays, since he carried them in his hand.

"Mighty pretty," I said, and bless God, if he didn't plump
them right down on the snowy double-damask tablecloth!

"Geraldine Humphreys will never forgive me if I don't
take you over to see her," Sam said after I had known the Partlows about an hour.

Thornton Wilder once wrote me that it was a gift straight
from the gods to be able to make friends quickly and *rightly.*
The gods were good to me in Liberty.

We drove to the Humphreys' house behind old brick walls,
with gnarled and tangled gardens around it. Large camellia
bushes were in bloom: "We fell in over camellias," Sam said.
Since the Partlows and I "fell in" over gardens, I knew it was the
opposite of "falling out." He helped take care of Mrs. Humphreys' valuable bushes by spraying and supervising their care
generally.

Mrs. Humphreys had suffered a long and crushing illness,
but even so, she lay back among her pillows and held her levée
like a queen. In her face there was a timeless, indestructible
kind of beauty.

"I am told that you studied painting with Whistler in Paris, Mrs. Humphreys," I said. "I have a strong hunch that he painted your portrait."

"Who on earth could have told you about Whistler painting me? No one knows it." Her voice is musical and quite unforgettable.

"You have the kind of face he *had* to paint."

"That clique of artists was stimulating." She smiled. "I remember Sarah Bernhardt coming to the *vernissages*, the first showings, wearing a coat of ostrich feathers and lemon-yellow gloves. I also remember when she had to perform in a tent in Dallas, Texas! Loie Fuller was the reigning beauty of Paris then. La Loie, the Law, the French called her."

I had heard something about Mrs. Humphreys' gay and varied life, and asked, "General Cós' grandson gave a ball for you in Mexico City, didn't he?"

"That was a very long time ago." She smiled. "It was because my people released the Mexican prisoners here after the surrender."

I knew that A. B. Hardin and his brother Franklin had managed to save the lives of the Mexican prisoners held captive in Liberty after the revolution. Franklin Hardin was commander of the post and released thirty-two Mexican officers upon their signatures, "the parole of honor." The last signature is that of General Perfecto de Cós. The Texans had scarcely enough food for themselves, much less for the prisoners, and were about to execute them when the Hardins intervened. Later Mrs. Humphreys gave me a photostatic copy of the surrender papers, a document I treasure.

How we got onto the American flag I cannot recall, but its mention brought a smile to Mrs. Humphreys' face: "Years ago in Paris, there was a dinner at the American Embassy, and the dessert was an ice in the form of an American flag, horribly red, white, and blue. 'Aren't you going to eat it?' my dinner partner asked. 'What? Eat Old Glory?' I laughed. 'Never!' "

"Mrs. Humphreys, I understand that oil companies are leasing new sections of your land holdings," I said.

Geraldine Humphreys chuckled.

"I suppose they are used to dealing with the illiterate. They came in bowing and scraping, spelling everything out for me, hinting around for me to produce an abstract for them. 'It's a real big paper, ma'am. Kinda bulky. You're bound to have a paper for the land. They're generally real large.'

" 'If you are referring to the deed,' I said, 'it will be quite short: there will be only three signatures on it: Grandpa's, Pa's — and mine.' "

She wages gentle but unremitting warfare against sloppy speech, jargon, pretentiousness of any kind, and most of all, against anything that interferes with plain speaking.

Henry, her houseman, came in with sleeping pills on a tray. "Forgive me," Mrs. Humphreys smiled, "it's time for my hush puppies."

Such spirit will not be kept under. It has been my good fortune to see the incredible recovery made by one of the Texican Great Ladies of all time. She was really ill when we met, but soon afterward, she flew to Dallas, had her hair cut short, bought a Cadillac I call "The Golden Goddess," opened her house in Galveston, and to top things off, bought a clear, citron-yellow pick-up truck for her country place at Hardin, "because there is no one to tell me I can't!"

Later, she said, "We need you, Mary. Come to Liberty. You can help us save the Thicket."

She loves the Thicket, and for the first time in my exploration of the Great Garden, I felt hopeful. To preserve even a portion of this beauty spot will require concerted action by many people, but if any one individual can "save" part of the Thicket, it is Geraldine Humphreys, in whose veins runs the same blood that "saved" the Mexican prisoners.

9. THE LAND AND THE MAN

I LEFT the Green East and came back to the Big Middle just in time to see the cataclysmic goings-on when the drouth broke. I had a ringside seat at the colossal struggle between man and Nature.

The one great inescapable fact in Texas is the weather. Everywhere I saw the results of the drouth, seven bitter biblical years of it. Groves of majestic live oaks died, oaks that had given a county its name. Farmers, cattlemen, and merchants went broke — or so far in debt to the bank that climbing out seemed impossible. Again, in the Empire of Extremes, there is too much or too little: drouth or flood.

Ten years ago the banks of the Pedernales River, a few miles out of Austin, were jeweled with giant cypress trees, tall and frondy. Today their gray ghosts stand in mute protest against the ravages of Nature and man.

First came the floods, covering the tops of the ferny trees, some of them thirty feet or more in height. Then the waters receded, leaving the roots washed bare. The bare roots were seared and scorched by the drouth, which finally killed the majestic cypresses and destroyed forever the lacy leafiness of the landscape.

From the top of a hard-packed, burned-out hill I looked down upon the dead trunks, standing like the tree stumps of Hell. I saw the story of the ravages of the past ten years: twigs and sticks borne by the flood still lodged in the branches of the dead trees thirty feet above ground, at the edge of the meager meander that was once a river. The whole east side of the dead trees was charred and black, the result of man's carelessness with fire. A chain of destruction had set in, each link clearly traceable.

The land is shifting about. The topsoil will blow away from one man's property and land over on another's, unless stopped by scientific soil conservation. But somehow the destructive forces of Nature will be stopped, for man is still the only animal who lives by controlling his environment and not by allowing it to control him. And people are getting wiser all the time: they plant more gardens in Texas than they used to, more flowers and vines. That makes the birds happy and the world a sweeter place to live in. Water and trees: the wealth of the world.

Texas people, trying to live with the weather, are taking part in a long enthralling serial, the last installment of which has not been completed. Sometimes it may look as though the last chapter had been written, but God and Nature always seem to think of another episode that must be tacked on. So the Texan asks "What next?" and life goes on like the *Thousand and One Nights,* because, like the teller of the tales, it spells death for him if he gives up. Giving up is not in the Texan's vocabulary — not even when it would be the wise thing to do.

He gives his family a Spanish supper (taking another notch in the belt), and digs his heels in resolved to toughen it out, come hell or high water.

In April 1957 the parched earth cried out for water — and got it. More than it bargained for. Torrential rains brought floods of disaster in their wake. Land, choking, powder-dry one week — and the next, coffins washed from their graves to perch obscenely twelve feet above the ground in the branches of trees. According to a Texas newspaper, several corpses were found at McGregor washed right out of their coffins, one corpse "as neat as the day of the funeral."

Contrast and contradiction. When Texas finally got disaster aid, relief from Washington for the drouth-stricken areas, before the checks could be cashed all the blanks that said DROUTH on the seven copies of everything had to be erased, and the word FLOOD printed in its place. Farmers are still figuring cagily how to collect for flood relief without losing their drouth money!

By the time I had explored the four cardinal points of the compass, I began to feel that I had found out what Texas is really like, and I think I know what the Texan is. Certainly he is not the popular conception, or what one man old enough to know better refers to as "The Eugene Manlove Rhodes Texan." The land has had a strong effect on the man, and instead of making generalities, I am trying to provide a few specific examples of "bonified" (Texas newspaper spelling) Texans. The man has affected the land, too. People make places — and in Texas, person and place are sometimes almost inseparable. It would be hard to imagine the Kings without the ranch. John Knight without the Thicket. Shanghai Pierce without the Gulf Coast cattle ranges. Charles Goodnight without the Palo Duro Canyon.

The land of Texas, when seen piecemeal, is like a view through a knothole, observed by someone who thinks the whole is like the small portion before the eye. People living out of Texas tend to think "the Texan," male or female, is like the isolated Texan or Texans they have known.

The six blind men who ran across an elephant were much like a man trying to get a clear picture of Texas and Texans. One said, "An elephant is like a string." He had taken hold of the tail. The second said, "An elephant is like a snake." He had the trunk in his hand. "You're wrong," shouted the third, "an elephant is like a tree." His arm was around the elephant's leg. The fourth, fifth, and sixth blind men said something else again. "An elephant is like a fan," insisted the one holding the ear. "No! Like a saber," cried the one holding a tusk. "You're all wrong," cried the sixth, "an elephant is like a wall." He leaned against the side of the elephant and went to sleep. They were *all* right in the descriptions . . . as far as they knew.

A man driving into Texas from the Louisiana border soon hits the Piney Woods. So this is Texas, he thinks, all lush green forests and shrubs. If he enters the state from El Paso on his way from California, he will say that Texas is an endless desert, more of the same he has traversed on the way. Should a tourist drive down from Alberta on the Canadian Border, keeping parallel to the 98th meridian, he will find that Texas is a continuation of the Great Plains. The traveler who enters Texas at Brownsville, coming from Mexico, will say: "Texas is a subtropical country. Palms, bananas, guavas." Like the blind men and the elephant, each of these travelers is correct . . . as far as he knows! Texas combines examples of practically every form of topographical territory found in the United States.

After exploring Texas over a period of three years, I am forced to conclude that God made Texas on His day off, for pure entertainment, just to prove what diversity could be crammed into one section of earth by a really Top Hand. When it comes to accounting for the diversity in Texans, I think God just outdid Himself!

Looking back from the top of the hill over thousands of miles of plains, prairies, forests, deserts, swamps, lakes, canyons, mountains, hills, jungles, caverns, oceans, bays, rivers, baygalls and creeks, the land, covering roughly one twelfth of the total area of the United States, is a giant jackpot.

The thinking observer cannot help feeling a fairy-tale quality in Texas. Some of the worst-looking, apparently godforsaken land is yielding vast wealth through its mineral content. The ragged dress to the stepsister, Beauty loving the Beast in spite of his surface ugliness, the lump of butter in the bottom of the Brownie's bowl all carried hidden rewards for accepting what was dealt out, and making the best of it. Only men and women of great stamina — physical and spiritual — could stand up under the trials by fire, flood, and drouth that have beset Texas over the years. It took endurance to participate in the Great Treasure Hunt. Whatever the old Texans got, they got the hard way. The land was enough for them. All they expected from beneath the earth was water — and even that was scarce.

The land made the man. No one who has not traveled over a large portion of Texas can conceive of the variety of climates and conditions man has always had to contend with in this empire of contrasts and contradictions. Varied soils and scenes, tumbling oceans and towering mountains. Rivers, a brown trickle one moment, a raging, racing wall of water the next. Unbroken flat gray plains, unrolling before the eye in apparently endless monotony, change suddenly to thick waving green fields, sparkling under the ever living stream of crystal water from vast artesian treasures hidden under the earth, brought forth by the hand and mind of man, the life-giving blood of a region that is literally the embodiment of the desert made to blossom and bear. To see the sun playing on the great streams of clear water gushing from the pipes into irrigation canals is a profoundly moving experience.

Despite the lively and flattering interest that the world has shown in Texas of recent years, few people set themselves up as authorities on the land. It is one of the few subjects that call forth an honest "I don't know." Most people will say: "I only know about the part I drove through on my way to California." An occasional embittered serviceman will say: "I was there in training. Don't mention the word Texas in my presence." Honest Texans are not loath to admit that they don't know their own country: "There's just too damned much of it."

On the other hand, everyone with a set of vocal cords, and probably some who lack them, knows of a certainty, with utmost positiveness exactly what the Texan is like. He may confess ignorance of the land with perfect aplomb, but he will fight to the finish to defend his concept of a Texan.

The myth of the Typical Texan seems to me to be the result of man's eternal desire to believe that there is in existence, somewhere, the man he would like to be: a man of super vitality, of monumental size, gargantuan appetites, and epic bravery. Who wants intellect? Intellect is for men peering into microscopes. The mythomaniacs are like God, in a sense, for they have created the Typical Texan in their own image: their dream image. The Walter Mittys create a man who is all the things they are not. This is the myth I call Ol' Typ, the Texan.

To the unrealistic dreamers who invented him, Ol' Typ is a composite of Owen Wister's Virginian, Gary Cooper, and that newcomer of dubious origin and authenticity, Pecos Bill.

Ol' Typ wears a ten-gallon hat, painfully tight blue jeans, high-heeled boots with sides of spotted bob-cat hide, fancy shirt and string tie, cartridge belt and two guns a-smokin'.

"If I were like him," the mouse-men of the world swear silently, "I'd really spit in the boss's face."

Even in the South Pacific, American Samoa, on Robert Louis Stevenson's Tutuila, where there are few mouse-men and fewer intellectual Herculeses, I found that Ol' Typ reigns supreme. Eighty per cent of the books in the Samoan Library are Westerns, Western movies are the most popular, but few of the natives have ever seen a live horse.

I saw the garb of Ol' Typ, with certain Samoan modifications, worn by all who could raise the price. His "Howdy, podner!" sometimes replaces the musical native greeting "Talofa." True, Ol' Typ goes barefoot in the tropics and wears a lava-lava, or sarong, instead of high-heeled boots and skin-tight blue jeans. His torso is bare; no satin rodeo shirt with fancy yoke and pocket flaps — but he wears a coat of Samoan coconut oil and a cartridge belt with two toy guns in the holsters. Leather wristlets at the end of bare arms and a red bandanna round his neck add to his elegance. His ten-gallon hat is Sears, Roebuck or Montgomery Ward's best, worn at the same reckless slant Pecos Bill probably affected. Behind Ol' Typ's Samoan ear is a large red hibiscus, a signal that he is on the prowl for female companionship. Since he has difficulty in pronouncing the letter *b*, the bronze version of Ol' Typ shouts: "Pang! Pang! Reach for the sky, podner."

He's rough and tough and full o' fleas . . . and hard to curry above the knees.

I think most likely the Laplanders have a native version of the Typical Texan, but wherever his myth materializes, like Topper's ectoplasm, Ol' Typ wipes his mouth with the leaf of a prickly pear. Where he spits, no grass grows. But he is always a gentleman.

The female race has done some daydreaming, too. Timid spinsters love him. Dowagers adore him, because nothing about him reminds them of their fifty-year-old sons. Quiet little gray ladies revel in dream-abductions by Ol' Typ to the rocky ledges of the Chisos Basin much as the women of the adolescent twenties reveled in dreams of abduction by the Sheik. Ol' Typ is their escape from the feasible, the achievable prospect: the balding, paunchy man who occasionally shares his umbrella with them on rainy nights after the New Thought

Meeting breaks up. He is always a bachelor. Being a myth, Ol' Typ is never married and the hardworking father of five.

Children, too close to reality for daydreaming, understand him and appreciate him. They understand that paradox is the truth from both sides: they love his extremes, mental and physical.

Perhaps it was Ol' Typ who placed a Santa Claus big enough to hold a Chevrolet sedan on his lap on top of a skyscraper in Dallas at Christmas. Nothing in moderation, that's Ol' Typ. He is just as big and empty as the gigantic papiermâché "Texan" at the Dallas Fair Grounds.

Paul Bunyan to the men, Prince Charming to the women, and Santa Claus to the children: is it any wonder that along with Sam Slick, the Typical Texan was one of the first and best-loved regional characters to emerge from the United States? He will probably be the last to die. He is the man everybody wants, or wants to be. Song and story, poetry and plays, movies and television have made the word incarnate. I claim he is one of the world's most enduring and lucrative myths. No one in his right mind is going to kill a myth — certainly not one he can sell!

There is just no such thing as a Typical Texan any more than there is a typical thumbprint. Texas is too big to be uniform in anything.

The Mexican Border Texan differs so radically from an East Texan that they might as well come from different hemispheres. How does an East Texan differ from a West Texas plainsman? The old answer is, the East Texan is lazier. Fifty-one inches of rainfall make a difference in a man's way of life, and even in his looks. A Fredericksburg Texan, of German origin, will ask you if you want a "weal cutlet" or a "walve job." A Brownsville Texan will ask for *pilón,* while an Orange Texan will demand *lagniappe,* a handful of candy thrown in free with a purchase. Spanish influence on the Border, the French influence in the other section owing to the proximity to Louisiana.

There is, however, a Representative Texan whose habitat is known to cover most towns in Texas. This is the man I call Ol' Rep. The genus has three common characteristics. While not highly colored, three distinguishing qualities are present in all these specimens: piety, patriotism, and politeness. At least one such specimen can be found even in Frijole, Dreamland, or Babyhead, Texas.

In physical appearance the Representative Texan is apt to look pretty much like the Mayor of Livingston, in the Piney Woods, the place where "the tall pines tickle the angels' toes." He is a man of middle height, fifty-ish, with crinkly graying hair. He wears a seersucker suit in hot weather, rimless glasses all the year round. Put him down in the middle of a cocktail party on Beacon Hill and he would pass for the president of a Boston bank. His speech would give him away to only a very keen ear, for he has scarcely any regional accent. He might start "talking Texas" for fun, and jokingly mention that he drips "rozzum" instead of rosin from the Piney Woods. He takes care of his teeth and does not always use a toothpick in private; but his fingernails are clean. He cleans them with his pocketknife, anywhere, anytime he thinks they need it.

This unsung Texan has been to college, more than likely to a denominational one. A large percentage of these unspectacular men are college graduates. Most of them are the efficient owners of a small business of some sort. They drink Coca-Cola and sing songs at the Rotary Club just as similar men do in Wisconsin. They pay their taxes promptly, take their hats off to women in elevators, and take part in all wars. They have an intelligent interest in finance, investment programs, and insurance.

Most of them are notoriously early risers. Recently I saw one come into a coffee shop in Marshall about 6 A.M. "What you doin' here this time o' day?" he was asked. "I slep' in," he said shamefacedly. "Got up too late an' missed breakfast at home." Even in Austin, a city of 181,000, a great many Ol' Reps go home to dinner in the middle of the day. An astonishing number of these men like their steak well done.

Some of them are constructively self-critical, especially those who became acquainted with other portions of the globe during wartime.

One Representative Texan met many foreign engineers during World War II, men from Brussels and Belgrade, Milan and Melbourne. His own engineering degree stood up alongside the best of them. "But what have they got that I haven't?" he mused. "There is greater depth and breadth to their background of knowledge than our system of education seems to provide." For months he analyzed and reasoned. Then one day he saw the obvious answer: the foreigners had a background in the arts and sciences, philosophy and history of ideas that he lacked. Being a Texan, resolution and action were simultaneous. He got Brentano's on the phone in New York and said: "Send me a thousand dollars worth of books on the Humanities."

Ol' Rep reads *Time* Magazine or *Newsweek;* he is also addicted to *Readers' Digest*, and oddly enough — to *The Ladies' Home Journal*. He usually belongs to a small country club, even if he only takes his family there for twelve o'clock dinner, right after church on Sunday. He never misses the $64,000 Question on television if he can help it. Groucho Marx is a favorite of his, and he believes that Bob Hope and Gracie Allen *ad lib* most of their quips. If he is laid up, he hopes it will be at a time when he can watch the Worlds Series or Southwest Conference Games on television. At parties he gangs up with the other men out on the porch or in the den, while his womenfolk go into a huddle over diet or dress in another room.

The Representative Texan frequently likes to garden and when he breaks out with azalea or camellia fever, he is likely to be out for blood. He joins camellia societies and walks up to the Judges' stand to claim his silver cup looking only slightly sheepish. I know one who has been known to take the big umbrella off his tractor and put it over a prize camellia bush when bad weather was predicted a day or so before the show.

A burly, prosperous Dallas Texan, who handles two-hundred-pound cakes of ice all day, raises orchids in his spare time. He owns and displays many rare "plaints" and has been President of the Orchid Growers' Society.

A retired Chamber of Commerce manager raises night-blooming cereus in an effective and imaginative manner. The plants bloom once a year: they work 365 days to produce one dazzling night. Two days before the blooms are to open, some hundred-odd letters go out telling the approximate time, the day and hour the gorgeous blooms are expected to open. A self-addressed postcard is enclosed for the guests' acceptance;

the guest writes his telephone number on the postcard and is kept posted as to the progress of the blooms. Cloudy weather may delay the opening two or more days. Finally, around ten in the morning, the call comes saying they will open that night for sure. Around nine o'clock in the evening, the guests gather in the garden and look up toward a landing at the head of a flight of stairs that lead up to it from either side. Cereus plants are stiff and leggy, require much staking, and are a real challenge to the exhibitor. Not to this Representative Texan! He places the great earthenware pots on the paving at the foot of both stairways and trains the sprawling, cactus-y cereus right up both banisters in a pyramid of living green. The great oval feathery buds look like doves resting on the branches. The floodlights in the garden are turned on to give the guests a chance to study the flowers and to photograph them in various stages of their development. The light arrests the opening of the buds. When the lights are turned off, the slow unfolding begins again. The entire process takes about an hour: from egg-shaped tightly folded bud to dinner-plate size, frondy waterlily. A hundred or more blooms unfolded on those banisters last year, gleaming like moons of delight, smelling as though all the perfume in the tropics had been spilled at once. The guests sat for a while in the dark, steeped in enchantment. There was a choice of sherry or lemonade, a flower to take home, and a memory too that would shine like a candle.

It is safe to assume that few of the Texans attending this watch party were invited to attend the opening of the Shamrock Hotel in Houston.

The Representative Texan carries much religious, civic, and personal responsibility. In a few widely scattered instances, he may be irreligious himself, but he respects the concept of religion as a civilizing force. He will shoot to kill, if necessary, when anyone tries to interfere with any other man's right to worship whomsoever and howsoever he pleases.

If he is one of the many Latin-American Representative Texans, he knows that some of his ancestors were once subjugated by the missionaries of His Catholic Majesty, the King of Spain, sovereign owner of all the Texas earth and all that lay beneath it . . . even in its waters. For the salt of the earth belonged to the King; El Sal del Rey, a salt lake that has been much fought over, played a significant role in the history of Texas mineral law. Once all Texicans had to pay tribute, civil to the King of Spain, and religious to the Roman Church. They had to embrace the Catholic religion to make their land titles good, but the conversion was usually from the teeth out. For that reason religious freedom is as vital as fresh air to most of their descendants.

Texans have bolted the Democratic Party three times in eighty-four years. A lot of Representative Texans, those solid men who read the *Wall Street Journal* with one eye and the Bible with the other, may very well have been quietly voting the Republican ticket all along. They are ultraconservative and opposed to the New Deal or its descendant policies. The proof of their Texanship lies in the fact that they are beset by contradictions and paradoxical emotions. They will defend any man's right to any religious faith he chooses to believe in or is born into, but they will not elect him President of the United States. In 1928 "yellow dog Democrats" — those pledged to support a yellow dog should he win the nomination in the primaries — elected Herbert Hoover over Al Smith, a Roman Catholic, by a substantial majority.

In 1952, Ol' Rep put man over party. How great a part war played in the decision would be hard to say. The significant factor is that more Representative Texans every day are thinking and acting independently on personal issues. It is a small grain of comfort to glean from world-wide conflict, but the broadening effect of widened perceptions and fields of knowledge, the opportunity to observe other civilizations and cultures at first hand, is showing its effect, in a palpable degree, on the minds of Representative Texans. Many of them wage daily war with themselves trying sincerely and honestly to be Americans first and Texans second. It is certainly not an easy thing to do, in the light of Texas' history and tradition. After all, Robert E. Lee himself had said: "If I had twenty thousand Texans, I need not retreat!"

Threats of secession and proposals to meet the United States forces of law enforcement at the Red River with Texas Rangers are heard, but infrequently. In Texas, even as in the rest of the United States, the majority rules. The cool heads, those true conservatives who want to preserve all that is good of the past while adopting the best that the future promises, see to it at the polls that the fire-eating doesn't go much beyond the speechifying stage.

When it comes to a question of his rights, Ol' Rep is going to see that he gets them, just as his great-grandpaw did one hundred and fifty years ago when he said: "I'm from Tennessee, an' I come to Texas to fight for my rights." He is a State's Rights man, regardless of his voting politics. When President Eisenhower vetoed the Natural Gas Bill after signing the Tidelands Bill, the cry was quickly taken up: "He didn't do right by Texas!" The long-headed founding fathers, direct progenitors of the Representative Texan, held out sundry properties and privileges when they entered the Union in 1845. Public lands, tidelands, and the right to divide into five states should Texans ever decide to do so. Special privilege? It was "so nominated in the bond." Texas was the only state to enter as an independent Republic, and she made the most of it. The Representative Texan is unlikely to be cajoled into dividing the state any time soon. "Who would get the Alamo?" Most of these men, during their schooldays, declaimed on one platform or another to the proud delight of their relatives a poem called "Divide the State?" It is an impassioned plea for unity and ran second only to Travis' appeal for help at the Alamo, a document so simple and moving in its forlorn and gallant hope that it still brings a lump to Texan throats. "My country, right or wrong!" That is what the Alamo stands for to Texans who remember that there were loyal Mexicans fighting their own blood kin for the Texan cause. Frank Dobie said that the hero-making fall of the Alamo came along just in time to save a lot of reputations. The Representative Texan feels that most any kind of life can be redeemed by a heroic death.

When it comes to defending Texas, there is one body of Representative Texans whose fame rings round the world: the Texas Rangers. Robert A. Crowder is chief of the corps, the first full-time chief of the celebrated organization in modern times. He is the personification of the universal image of the Texas Ranger. Lean, muscular, and laconic, Crowder wears steel-rimmed spectacles — a comforting touch, somehow — along with his conventional Ranger western attire. Fifty-five, a Ranger for nearly twenty years, Crowder is a man to tie to in time of trouble. When he puts his booted foot up on a stump and starts to whittle, law and order has arrived. Chief Crowder, six Captains, and forty-five Rangers scattered across the state add up to a small force — numerically. But seeing any one of them at work is ample corroboration of the old saying: "One riot, one Ranger." One Ranger is all that's needed.

Texas survived the domination of the French, the Spanish, the Mexicans, also the depredations of the carpetbaggers during Reconstruction. The Indians were more gory in their raids, but less cordially hated than the carpetbaggers by Texans. The last Indian massacres took place in the Texas Big Bend Country in the far from gay nineties. You can still find a few old people in Texas today who remember those raids. Mexican nationals killed Texans on Texas soil as late as 1917.

Sharing physical dangers and hardships sets any group of

people apart, especially when they are aroused on their home diamond. It would be almost impossible for such people not to feel the equal of any man — and maybe just a little superior to some. Texans feel self-sufficient because they wrested their land and survival from enemy invaders instead of merely having inherited peace and plenty. It is quite likely that there are still citizens of Vermont who believe the Green Mountain Boys could lick the H-bomb. Both of these groups have made it the hard way. They cannot help loving their own land best: thin, rocky, eroded, or powder dry. The fact that some of the most worthless-looking land in Texas covers unmeasured wealth, has little to do with a Texan's passionate love for his "country." He and his fathers before him thought it was the "finest country in the world" long before 1901 when old Spindletop blew in. The men who blazed the cattle trails and started the early herds of longhorns on isolated ranches under what now seem almost insurmountable difficulties felt the same way about Texas that the man in Liberty, Texas, who has three hundred oil wells in his pasture feels today.

If all the oil wells and the minerals were to disappear tomorrow, the way they came — by magic, like a giant prize in a box of crackerjack, a reward for the lean years of toughening it out, when folks were dead, maybe, but not defeated — the principal personality trait of all Texans, Ol' Typs or Ol' Reps of both genders, their overweening love of Texas, would not change one bit.

Oil has affected most phases of life in Texas, in many cases indirectly, funneling down from the top to the bottom. Imagine the impact on a returning Texan of a great number of signs reading WATER WELLS DUG. Within the last thirty years, the word "well" has come to have the connotation of "oil well" in Texas. Thirty years ago a man could speak happily about the fine well he drove down, and it would be understood that he referred to water. People digging for sorely needed water not infrequently hit oil. Naturally they don't refuse to sell it, but in many cases they would honestly prefer water for their stock. Travelers seeing a sign BULK MUD DELIVERED ANY HOUR OF THE DAY OR NIGHT are mystified. They think it is another of the gigantic Texan brags: the children want to make bigger and better mud pies in the middle of the night. The "mud" is actually used for weight in the drilling process, when gas is encountered and forces the boring bit and accessories back up the hole. The mud weights down the gas, offsets pressure, and allows the drilling to continue.

It is possible to drive better than thirty thousand miles in Texas and seldom be out of the sight or sound of an oil well. The Big Bend region is one of the regions where the clunk CLONK, clunk CLONK of the oil pump is not heard. Over the rest of the state, through the vegetable fields and the citrus orchards, the pumps and derricks stand incongruous, but valuable. A hard freeze doesn't kill an oil well.

On the coastal prairies and the vast ranches of the plains, the oil wells contribute much to the welfare of the livestock. There is nothing in the world that will make a cow so sleek and fat as an oil well. Steers seem to thrive better when they lie down to ruminate in the shade of a clump of oil derricks. The owner of the land, and the wells, has "repaired" the fences, ten costly new steel posts to one almost "wore out" cedar post in the name of repair deductions to his farm. He installs expensive aluminum gates, known in the hill country as "Houston gates." Some rich oil man from Houston owns the land

and the cattle. How much time he spends "raising cattle" is a matter for conjecture, and the T Men. The fact remains that "land is a scarce item in Texas," for the serious farmer or rancher. Cattlemen sometimes rent the top of the land that the owner has already leased for oil: "They've got the oil. I've got the grass." Oil provides, I was told by a reliable source in Odessa, out in West Texas, football coaches for the primary grades. Not just overall strategy coaches, but line and back-field; coaches for every position. Santa Rita, the discovery well of the University, provides much of the wealth for the University of Texas and allied schools, but with such ham-stringing restrictions as to be of little use except for buildings. These funds cannot be used legally to obtain top-flight pro-fessors or lecturers. It's agin the law. Jim Ferguson, one of the "Heroes of Education" in Texas, said Texas had gone hog-wild on higher education. But there is a relatively small group of dogged and determined men who differ with the former Governor on that point, and they are working unremittingly and quietly to loosen the stranglehold on the moneybags that is indirectly causing many of the intelligentsia of Texas to go into almost any field but that of education. The tight-fisted gripsters have a convenient way of forgetting their Scripture, namely the passage that says "The laborer is worthy of his hire." Yet 90 per cent of the obstructionists, and any candi-date for public office, when asked who had exerted the greatest influence on his life, will reply: "An old schoolteacher I had one time." Then remembering the votes, he will add: "Of course, that's outside of my mother, you understand."

In the general criticism of Texas' oil wealth, her cotton, cat-tle, and other minerals are often overlooked. The wealth and scope of shipping, her newly developed shrimp industry, plus the rich chemical industries now operating within the state will doubtless soon draw comment from the "crimmicks." The word was coined by a Texan to express his opinion in a hybrid manner, a cross between criminals and critics. The new noun is spreading to Mexico, just the word they needed to tag their own "crímicos." Texans, like most people who are coming of age, find it difficult to swallow criticism from respected sources of their own — even when made politely, that is to say, privately. They believe that a public insult demands a public apology, and not infrequently, they get it.

The statement has been made that there is billionaire support of and allegiance to fanatical causes outside the state. The percentage of billionaires, even in Texas, is not large. Of course a very rich man gets more publicity throughout the nation than the other millions of hardworking, level-headed Texas citizens all put together. The Representative Texans have, by and large, worked hard all their lives, few have ever been sold Brooklyn Bridge, and most of them have heeded the East Texas admonition to "Keep the forkèd end down."

In Texas it is possible to find a man who can stand up and say: "I will donate eighty million dollars and my wife will donate a like sum" — and actually do it. Down the road a piece in the same county they have an economical elderly lady whose hens nests are being robbed daily of the fresh eggs by snakes. She cannily fills an egg with arsenic and poisons the snake. Then she remembers that where there is one snake, there are two. She squeezes the dead snake in the right places, takes a razor blade and slits the snake's belly open and removes the poisoned egg. "No need to waste money buying more poison." She kills two more snakes with the same egg.

I have heard it said that the natives of the Empire of Extremes have a tendency to put comfort and expediency ahead of appearance. In one of the flossy banks in Dallas, the receptionists have been seen with their hair done up in pincurls while on duty. An Eastern woman asked the personnel manager how he accounted for such informal custom.

"Well, I tell you," the efficiency expert said, "we have loads of Big Rich coming in here to deposit money. Just loads of them. They drive up and come pounding in. Never give the girls a thought or second look. Their pockets are bulging and they want to get rid of the money. BUT, we have the Little Man: our small depositor, and we want many more like him. Ten to one he's overawed by the Board of Directors, the magnificence of the building, and the beauty of the receptionists . . . he might feel uncomfortable and a little out of place in such glamorous surroundings. But when he sees that gorgeously stacked beauty with her hair up in pincurls, why, he feels right at home!"

Much of the Representative Texan's native politeness stems from the progenitors of the present breed. The chivalry of the Old South, the novels of Sir Walter Scott, and the intrinsic gallantry of men who were brought up in an age when women were a scarce commodity have all combined to make the Texan polite. It is handed down from father to son. Maiden aunts have pounded politeness into the recalcitrant. The men are even polite to each other. And they revere Momma and Poppa. I know of no more mildly amusing pastime than to listen to two Texans, gray-haired men well into their sixties, conversing solemnly about the "time my poppa and your poppa were law partners."

The influence of Latin Americans, who pay open, intentionally audible compliments to the passer-by, has colored the manners of many Texans. Then the Irish contingent, who settled San Patricio County and other sections, brought their blarney with them, and when they intermarried with the Latin Americans, the desert flowered indeed. The early German settlers brought grace and dignity to the frontier. The kind of German family influenced by Prince Solms von Braunfels to come to the Republic of Texas was of a very high order, some of them of noble birth. Their dignity and somewhat formal

bearing are in evidence today in predominantly German settlements like Cuero, Fredericksburg, and Seguin.

A third factor that had considerable influence on the manners of the Texan is the influence of the Negro slaves and servants that "raised" him. They had almost complete charge of
the children. In sections of Texas where plantation life was
lived much as it was in the Old South, it is interesting to note
that many whites speak exactly like Negroes, but few Negroes
speak like whites. The Southern Negro's own natural affability and love of elegant manners has "rubbed off" on many of
their charges.

In early Texas, women were at a premium, numerically
speaking, for a long time. They are still prized, emotionally
speaking. A somewhat embittered defendant in a divorce case
was heard to remark: "You don't have to worry about *The
Woman* in Texas!" In the little towns of Texas, a woman
alighting from a car will be greeted by raised hats and
"Howdy-do, ma'am" from practically every male in the block.

If you change the time of an appointment, it is customary to
hear "The time doesn't make a bit of difference just so long as
you come back."

I once overheard a postal clerk cashing a money order for a
woman saying gently: "I'm sure sorry it's not more!"

The most backwoods boy in Texas can "Ma'am" with grace
and naturalness. Many families in other states send their sons
to Groton, Exeter, and St. George's to learn how to say it. The
backwoods boy would "jus' nacherly" know how to address
the Queen of England.

Offered a drink, one Texas woodsman, the only Jewish fox
hunter in the Piney Woods, replied: "I thank you. I was too
well raised to refuse."

A Mexican radio program emanating from San Antonio encourages politeness in its Spanish-speaking listeners. The announcer has a kind voice, full of pathos: "If you see a man

stopped by the side of the road with a 'flet,' stop at least and inquire: 'Are you lacking anything, buddy? *Un parche?* Un yack?' Of course, we know you haven't got a cold patch or a jack in your own car for yourself! But stop anyway! It will keep him from feeling so abandoned, so disconsolate."

If a traveler asks road directions in Texas the answer is frequently: "Follow me." Men and women will drive blocks, often several miles, out of their way to set the stranger on the right road. Drivers who get in the wrong lane, due to ignorance of the route, signaling their distress and embarrassment, meet with more help and less honking than one would expect in the heavy traffic. A man in a panel truck in the left lane calls out to the erring driver who is trying to make a left turn from a right-hand lane, "You fade forward, and I'll fade back. Soon as the light changes, make you a left turn and keep a-goin'. You can't miss."

When motorcycle policemen see a funeral procession coming, they unostentatiously clear a way through the traffic. Many drivers pull over to the curb and stop their cars out of respect to the cortège. I am told there is no regulation requiring this gesture.

Holding on to a telephone for a business call, the switchboard operator often cuts in to say: "I haven't forgotten you. I'm holding on for you, honey."

I went into the Walker County Hardware Store to browse — "prowl" is the word in Texas. I was entranced by three objects: a cast-iron cookstove, a glass electric churn, and an electric ice-cream freezer. A voice behind me crooned gently, but so unexpectedly that I jumped: "HAow do yew FEEL, MA'AM?" A long, tall drink-of-water with a honey-pouring voice had slipped up behind me and his tone would have done credit to a rabid Republican mustering all his concern and solicitude as he inquired about the state of the President's health.

I have mentioned several of the elements that are responsible for the Texan's politeness: namely Latin American, Deep South, and African. They have been known to get blended into a single, distinctive dialect and phraseology. One case in point was reported by a woman whose elderly Mexican fish merchant addresses her as "LEETLE LADY, HAWNEY" (honey).

In his politeness, the Texan likes to do what is expected of him. He has been known to buy his first cowboy boots and ten-gallon hat for a trip to New York.

"How many oil wells have you got?" That question is put to visiting Texans all over the country from Georgia to the Gaspé. Texans, as has been said earlier, sometimes own a great many oil wells and seldom mention the fact. "Aw, come on," the inquisitor says, mistaking diffidence for poverty, "lie a little, won't you? We just naturally expect Texans to have oil wells."

"What are you doing these days?" a Texan was asked in the East.

"Improving some land I have in East Texas."

"Yeah, with gas and oil wells, I guess."

It is going to come as a real shock to many, but contrary to public opinion, the poor but proud Texan is not extinct. Texas is still a good place to find "a penniless lass wi' a lang pedigree." Salaries are low in comparison with other sections of the United States, but the Texan is willing to pay for the privilege of living in his state.

And not all Texans are polite. There are oafs and boors in Texas, too. They stand out more noticeably than they do in other parts of the United States, first by their scarcity, and second, by contrast to the general courtesy of the people. True to Texas tradition, the oafs and boors are the "biggest and best" of their kind.

Colored Texans have a culture, a way of speaking and an individual outlook of their own, as distinctive as those of the Thicket Texans or the men of the Border.

An Austin friend of mine lost her maid temporarily. The

lure of cotton picking was too strong. "Don't you miss your home comforts, Beulah?" the lady asked.

"No, ma'am. We jis' rolls 'em up an' takes 'em wid us."

An elderly colored woman was discussing religion with her employer: "If you sees any colored folks what ain't Baptists, they's had they religion tampered wif!"

A man inquired of an elderly Negro stockman if he belonged to a church that had a good hell-fire-and-brimstone preacher. "Nossuh," the old man shook his head. "But some folks emotionally DO cut up!"

Over in East Texas, I asked a colored school principal of many years' experience to characterize briefly the present generation of his charges.

"They do not clamor for the fundamentals," he said. But I found evidence to the contrary when I heard that Dr. Aaron Shaffer, Chairman of the Romance Language Department of the University, distinguished scholar and author, got up on Saturday mornings in time to meet an eight o'clock class in French Literature for the benefit of a car pool of colored teachers from Houston who left that city at 4 A.M. They bewailed the lack of "conference time" and offered to leave Houston at three in the morning if necessary. Aside from his intellectual attainments, Dr. Shaffer's human kindness could have earned him the Légion d'Honneur.

The vivid, graphic expressions in use among the colored folk of Texas add to the gaiety of nations. When they are desperately ill, they are "low sick." High blood pressure and low blood pressure transmute into "He's got de low-blood," or "She got de high-blood." There is even a song called "The Low Blood Blues." They suffer from "de pressures," as who doesn't? When they die they "pass," and when they are buried they have a "funeralization." Messages come: "Poppa done pass. We gonna funeralize Poppa on Monday."

Some of their imagery is poetic. On a bitter morning in a

blue norther a high tenor voice can be heard in the Piney
Woods: "It's so co-o-o-ld in China, dat de b-u-u-u-r-ds cain't
hardly sing!" On a bright sunny afternoon, a rich voice will
soar in joy: "Roberta got a gold toof, shine like de mawnin'
star!" A cotton picker in the Trinity bottom, raising up to
ease his bent back, looks up and sees a buzzard floating lazily
in the sky. Somehow his restless soul knows what the bird is
thinking and he "opes his mouf' an' hollers":

> Ol' King Buzzard flyin' mighty high,
> Wishin' to de Lawd some cow would die.

A daughter complains of her recalcitrant father who is leery
about turning his old-age pension checks over to her: "Poppa
don' wanna X his checks!"

The colored Texans own a peculiar treasure in their speech.
As they would say: "They's so much valiance in it." "Man,
you ain't got no compeltry over me!" And again, "I don' blame
you fo' bein' precautious." Of anything watery or lacking in
substance they say, "It ain't got no suction to it!"

Texas radio programs aimed directly at the colored population are interesting, both the sacred and secular. One of the
most popular is one in which the minister exhorts his listeners
to "put one han' on yo' misery, an' the other han' on the radio.
Let your kingdom come tonight! Precious God, tonight! Jesus
will help you. He has kep' us clothed in our right mind. Jesus,
touch those sufferers tonight! Let sin give away tonight! Hal-
lelujah to God, for He is a mind revelator. A consolator!" Web-
ster's Unabridged Dictionary recognizes consolator as a syno-
nym for consoler.

A recent sermon delivered by a colored minister contained
this simile. The substance of the sermon was that Eternity was
too long a time to have God's wrath turned against a sinner.
A small boy, he said, was standing on the shore seeing the
ocean for the first time, watching its endless come and go, its

ceaseless rise and fall. He walked up to a man standing by and said: "Sir, how long is Eternity?" "Lad," the man said, "you see that bird on that willow tree over yonder? If that bird was to fly up to Heaven carrying a willow leaf in its beak and stay a million years, and then come back and get another leaf and stay another million years — and so on until every leaf was gone from that tree, that would not even be the beginning of Eternity." The boy shook his head in wonder.

"And, son," the man continued, "you see that ocean out there? If an angel came down from Heaven and took one drop of water out of that ocean back to Heaven and stayed a billion years, and then came back and got another drop of water and stayed another billion years — and so on until every drop of water was gone from the ocean and the land left dry, that, son, would be only the beginning of the edge of Eternity."

The devotion and loyalty human hearts are capable of is explicit in a statement by Uncle Row, ex-slave, sage, and philosopher, father of seventeen legitimate children and "one bresh colt." He was a fine horseman and an excellent hand with a rope at round-up and branding time. The searing burn of a rope pulling the skin off his palms as it was dragged through his clenched fists by a frantic animal at the other end of the rope was nothing new to Uncle Row. A man remarked that he seemed devoted to a white friend of his: "Oh, yassuh," Uncle Row replied, "I'll stick wid Mr. Bob till de skin slips."

Texas is literally a land of caviar and clabber. With the prevalence of pasteurization and the advent of the cream separator, caviar is easier to find than clabber. Most chain stores in Texas carry caviar. In the next bin, there will very likely be bundles of sassafras roots for sale. They taste like wintergreen and many people still use them for making tea in the spring.

The sophisticated and the primitive side by side. That's Texas.

Milk for making butter was poured into big crocks to let the cream rise. By the time the cream was right, the milk underneath had soured and congealed into a milky white, shivering Liz jellified mass. Clabber was cooling, and better tasting than its cultured cousin, yogurt. There is no better milk with which to make cornbread. Dogs and chickens were fed scraps of cornbread soaked in clabber. The old-timy people used to hang clabber up in a clean dishtowel to drip dry. The resulting cottage cheese was a memorable dish, as Texan as frijoles or cowboy coffee. There are two schools of thought on the cottage cheese: one side is for salt and lots of black pepper, a ripe tomato and a few green onions. The other side is for cottage cheese sprinkled with sugar and nutmeg, with thick sweet cream slurped over it. The old Texans will take both: first one, and then the other. The younger generation, used to the exotic in foods may say: "I've saved you a wonderful alligator steak in the deep freeze," but Poppa is sure to speak up: "Got plenty chicken, beef, an' hawg . . . don't see no call to go messin' with no 'gator steak."

When I considered the original sources and motives of early Texas settlers, I saw that such a conglomerate could not fail to produce an interesting breed.

A large proportion of Texas pioneers were solid, righteous stand-fasters and last-ditchers. Today they are fighting tougher issues than the relatively uncomplicated physical dangers of the frontier: they are fighting on the battleground of the mind, struggling to overcome deeply grooved inherited patterns of thinking and behaving, showing a reassuring rapidity of growth by changing with surprising elasticity to meet the needs of an almost hourly changing world.

I have seen the myth and the reality, Ol' Typ and Ol' Rep, both male and female. In the reality there are many subdivisions, but two stand out in bold relief because they are present in all races and breeds: Types and Originals. The greatest originality of thought and action, even a certain elegance, is added to any society by its eccentrics, those outside the circle of commonplace behavior.

Coral Bean

In Texas, the Types go right on fulfilling their stereotyped destinies, happy when their protective coloration blends them unnoticed into the grayish mass of the herd. They are a steady, industrious bunch, seldom out of character. They eat when it is conventional to eat, wear what everyone else wears, read only books that everyone else is reading, think only thoughts that are predigested for them, and live in mortal peril of appearing to be different in any way from their rubber stamp brothers and sisters, complete with blue-rinsed hair. They truly work hard at achieving mediocrity and never miss an opportunity to be like everyone else that they happen to approve of. Types behave much as Bores do, giving their lives to their careers: getting up at dawn, always the first at the party, always the last to leave. Just as Bores never want to miss one precious moment of boring, so the Types, with admirable singleness of purpose, give a full day's work to being their own prefabricated selves.

Originals in Texas are largely of aborigine stock. They are full-blooded Originals. That does not mean that they are necessarily plethoric or sanguine: in Texas, "full blooded" means purebred, like a full-blooded Cherokee or a full-blooded Irishman. Where else would the thoroughbred Original find such favorable soil and climate? The weather, the landscape, the very temperament of the country are highly original in themselves. Unpredictable. Did the climate produce the Originals? Or did they produce the climate? Since this business of the atom, the problem becomes more than ever one of which came first: the chicken or the egg?

Picture, then, in the rich loam of Texas history, the seed sprouting and flourishing, burgeoning and blooming, of a race founded by Simon-pure, double-dyed Originals. Those who came to Texas before the revolution in 1836 are privileged to call themselves Texicans. Those men and women were Originals of purest distillation. Almost without exception, their descendants are true to form. Those who followed, and were here in time for the Civil War, are called Texians, and they too assayed a very high percentage of Originals. The plain Texan, whose people came along after the Civil War, is likely to show an impressive number of Originals among his scions. No matter when or how their forebears got here, it is safe to say that at least 75 per cent of the genu-WINE Texans are Originals. Good or bad, the people who settled early Texas were characters!

The Texas Original has a certain pride in being himself. Physical comfort, while not assuring a good disposition, does remove certain pains to which the flesh is heir and thus releases tension, erases frowns from the forehead, and cross lines about the mouth. It is human to like men or women who are "comfortable people to be around." The compliment, "as plain as an old shoe," is one that is esteemed by Texans.

At a coffee this fall an elderly, impressively gowned lady marched in wearing a sable cape. Like the peacock of fable, she stopped strutting when she looked down at her feet. To the unfeeling, they could easily have suggested Clementine's "herring boxes without topses." Her shoes were large, orthopedic, and expensive. She had not slashed them nonchalantly, as the colored folk do; she had gone them one better and cut out great lozenge-shaped windows wherever she happened to have a protuberance. She was, nevertheless, a good-looking woman, from bangs to bunions. Her disposition was and is delightful. "Aren't my feet awful?" she sighed. "I had the most terrible accident to them as a baby." Sympathetic eyebrows went up. "I got my brother's feet and he got mine." It frequently happens with hair: a boy gets the ringlets and his sister gets the rat tails. Why shouldn't genes get mixed up about feet?

A small Texican lady runs a ranch near Marble Falls. Her children have grown up and left. She was handicapped by not being able to drive a car. In the first place she didn't know how and in the second place, she was barely over four feet tall. Short, but not for long, the Irish would say. She wired four-inch blocks of wood to the pedals of her Model T Ford and set out for the loose sandy ground of the pasture to teach herself to drive, all alone.

"I'm ready for Marble," she announced a week later to her horrified friends.

"You can't take the car out on the highway! You don't know how to drive and you haven't even got a license."

"I'll get one," she said. "I can now give a jackrabbit a hit or a miss at will. I figure I'm ready for Marble."

She wears cowboy boots, tight blue jeans, a blue hickory shirt and a sunbonnet. What gives fillip to her outfit is the frilly, rounded short white apron she wears tied around her waist.

She decided it was time to wire her house for electric light, so she did. The authorities in Marble Falls told her she hadn't orta done it.

"It's done did," she said. The least they could do, the authorities said, was to inspect the job. It was a violation; they would be willing to go along a little bit, but inspect they must.

"Come ahead on," she said. The inspectors found thirteen drop lights in her house, well installed, and all but one in perfect working order. "You did a real good job. Thirteen lights and only one that doesn't work. Yes'm. Real good!" the inspector said.

"What do you mean doesn't work?"

"No light," the inspector flipped the switch.

She dragged out a stepladder:

"Wait a minute," she replaced the bulb, hopped down and turned on the switch: "Faulty bul-lub."

A few weeks later her goats were busy increasing her herd for her. She drove to the pasture to check up on them. A young woman from the University at Austin was visiting at the ranch on vacation, so she went with her. The lady rancher spied a goat down under a small live-oak tree. Her experienced eye saw that the goat was sick.

"Get out and pick him up," she said. "Put him in the back seat."

"I couldn't do that," the girl said. "Scare me silly! I'll drive the car and you get him."

"You can't drive the car. Don't you see my contraptions? The blocks on the pedals? You're too big. Pick up the goat!"

"I've never picked up a goat in my life," the girl was sweating, "I can't do it."

"I tell you to pick him up! Nothin' to it. Git goin'!"

There was nothing else to do; the girl got out and picked up the goat and put him in the back seat.

"What'd I tell you?" the driver said. "An' don't you forget: next time you're feelin' inferior an' low in the self-efficiency, just remember an' tell yourself: 'I picked up a goat when I knew I couldn't do it!'"

Two women I know, in their forties, had been to Dallas to the opera. They live in Odessa and decided that, since there was a full moon and the Cadillac was filled up, they would haul off and drive on home that night, a nice jaunt even by Texas standards. The highway was good and the night cool. They still wore their handsome evening gowns and furs. When they had gone about four hundred miles, one of the women remembered that a friend of hers lived on a rather isolated ranch not too far from Abilene.

"Let's stop by and see Louise."

They drove in the gate of the ranch as day was breaking. Nobody came out to meet them, and their prospective hosts' car was gone. They decided that the best thing to do was to go in and fix themselves some coffee as any sensible person would.

They found Louise in a bad fix. Her husband had gone after the doctor when her labor pains started, and he must have had a flat.

The woman who owned the car rolled up the sleeves of her ermine coat and plunged her arms, loaded with more diamond bracelets than Peggy Hopkins Joyce had service stripes, into a sinkful of hot water and started scrubbing with Ivory soap.

Louise moaned on the bed and the baby squalled.

"Boil me a razor blade, honey," the impromptu midwife instructed her friend, still scrubbing her hands, "I'll need it to cut the cord."

The blood of the Texican woman who killed an Indian, scalped him, and stuck his head on a pole to scare off the rest of the band is not thinning out too badly.

Up in Somervell County, at Glenrose, lives Dr. Bull Adams. Ernest Adams was the first Rhodes Scholar from Baylor University. He was outstanding in all branches of athletics, in America and in England. He can still get into his 1911 football suit — the only one of the team who can! He headed his

classes in all his studies at Baylor and at Oxford, in addition
to starring in British sports, he distinguished himself in the
British Expeditionary Force and the American Army.

Dr. Adams has an earned doctorate of what one Texan calls
"Judas-prudence." No disrespect to Bull Adams, because he is
a good lawyer. He lives in a crude rock structure, a cross between a cave and a dugout, where he relives as much as he
can the life of the primitive caveman. He cooks out between
rocks, and keeps his condiments in a box nailed high up on a
pole out of the reach of varmints. He has built a river bed of
stones, with a small rustic bridge spanning its lily studded
depths. Periwinkle clambers over the rocky banks and carpets
the ground under the trees.

His study was the law, but he also pursued archeology and
anthropology. He has long worked on a study as to whether
man or the bison was here first. He is Honorary Curator of the
Baylor University Museum, and is said to have unearthed the
jawbone of a giant woman whom he contends lived on the
Brazos 30,000 years ago. He claims that she was seven feet
tall, that she died in childbirth and that her remains were in
a sleeping compartment that could be warmed from beneath.

Returning to primitive Somervell County, Dr. Adams found
himself the only lawyer in the county and the office of County
Attorney was forced upon him by the needful citizens. While
chatting with visitors, Dr. Adams keeps a weather eye peeled
on the road, and any approaching car he can see over the
wreckage of old car bodies that obscures the view from his
yard.

"Excuse me," he says, "I don't want that fellow to see me.
He will want me to take a case for him. I don't want any
cases. I wish to go on exploring my Indian mounds without
interruption. I keep out of my office as much as possible."
This last statement is not news to anyone who has ever tried
to locate him for any reason. Natives when approached say:

"Bull Adams? He was in here drinkin' ice tea a minute ago. Look around, and if you see a little black and white dog, he's inside. Or else out diggin' in his old Indian mounds."

Dr. Adams' speech is cultivated and polished. His head is proud and impressive, like the head of a lion. No one can mistake the fact that he is in the presence of a personage when he talks to Bull Adams. He knows what he wants to do and does it.

A Dallas lawyer, waiting to try a case, tells a story about Bull Adams before a jury in the courthouse. Without thinking, Dr. Adams removed his shoes, and continued his interpretation of the law barefooted, for he wore no socks.

Sometimes Dr. Ernest Adams likes to make arrowheads. Some of them fooled the Smithsonian Institute.

One of Texas' Originals ran a boardinghouse for boys at Baylor University. Those who lived there would characterize themselves as "the rough ELEMENT." They were, almost without exception, men who achieved distinction on the campus, and later. Many athletes lived at Maw Greer's and that redoubtable lady kept order with a buggy whip. When the gilded youths were called to the telephone in the downstairs hall, they would occasionally be provoked to forthright language and frequently blued-up the air, to Mrs. Greer's displeasure. She would admonish them to cease such talk in her house. If they did not do so at once, she would emerge in stiffly rustling starched petticoats, full-skirted dress, and crackling crisp white apron, buggy whip in hand and proceed to lash the offender soundly, particularly if he happened to be in his bathrobe and his bare shanks offered a handy target.

A teacher of education in Baylor, white-haired and fragile, came to live at Maw Greer's, ostensibly because the food was of such high quality. Anyone who has ever been fortunate enough to be in the presence of Miss Lily Louise knows that nothing so earthbound as food could have lured her to that bulging household, overflowing with youthful spirits and high jinks. She loved life with a deep, serene passion. She is filled with infinite charity and benign wisdom. And a good thing it was that she had it! The hellions adored her and took the usual way of showing it: by tormenting her. Many mornings they piled up trunks in front of her door so high that she could not get out of her room to go down to breakfast, until the colored porter came up and rescued her.

Miss Lily Louise taught a Sunday School class; every Sunday morning she would take up her Bible and parasol to meet a group of her young lady students and walk to church with them. Sweet Miss Lily Louise never protested at the shower of sinful playing cards that fell out of her parasol when she opened it, or were found wedged in the pages of her Bible when she started to read to her class. How many times she was awakened in the middle of the night to eat a hog-ear sandwich that one of the lads, returning from a midnight prowl, had brought her, would be hard to say. Late one night she received a telephone call from a man who told her one of her prime favorites was held in the city jail. No word of surprise or condemnation: "Tell him I'll be right down as soon as I can get dressed."

"No need to come down, Miss Lily Louise; we just wanted you to know where he was," the voice continued, struggling for control, because it was the very villain who was supposed to be in jail, changing his voice and trying to keep the laughter out of it. "Oh, but I must! He is my friend," Miss Lily Louise insisted. "It won't take me long." Finally the demon had to break down and confess that it was only a joke, and Miss Lily Louise went back to bed, no doubt to pray for the rapscallion and to ask God to bless him.

At almost ninety, she was removed to the hospital, more for safekeeping than anything else, and by some accident was placed in a wing that bore on its glass swinging door the words: MATERNITY WARD. In her room there was not space enough to stand a greeting card up edgewise: flowers, gifts, toiletries enough to stock a gift shop. Her irrepressible tormentors were still at it after thirty-five years: "Miss Lily Louise, is there something you want to tell us? Have you been keeping some little secret from us?" Then one leaned over and whispered in her ear. The tiny white-haired figure smiled and blushed, blinked her eyes rapidly at them and murmured: "Boys! Boys!"

Over in Milam County, one beloved Original, a veteran of Hood's Brigade, lived a long time, rocking out his days on the front porch in a quiet little Texas town. He had lost touch with the present, but the past was vivid to him. Day after day he put on his tattered uniform of Confederate gray and sat with his shotgun by his side. He might go rabbit hunting, if he didn't fall asleep.

Then one day Mr. Mackay opened a spandy new office in the town, a branch of his Postal Telegraph. Someone in a distant city sent a telegraph message to the family of the senescent veteran. In due time it was delivered to the house where the last remnant of Hood's gallant band snoozed in the sunshine. At the sound of the gate, the old man woke with a start. His mind raced back thirty-five years: here in his front yard was the hated Yankee uniform, blue with brass buttons! Conditioned reflex did the rest. He fired point-blank and peppered the Postal Telegraph delivery boy with birdshot from the ever present gun at his side.

In the same sleepy town, an Original sheriff decided that he needed a diamond-studded badge. He poked his six-shooter in the belly of each male passer-by: "Gimme ten dollars!" he said. It didn't take long to get the badge.

San Antonio Originals, romantic and glamorous to the outsider, but hard-bitten, realistic, and reactionary to the old mossy-horn natives, produced an example of "making do" that would do credit to a New Englander of the breed who is said to take anything anybody else throws away and make a chowder out of it.

Museums are associated in most minds with mummies and wax-works, stuffy relics of the past. Not in San Antonio. Keeping the Witte Museum open during the depression was a real challenge. The women of the Board decided that nothing commonplace would part the citizenry from a dime. They scorned the idea of fish fries, steak fries, and all the other usual fries. They decided to hold snake fries, and did. The public came and paid well to eat fried rattlesnake. The commonality would not pay to examine the treasures of the Museum, but they would pay ten cents to see snakes without benefit of booze. The board kept a snake show running for some time and exhibited the living reptiles in a pen. One day the snakes got loose and the Grant Wood girls, imitating their ancestors, sensibly took to the trees. No one ever has a camera at the right time.

In Madisonville, home of the Sidewalk Cattleman's Association, a real Texican Original stood one winter day not long ago warming his hands at the pot-bellied stove where the Spit and Whittle Club holds sway. His pale blue eye lit on a personable young man sitting quietly listening to his elders discourse.

"You married, son?" the old Texican said.

"No, sir," the young man replied.

"Why not?"

"Oh, . . . I dunno. I might, some day."

"What's holdin' you back?" the old man persisted.

"Nothin' much, I reckon. Kinda fear'd o' women," he smiled.

"Nothin' to be fear'd of, son. I ben married fifty-five years, myself."

"Ever have any trouble?"

"Yeup." The old man spat. "One time."

"What kinda trouble?"

"Well, I married Amy, my young bride, an' brought her home. On my weddin' night, she wouldn't lemme come near her."

"What'd you do?"

"Next mawnin' I hitched up the wagon an' drove roun' to the front o' the house. 'Come on, Amy,' I says. 'Git in.'"

"Where?" she says.

"I'm takin' you back to yer paw."

"Whut fer?" she says.

"You know good'n well what fer, Amy!" I says. "Right then an' there she promised to do better. An' furthermore, son, she DONE better! See them ten boys?" He pointed to his ten stalwart sons leaning against the wall. "No call to be fear'd o' women, son."

There are some subtle Originals who will show you, with joy, the clipping from the Houston paper about Little Sammy Snide having the water for his christening flown especially from the River Jordan. The discoverer of this rare treasure in "social notes from all over" may even send a telegram of congratulations addressed to the proud parents in care of Saint David's "Christening Parlors," stating that he knew the drouth was bad, but hadn't realized things were at such a pass.

Originals delight in dramatic and picturesque language. I had to have my car reinspected when I took out Texas registration. "Where can I get that done?" I asked. "Stop any man with a gun!" was the reply. "Ask any policeman" would have been too tame.

Inquire about the health of a man's mother and he is likely to reply: "You couldn't kill her if you hit her in the head with a pine knot!"

"How is Homer?" a friend asks.

"He's in a manner dead."

"Which car is yours?" a boy in a supermarket inquires.

"I'm on foot," is the reply, the result of years of horseback travel.

Teen-age girls are referred to as "frying size, ready for the axe."

Financial stringency is known as being on "short grass."

An elevator button is not pressed: "Maish the button, honey! Maish it good!"

A man, now well heeled with oil money, worked his way through grammar school picking cotton. His wife decided to eat at a very plush club every day — and the husband said: "Guess I'll have to get me a longer sack!"

Whatever else may be said of Types or Originals, they are both graphic.

And just to add to the confusion, like everywhere else in nature there pops up the occasional hybrid. One Type (he could pass with his rimless glasses, watery blue eyes, and round pale pink cheeks for one of the wax dummies seen in old-fashioned tailor shops) is a paragon of sartorial perfection: polished derby, Ivy league collar carefully buttoned down, restrained Sulka tie, navy blue cashmere Chesterfield, knife-creased trousers, gray spats, and lemon-yellow gloves. Standing on the corner of Main and Akaard in Dallas he was asked if his coat was vicuña. "No," he said, "but I got me a vicuña-lined pouch for my chewing tobacco."

And since a woman usually has the last word in anything, there is the great Texas lady of ninety-three, an Original of the first water, who has the finest sense of values it has ever been my privilege to encounter. Mrs. Ben Rice, wife of a Texas judge, and mother of a federal one, had eight children, "like the pipes of an organ in size," my friend the saint-seller would say. She also had a jewel of a nursemaid, perfect with the high-strung small Rices. The jewel had one serious flaw: she took things that did not belong to her. From time to time Mrs.

Rice had to rescue various articles of value from the nurse-maid's trunk, where she had put them "until she got a chance to put 'em back where dey belonged." It was the girl's custom to send money orders to her relatives, but one day the process was reversed and the nursemaid began to get money in the mail.

Dressing for some special occasion, Mrs. Rice was unable to find a valuable diamond ring that she kept in her jewel case. The most diligent search failed to turn up the ring. Things looked very serious for the nursemaid, so completely reliable in every respect but one.

"What are you going to do about it?" Judge Rice asked.

Mrs. Rice studied for a while, then said gravely: "I haven't got a bit of use in the world for a diamond!"

The variety of territories and racial backgrounds in Texas have combined to produce these men and women whom I think of as Originals. While none of their features of character may be absolutely unique, it is unlikely that many of them exist in other parts of the world because the combination of circumstances is so unusual. It is not often possible to find all the component parts at the same time in one locality. There is a slangy Mexican verse of the people called "Mi Tierra Es Así," "My Country's Like That." The unknown author ends up by characterizing Texas Originals better than I can. *"Yo soy como soy. No me parezco a naiden!"* ("I am the way I AM. I don't resemble nobody!")

10. THE HELL-RIDIN' STARS

PEOPLE love danger to another's life. It is especially dear to those who pass their lives removed from any risk. Ol' Typ and Ol' Rep like excitement too. Since they no longer have to battle daily for their lives, to save their scalps from Indians, they are passionate devotees of any contest involving risk of life and limb.

"You haven't seen Texas until you've seen the Prison Rodeo at Huntsville," I was told. It seemed like a good place to watch the reactions of Texans. The word *rodeo*, basically, means "beating about the bush," avoiding a direct approach to anything. From there it developed into roundup, and by extension, from roundup to the exhibition of skill and daring the word now means. Born of the Southwest, transplanted to the heart of the Piney Woods, a physical contest, outlaw man against outlaw beast, neither with anything to lose, both hating to be deprived of their liberty, the Texas Prison Rodeo is the wildest outdoor spectacle put on since they threw the lions to the Christians. It is held every Sunday in October, and the convicts know of a certainty what years have five Sundays in that month!

I used to think crime didn't pay, but at Huntsville it pays to the tune of one hundred thousand dollars annually. Crime provides the headliners for the spectacle that pays all the bills for the entire educational and recreational program for all the wards of the state without a cent of cost to the taxpayer. It pays for glasses, dentures, hearing aids, teachers, and coaches. To say that the show has increased the rate of crime in Texas would be misleading, but it is well known to inmates that former rodeo participants, once released, have tried to get back into prison in time to take part in the show. With all due respect to the Confederacy, I think the production could be called Stars and Bars.

Texans are enthusiastic about the outdoors. That fact struck me as odd, since so much of Texas is "outdoors." I always thought the people cooped up in New York and Chicago loved the outdoors more than other Americans. But the pathetic lines of Sunday drivers on the Merritt Parkway and the hordes on the grass in Central Park have nothing on Texans when it comes to open-air activities!

I was eating breakfast in a crowded Huntsville restaurant on a blazing blue October Sunday, and I didn't have my mind on my vittles. The other customers ate with one ear cocked, listening for something important. The proprietor picked his teeth vigorously and looked at the clock a lot. Excitement amounting to frenzy filled the air.

"People lined up in cars along the highway all the way to Conroe . . . mebbe further, to watch 'em bring 'em in. Cain't imagine what's holdin' 'em." The speaker got up and strolled out to push himself a place among the crowd on the sidewalk. Prison officials say "delivery" of this captive audience, over distances varying from five to one hundred and eighty-two miles from all parts of the 46,000-acre Prison Farm System, is one of the most difficult phases of the Rodeo production.

The hair-raising howl of the police sirens galvanized the last of the die-hard coffee drinkers out into the street. "Here they come!" The wavy heat of the highway was splintered by the roar and crash of trucks laden with wild cargo: convicts.

Quietly, almost invisibly, motorcycle police, constables in Fords, and other peace officers materialized at every street crossing and corner. The crowd was tense and silent, filled with sinister curiosity, a morbid fear of missing any excitement that might come with the arrival of the human freight. The convicts were being delivered, hauled in, for the Prison Rodeo, some as participants and some as spectators.

Most of the convicts were shut-faced: grim-eyed and cold-mouthed. They rode with arms folded over their uniforms, tight-lipped, looking straight ahead. One or two show-offs grinned defiantly. They rode in trucks, vans, ambulancelike contraptions loaded to the gunwales, locked in like rats in an old-fashioned wire rattrap. Cages of rat wire and chicken wire speeding by on rubber-tired wheels. Steely-eyed guards, each with a sawed-off shotgun in his hand and a pistol in his belt, sat fore and aft in each vehicle. Between every conveyance a motorcycle policeman, primed and loaded, rode herd. A police car cruised behind each motor cop.

"The bad un's goes to the farms," a red-necked snuff dipper commented to his son. "Ramsey One's where they send the meanest. Some of em's three-time losers. Ain't them mean lookin' boogers?"

They were, too.

Whites, some shifty-looking, some sullen, some impudent. Mexicans, a few defiant, others shamefaced, mostly stoic. Negroes, their eyes rolling like the eyes of frightened horses, or insolent, or merely sorrowful. All carefully segregated: black, brown, and white. Even going by at a good fifty miles an hour their faces were studies by Hogarth. The truckloads of criminals continued to whip by for more than twenty minutes, prodded on by the businesslike law officers. Dawdling was out.

The Prison Rodeo is good for Huntsville. Everyone in town benefits. The place is jammed. Many spectators have to get rooms in Conroe and Livingston, or other towns within a radius of fifty miles, as the reservations in Huntsville are booked for months in advance. The restaurants do a land-office business, although hundreds of families bring their own food. Lots of them cook out by the side of the road or at one of the beautifully kept roadside parks.

The townspeople make money by turning their yards into makeshift parking lots, and they really make you shift! Little Negroes hop on the car bumpers and guide the visitors to the lots. Sometimes they get to keep the quarter they earn. The cars are bumper to bumper in the street and in the yards. The only comfort stations to be found for blocks are flimsy bits of burlap tacked onto filthy open goat pens, where white and colored stand to ease themselves like so many head of cattle. The town and the Prison System are working for better comfort stations.

It would be unwise to fix a definite hour to be somewhere upon leaving the Rodeo. In spite of the skillful and courteous management of the traffic police, the break-up is a long hot nerve-racking business. The traffic problem grows with the Rodeo and must soon be solved, unless people are to become discouraged and decide to forego the show.

Texans come to the show armed with pillows and backrests, sun visors, and dark glasses, for the glare of the mad October sunshine is formidable. Most people wear old and very comfortable clothes. Much Western dress is worn by men, women, and children. The prisoners sell squirrelly hats of every description and the children cry for them. The box lunches at the Prison, usually barbecued chicken or beef, potato salad and baked beans, aren't too bad, and the fresh air and the excitement is sauce enough to make you eat the leg off a chair. Trusty prisoners circulate freely out in the open, selling food and souvenirs, visiting with the crowd, talking just a little longer to pretty girls than the buying of a box lunch actually requires. A loud speaker blares out the latest convict recording and the proud composer is on hand to sell and autograph phonograph records and printed song sheets of the words to his song. The souvenir booths are swamped: they make about $8500 annually.

Since only inmates with good conduct records are allowed to participate and to attend — "You gotta be a good co-operatin' con!" — the Rodeo is a powerful stimulant to good behavior and a real godsend to the entire Prison System. Nothing short of a pardon is more important to a convict than a chance to be in the Rodeo or to attend the show. The convicts who are sick in the hospital (which they call the "Little Shamrock") watch the show on television.

The show developed almost by accident under the direction of the man who raised the chute on the first head of stock that was ever ridden at the penitentiary: Albert Moore. For twenty-four years he has managed the spectacle, which grew from an experiment of turning a few head of wild stock loose in the baseball diamond and allowing some of the prisoners to try their luck at bronc busting, calf roping, and bull riding into a standing-room-only event: the wildest and fastest show on earth. The prisoners' feats have paid for the building of an enormous stadium. At least 100,000 persons every year see the show staged by convicted murderers, bank robbers, forgers, thieves, and confidence men. That same something, the reck-

less daring perhaps, that makes men defy the laws and rules
of society makes them unable to resist the challenge of a snorting horse or a bellowing bull that refuses to be ridden. A spirit
of bone-breaking defiance characterizes the performance and
makes it unique. The same spirit that got the men into trouble
in the Free World serves as an asset in the Pen. More than
one hundred convicts participate every year, while better than
six thousand prisoners watch it from the bleachers.

Albert Moore screens the contestants carefully for riding
ability and showmanship. These are prime requisites. Long-
termers, who compete year after year, have no trouble getting
on the list. Each participant is paid a small amount of "day
money." They love the spotlight — and the chance to compete for prize money. New talent presents more of a problem.
Many of the prisoners have had no closer contact with life on
the range than a Western motion picture viewed from the up-
holstered seat of a movie palace. Many tyros try out . . .
more guts than brains is their trouble. All contestants are sub-
jected to a rigid physical examination before being allowed to
enter and must sign a waiver of all claims against the state in
case of injury during the show. What have they got to lose?

One contestant, known to the inmates, I was told, as the
Old Man by virtue of his eleven years in the Rodeo, is getting
a reputation for being jinxed. Assigned as a stockman at the
Ramsey farm unit, he broke his leg just before the 1950 rodeo,
broke a collarbone two weeks before last year's show, and was
struck by lightning last August. He's still in there pitching.
He has a lifetime in which to try.

Most interesting to me out of the whole incredible performance is the unforeseen interest and response on the part of
the public. To many people there is an element of spine-chill-
ing thrill in being inside the stadium of the prison, surrounded
by dangerous men. They can talk to the trusties, and sit close
enough to the prisoners to hear what they are saying. To many
of the weak, there is a certain reassurance in the fact that they

are still at large while these strong, desperate men are heavily guarded behind bars, or stout steel mesh. While the temper of the crowd is good-natured and gay, there is an atmosphere of wariness. The presence of the guards contributes something to the feeling of cautious behavior. There are no left-handed men among the guards!

The Texas Prison System is a steely strait jacket of punishment for wrongdoing in the toughest Texas tradition. Take one look at the faces of the prison guards. Look into those motionless eyes that see out, but won't let you see in — eyes so hard they could flatten a steel bullet with one wink, and you will accept the fact that the Texas Prison System is no dude ranch. The air is filled with the tingling sensation that violence may occur at any minute.

In the arena, you can *depend* on violence. Resentful men trying to break resentful beasts. They take their meanness out on the stock and the four-footed contenders win most of the rounds. When it comes to pure dee toughness, it's a draw. Man and mount are equally wild.

The October sun sizzles down on the many thousands seated in the stadium, making an unforgettable picture. The stadium is shaped like a giant U, with the high bars of the thick gate closing the open end of the U. The best seats are at the bottom of the U. The announcer's stand is there, and Roy Dillon does a prodigious job of keeping the public informed as to what is taking place. The audience must be told instantly and constantly, for many events are over before they are started. Prizefight announcers have to be quick, but the announcer at the Huntsville Prison Rodeo must have a tongue quicker than the eye, he must be clairvoyant, and have a tape-recorder memory, because the next hell-breathing fury is halfway over the fence and out of the chute before the handlers can open the gate or the announcer has had time to say who was riding what. The events are short and seldom sweet.

The important guests of the Prison System sit just behind

the announcer's platform, as they command a straightaway view of the full length of the arena. Up above, in a small wire cage, the prison band of about sixty men plays almost continuously. The total enrollment of the musicians' time adds up to 6008 years of penal servitude.

To the right of these desirable places is a large section for colored spectators. Toulouse-Lautrec's brush was a little too fine for this watercolor. Gauguin might have been able to do the mixture of skin tones, but I thought it a pity that neither painter had seen this sight: either one of them would have blown a fuse at the barbaric dazzle of colored silk sport shirts and dresses splattered over the stadium in a palette loud enough to cause spots in front of the strongest eyes.

The circus-poster color on the right stands out all the more when the spectator looks to the left to see six thousand convicts penned in a giant steel mesh box. "Those men in white ain't sailors," a man tells his wife. They are a study in white. White clothes. White faces. White hair. All different, yet all somehow the same. Reduced to a common denominator by the prison uniform.

The crowded stadium last October experienced one of those infrequent pin-dropping lulls that occur inexplicably and spontaneously in large herds of humanity. Frequently a humorous, irrelevant scrap of conversation floats above the silence; the female voice in the *luft-pause* of the symphony: "We cook ours with onions."

The accidental silence at the Rodeo in Huntsville Penitentiary was broken by a sound as far from humorous as any I have ever heard. Six motorcycle policemen walked gingerly in front of the six thousand caged men, looking neither to the right nor to the left, to reach their designated places. The eyes of the spectators from the Free World focused instantly on the small, wooden procession. The six thousand prisoners, watching the cops, let out a strange hoarse roar, a threatening sound that came on quickly, low and somber like the rumble that precedes the eruption of a volcano, growing louder as it rises from the earth. The police officers stiffened noticeably. The few hundred yards they had to walk must have seemed a mile to them.

I have heard some eerie sounds in my life: a newspaper-editor neighbor with the DT's; Samoans at a hanging; Mexican funerals; a Sicilian wake; the shriek of a giant magnolia as the power saw ripped its heart open; the fury of the wind as it hurled away the leper-colony huts at Pago Pago in a hurricane; the vicious Spanish cursing of a crowd turned enemy of the bullfighter. They were all bland as Brahms' Lullaby compared to the sound that engulfed the six cops at the Rodeo. The sustained, sinister distillate of menace and hate, that grisly growl was much like the sound Marie Antoinette must have heard as she was borne away in the tumbril.

The universal tension among the spectators was broken by an unconscious comedienne with a carrying voice: "Them cops walk jus' like a barefoot nigger walkin' on hard-froze ground!"

The band began to play for the Grand Entry, a sight that will bring a lump to the most blasé throat. The panoply of flags, pennants and streamers, the graceful, proud horses and handsome, rugged riders combine to stir the blood to an unexpected degree. The color and motion in such a display of power suggested to me the most moving scene I can remember: the ships of Shakespeare's Henry the Fifth curvetting and tossing on the waters of Southampton as they made ready to sail the troops to France for the Battle of Agincourt in Laurence Olivier's film.

Throughout the performance, the "world's largest rodeo stadium" is a scene of glory. The show is a triumph of wit and ingenuity, an everlasting tribute to those bent on sublimating the bitterness of "man's inhumanity to man."

The cattle chutes are just below and in front of the best

seats. "None of these contestants," says the announcer, "were flown in for the performance by the airlines! They all live right here. Good co-operating boys."

The stock is as fierce and homicidal as the riders. No professional rodeo performer would risk his neck riding the stock that stars in the hair-raisers at the Prison Rodeo. The Brahma bulls have murder in their hearts long before they rocket out of the chutes. The horses are wild, malevolent, and cunning.

"Yes, ladies and gentlemen," the announcer bleats in a voice of doom, "men and women everywhere, there'll be some sore behinds tonight!"

Many of the horses are fence-worms, whose specialty is dashing to the spiky fence to try to scrape the rider off if they can't dislodge him any other way. The animals have been on the range eleven months, without the sight of a human being since the previous year's rodeo. When they are choused about, herded into the chutes with electric prods and goads, plus the final indignity of a canvas "kitchen" strapped around them to enrage them further, you can stand by for action — and get it. Eighty head of bad stock ridden in a total riding time of thirty-five minutes is a fast rodeo, even in Texas.

The clowns deserve special credit. Their antics seem funny, but in reality they risk their lives in an effort to divert the course of the angry, frustrated horns and hoofs. They maneuver maniacal Brahmas away from a fallen rider, often just as the bull is about to hook him to death. Another dangerous task is to divert the iron heels of a mean, kicking horse, biting and snorting over a rider. The clowns in their ridiculous tramp costumes, or dressed as old women in mother hubbards and sunbonnets, sometimes in wildly striped convict garb, tear in, picador fashion, to draw the attention of the animal away from the tumbled contestant long enough for him to escape to the relative safety of the fence.

The clowns have an invention called the Bull-Mobile. It is a small one-man chariot with two big wheels and thick rubber tires, drawn by a roaring, snorting Brahma. It is harnessed to a surcingle around the bull's middle by an iron pipe that forms an inverted U connecting it with the chariot. The clowns pretend to lose a hubcap from the Bull-mobile. They get out and search the sand for it, picking up many round objects, including one just left by a frightened bull. The clown holds it up and his partner roars over the loudspeaker: "Not that! Not that!" The audience, salty and earthy, few of them strangers to the cowpen, loves it.

Snuffy Garrett is a famous clown. He gets his nickname from Garrett's Snuff. There is an apocryphal story around that Snuffy's mule pitched him into the Governor's Box at one rodeo and he said, "Pardon me, sir."

Rider, clown, and animal trainer, Marion Frazier is a lifer from Montague. He prepares charming animal acts, a particularly popular one involving a monkey that rides a trained fawn that works in harness. Marion hasn't much hair. The announcer offered to give him a Davy Crockett cap "so he would have something to comb and brush."

Mickey Mitchell from Matador is the clown making a life-work, at least during the month of October, of rolling around the arena in a big red barrel, offering himself as a target to the charging bulls.

A man lies on the ground. The clowns rush up. "Is he hurt or drunk?" "He's lyin' on a sand bar, not a whiskey bar." "Is he hurt bad?" "Just a simple fracture: he wasn't hit by a Houston driver."

One of the clowns came to the microphone and inquired if there was a doctor in the house. A lady in Section A had just informed him that the man next to her had a dislocated hand.

Women convicts, the Goree Girls, take part in the entertainment between the acts, and their name gives rise to considerable punning. Recently women of the Goree unit went into a garden club project; they did everything from gardening to making hand-painted sachet bags. The club was sponsored by a civilian garden club, the first in penal history to gain national recognition as a result of this rehabilitative project.

The Goree Girls have a string band and look well in their cowgirl outfits. They were less happy in gypsy costumes and songs. A soloist stepped forward to the mike and the announcer said: "This little lady has made quite a name for herself. She wrote it on the wrong check. But she's a nice girl with very taking ways or she wouldn't be in here." They play rough at Huntsville. Nobody can say that the prisoners can't take it. They get their turn, and one of the girls announces over the microphone that she is going to run a skunk farm: she doesn't want the state government sticking its nose in her business.

Throughout the show the performers, the audience, the announcer, and the venders of hot dogs and pop in the stands all make cracks involving time.

"Time!" the performers demand of the timekeeper in an event. "Hell, he's got a hundred and one years now."

"Hot dogs! Hot dogs! Buy 'em now. I'm gettin' out any minute!" cries a mournful-faced trusty. When a particularly dangerous beast comes ripping and staving out of the chute the crowd roars: "Stay a long time, cowboy." "Don't worry," says the announcer, "he got ninety-nine years to try. He's GOT his social security. When a man gets old enough to have money to burn, the pilot light goes out."

The program venders cry: "Get your program! Learn ALL about the inside of your prison. You might be in here someday yourself, and want to know who to get TO!" The program is an excellent job of writing, printing, and art work, all done by inmates. I was amazed to see in this souvenir program a bald-faced statement that "while 25 per cent of the inmates will behave themselves, 75 per cent will be aggressively homosexual if allowed to do so. Hence the need for new living quarters. Men cannot be rehabilitated while living in tanks where homosexuality is rampant. The weak are preyed upon by the strong and the vicious circle is ever widened." Texas has certainly come of age!

The director has wisely laced the more spectacular feats with acts billed as "special entertainment." Last October a woman rider did a Roman chariot leap, guiding her four magnificent horses over two flaming automobiles. Good as these acts are, they do not get the same response as the spontaneous, unrehearsed acts of daredevil heroics by the convicts.

Perhaps because the arteries can stand just so much, the crowd welcomes a spectacle like the Horseback Quadrille performed by men and women. Forty couples on perfectly matched horses, members of various riding clubs scattered over Texas, dance with the grace and spirit of the Ballet Russe. The lovely beasts are good, and they know it. The dainty, sure-footed swiftness of their movements is a delight: poetry in motion.

Everywhere in Texas that I see thoroughbred horses, beautiful, intelligent, loyal, and loving, I am reassured as to the rightness of the world. To see them enter the arena, ribbon bedecked, club colors and Texas flag flying, is an experience you can never forget. The poise and unself-conscious pride of thoroughbreds is a quality that has been denied too many human beings. Perhaps the noble animals have influenced their owners, for it seems to me that it requires disciplined individuals to train a pair of horses and to learn the routines themselves. It is pleasant to think of young, middle-aged, and elderly couples over Texas getting together with their beautifully paired mounts to practice dancing on horseback. There is an elegance and aristocratic quality about the idea that I admire tremendously.

The three outstanding events of the Rodeo are the Mad Scramble, the Wild Horse Race, and the Wild Bull Riding.

In the Mad Scramble, ten chutes are opened simultaneously spewing forth mad Brahma bulls, each intent on tossing and trampling the rider who has forked down on his back. Spills. Chills. Thrills. No one ever has enough eyes to take in all the spectacle. The pick-up men on horseback, a crew of experienced and top rodeo hands, have to look sharp to keep pace with the event that is erupting all around them. The cowboys bog their spurs into the sides of the beasts and hang on for dear life, one arm and one hand free, in compliance with the standard rules of rodeo. Few of the contestants stay glued on for more than a matter of seconds. The judges are rigorous in their standards of the acceptable. A man earns his time, more ways than one, in Huntsville. The Mad Scramble is a Neronian spectacle, dangerous from every point of view, and entirely unpredictable.

The Wild Horse Race calls for eight teams, three men to a team. Eight wild horses are turned loose simultaneously, and the eight teams have to rope and attempt to saddle the beasts before one of their team can ride him. Another act, Three Men on a Horse, is about as far away from the Broadway show of that name as anything the imagination can stretch to. It is vicious and dangerous. The greased-lightning activities of the contestants make the head swim just watching from the grandstand. When a cowboy mounts and rakes his spurs along the horse's sides from his neck to his flanks, the twisting, springing fury of the mount is like a tornado with hoofs. I have never understood why the horse doesn't break his own back in the frantic corkscrew effort to dislodge the hated human on his back. "Yessir, a little loud and comin' fast!" the announcer says. They are high rollers and no mistake. The enthusiasm of the spectators and the carelessness of life and limb of the participants build up into a frenzy.

With the excellent showmanship that characterizes the whole two-hour performance, the wildest Bull Riding is saved for last. Eight thundering mountains of meanness come out of the chutes one after the other with the rider tight-legging them for dear life. The frenzied animals twist and spiral, dive and kick in a frantic backlash, fighting like tigers and roaring like lions. Few riders last more than a couple of seconds. "Pancake!" the crowd roars as the cowboy hits the dust.

At the end of a long, breathtaking show last October the crowd was jumpy and edgy. One by one the gray menaces catapulted their riders to the ground, with a bone-breaking crash. The stretcher bearers carried most of them away to the Little Shamrock.

Then came Number Eight ridden by O'Neal Browning, a colored cowhand, a Lifer from Beaumont, the greatest rodeo performer I have ever seen. He can kick 'em forward and kick 'em back. If he lives to be eighty, he's got sixty-four more years to do. He was a cowman before he got into trouble and he will ride anything they can herd into the chutes. I saw him ride a bolt of greased lightning. From my seat at the south end of the stadium, just above the chutes, I watched him ride as a centaur rides. He and the leaping, twisting bull were one. The seconds passed and he still rode. The crowd had risen like puppets pulled by the same string. It couldn't be possible, but it was. The bull gave two leaps forward and one to the side. Then he changed his tactics to an angry, zigzag jump that must have wrenched every muscle in his body. Browning

stuck. The crowd screamed and whistled, unable to believe
what it was seeing. The bull soared into the air and brought
his feet together into a compact knot of four hard hoofs. But
he couldn't shake the enemy. Faster and faster he thundered,
bucking and pitching lethally, Browning riding him in rhythm
with his leaps and twists, toward the great heavy gate of
bridge timbers, planks perhaps twenty inches wide and not
less than four inches thick that form the safety barrier at the
north end of the stadium. Gathering a final reckless momen-
tum, the bull heaved his great massive fury at the gate, soared
like a giant porpoise rising from the ocean, smashed right
through the steely timbers of the first two bars on the top of
the gate, goaded by the relentless rider, leaving a great round
hole in the gate the size of the bull's belly. The gate might as
well have been made of cardboard. The bull landed with his
forelegs buckled under him. The crowd thought he had killed
himself and his rider. O'Neal Browning dismounted and stag-
gered to the fence to support himself to safety. The crowd
roared: "You flat-rode him, cowboy! You rode him all the
way!" It was Bonus Day for movie-camera fans, and I hope
nobody was out of film.

Thinking about the freakish leap of the bull through the
gate, I could not believe it had happened. The solid gate had
had a giant round bite taken out of it as though it had been a
gate in an old-time Keystone comedy. The next morning I saw
the picture of the hole in the gate and the bull down on his
knees on the front page of the Dallas *News* and I knew I had
not dreamed the great performance. "Stay a long time, cowboy!" was no college cheer this time. I saw it happen.

The next day A. C. Turner, then the Director of Rehabilitation, arranged for me to talk to some of the prisoners and to
witness an event as exciting to me in a musical way as the Rodeo had been in the way of sport. A trusty in neat white coat
and white duck trousers came to my attention because of the
elaborate tooled-leather cowboy boots he wore. They were

high-heeled and sharp-toed, trimmed with inlays of red and green leather, the fancy "hot-tamolly" blossoms that workers in tooled leather seem to love. The prisoner was putting away his stock of souvenirs left over from the Rodeo. "Five Sundays in October for the last three years. We're about sold outa saddles." There were handbags, briefcases, boots, belts, wallets, even ties made of satin-soft unborn calfskin. Hatbands, spectacle cases, and all the usual more or less useless articles that people buy for souvenirs.

"How'd you make out?" I asked.

"I have twenty-seven hundred dollars in bonds and twenty-two hundred in cash in the bank. I'da had more, but my sister got killed in a auto accident and they let me fly home. I left five hundred with the folks."

"What did you do before?"

"When I was in the Free World I worked in a filling station. I'm getting out next week."

"Were you a leather worker?"

"No'm. I learned this all Behind Walls on my spare time in the Craft Shop. We call it the Piddlin' Room. They give you a certain number of hours a day to work for yourself. In your free time they encourage you to do anything you want that's constructive. They get a teacher if they can, but we learn a lot from books and practice. We pay for all our own materials and if we sell anything, like at the Rodeo or to visitors, we keep the money."

"You seem to have a lot of privileges. What is your feeling about your sentence? Do you resent it?"

He never batted an eye: "Mrs. Lasswell, I'm not in here for but one reason in the world: I killed my wife."

It gave me an eerie feeling — and a great respect for law and order — to walk across that huge, concrete compound through various sets of very stout steel bars and highly polished solid brass bars, into the heart of the prison where few men and fewer women from the Free World have ever set foot. The dining room was quiet and orderly, and I had the feeling that everybody was on his best behavior.

Many of the men in prison are aware, for the first time in their lives, of what is going on in the Free World. Only now, when they are deprived of liberty and shut away from the world, do they know what the meaning of liberty is. They realize at last that they are not the sole occupants of the planet. Now the men have radios — and time to listen. "Time on My Hands," but no "you" in my arms.

The inmates knew they were being written about. There were two men from a Houston paper at the table with us and the white waiters listened openly to the conversation.

The food was country, coarse and plentiful. There were three kinds of meat: ham, chicken, and beef on the table. Eleven vegetables and many relishes. The strawberry pie for dessert was the most elaborate I have ever seen. It had custard, strawberries, meringue, and whipped cream on top. All the meats, vegetables, and dairy products used by the Prison System are raised on the prison farms. The farms located near the Gulf supply the Prison System with fresh fish, oysters, and shrimp in season.

"Come up to the Library," Mr. Turner said after lunch. "The men organized it and run it themselves. They read the Book Sections of the major Sunday papers and make their own selections. The range of their interests will amaze you." A lot of gray paint is in evidence at Huntsville. It is not much different from the gray paint used on warships. At the end of a long corridor I looked up, attracted by signs, as always. A framed beauty hung over the door of the library:

LET FICTION
EASE THE FRICTION
OF YOUR CONVICTION

Alexander Woollcott died too soon. He would have loved this sign for his collection.

There were several requests for books tacked to the bulletin board, among them Gibbon's *Decline and Fall of the Roman Empire*, Peale's *The Power of Positive Thinking*, and Jones' new *Life of Sigmund Freud* in three volumes.

"We try to keep *Forever Amber* and *Mamie Stover* out: what we call incendiary books."

The books on the shelves covered a wide range. The Librarian was an intelligent trusty, a coldly vicious murderer doing life, I was told. He was self-appointed and self-trained. His assistant was in for raping a colored baby-sitter while he was a student at S.M.U.

"The men in the band, trusties mostly," Mr. Turner said, "especially those from the farms, like to stay over for a jam session after the Rodeo. We let them do it as a reward for good behavior. They have a musical director from the College over in town, and they like to get together with their friends and play. They have done yeoman service for all five performances and we feel they are entitled to a little extra recreation. They're in the auditorium now . . . you heard them play the show yesterday. Would you . . ." Mr. Turner, a rather shy, gentle individual, hesitated a moment. "Would you come in and let them play for you? They'd like very much to do so." I feigned a decent hesitancy that deceived no one, but I didn't take any chances on him withdrawing the offer. The auditorium was surprisingly large and had a well-planned stage. The sound produced by a group of men warming up individually, tooting, twanging, scraping, and thumping is pretty much the same from Fifty-second Street to the Belgian Congo.

"Music is a powerful force over them," Mr. Turner said. "The band privilege is something they respect. They broadcast once a week over a Houston station. The Rotary Clubs of Houston and Beaumont sponsor the programs. It takes some of them away from the prison farms for the rehearsals and the broadcast, and of course they like that. They're invited to play in other towns sometimes, too. They have a kind of prestige and popularity that they value greatly. They're waiting for Pop, the piano player, now. He played bass fiddle with the trio at the Rodeo."

I remembered Pop, the guitar player, and the accordionist with special interest for they had played Lee Norton's accompaniment when he sang "Jalisco" at the opening of the Rodeo. "Pancho," as Lee Norton is known on the radio, sings "Jalisco" as well as I have ever heard it sung, even by Jorge Negrete. I knew from his singing that he must be a Mexican or an Anglo born in Mexico. He was born in Mexico, the son of missionaries, it turned out.

"Lee has done great things for the band and the prisoners at Huntsville," Mr. Turner said. "He helps the men in it to find jobs, arranges for the broadcasts every Saturday night 'Behind Prison Walls,' and urges the musicians to do original work. Several of them have composed songs, and Lee helps them make recordings that they sell. He plays them on the station to try to get big recording company scouts interested. Sometimes they hit. There is rejoicing in Huntsville when a prisoner writes a good one, and the juke boxes take over."

A tall, slender, graying man came in and sat down at the piano. There were about eighteen men in the outfit. A skinny Negro boy played drums with some of Cozy Cole's style and technique. The players looked slightly sheepish at first, but when Pop gave them the down beat, they were off to the races: "Muskrat Ramble."

There were only four in the audience, and I didn't know what to expect. I could sense the release, the unburdening of the soul, the loosing of pent-up emotions that music brought to these men. They had played a heavy show the day before, practically every moment of the entire Rodeo, but they put their hearts into what they were playing now. There is a strongly felt current that runs between people who love music. Some kind of antenna tells them when the listeners really

understand what it is they are trying to say and do. I silently
blessed whoever invented the seven notes of the scale, thinking
of the solace it has brought to those bereft of every other form
of beauty and means of expressing emotion.

They played "Stardust." It is not an easy number. It has
difficult intervals and covers a wide range. The piano har-
monies underneath it are subtle. I wasn't expecting much.
If they just managed to avoid discords, we would be lucky. It
is acutely embarrassing to me to have to listen to wrong notes
because I have a poor poker face. I know I looked down in my
lap that day, because my head snapped up at the sound of a
silvery trumpet, high, clear, like a waterfall of diamond dust.
Clean. Gleaming. Sustained. I was entranced by that beautiful articulation. The notes practically spoke the words of the
song.

The boy who played the trumpet like nobody this side of
Heaven was short and stocky. His skin was golden bronze and
he looked like an Indian cacique: blue-black hair and dimples
the size of jawbreakers. As he stood waiting for his next cue,
he held the trumpet poised against his copper chest with the
gleaming silver chain and crucifix hanging visible in the open
V of his white shirt.

"José Alvárez," Mr. Turner volunteered. "There's a deluge
of calls from name bands every time he plays over the air."

What had gone wrong? Why was this golden music shut
away behind bars for fifteen years? A knifing in a hot scuffle
over a girl? At a dance, perhaps? Some thoughtless girl probably flirting with the trumpet player in a big-name band, for
this music was strictly top-flight. She didn't know that the
Mexican male's proudest boast is: "*Con un Mexicano no se
juega.*" You don't play with a Mexican's emotions. Throw
down a gauntlet in that direction and it will be picked up . . .
quick.

The boy played with the sureness of the born musician, not

giving merely the sound of the single note that his instrument
confines him to, but giving the hearer the overtones of the
chord under that note; blowing a c major into that horn that
sounds different from a c minor, when actually they are the
same, single note, colored and differentiated only by a subtle
shading in the mind of the performer. Intonation can be
learned and improved — to a degree — but this was a gift
straight from the good fairies at the christening. It is art, but
not the kind that can be acquired, if art can ever be said to be
acquired. Science, perhaps — but not this art. Part of the gift
is feeling every note that the rest of the ensemble plays, leaning
on it with them, bearing down in the same places, blending
notes with a great sense of intimacy. The faces of the men in
the band showed they felt the same way I did about the trumpet solo. The boy stepped back and the saxophone took over.
When they reached the passage:

> But that was long ago, now my consolation
> Is in the stardust of a song . . .

the word *song* is, as everybody knows, a long sustained note at
the end of a cadence.

While the note was being held and played for its full value
by the saxophone, I heard a staccato, mischievous counterpoint
sotto voce on the trumpet: "Everybody loves a baby, that's
why I'm in love with you," the first six bars of "Pretty Baby"
blending in wit and wickedness with "Stardust." Johann Se-
bastian Bach could not have figured it out more tidily. The sly
rogue played the devilish descant with an innocent, "butter
wouldn't melt in my mouth" look on his face. There would be
no way to repress the good nature and high spirits of this prisoner.

When the band played a gospel hymn in swing time, I heard
the stuttering mutter of the saucy trumpet in the background,
making naughty comment on an alien music. He couldn't help
it. He is a star, and you can't put a veil over a star.

"We want José to play 'Brave Bulls,'" the piano player said to Mr. Turner. I began getting goose bumps before they even started because "La Macarena," a Flamenco paso doble, is the theme song of the movie, *The Brave Bulls*, from Tom Lea's novel. It is a favorite in all of the bull rings, named for La Virgen de la Macarena, the patroness of bullfighters.

It was evident that the other players liked José and wanted to show him off. He stepped out modestly and after the crashing chords that are the introduction had faded, a faint thread of pale gold tone spun from the trumpet into a comet tail of shimmering sound. He played the characteristic cadenza of Flamenco music with creative imagination and artistry. Here was musical imagery, the real gypsy gift for improvising embellishment, composing elaborate variations on a theme, making it up as he went along. The dazzling golden fireworks were almost painfully beautiful.

I had just come from visiting Tom Lea and was full of the power of his work. "I wish Tom Lea could hear you play that theme," I said to José. "If he were here, he would paint your picture."

"Tell him to come," he smiled, "*I'll* be here!"

Fifteen years. What would they do to the golden trumpet and the bronze boy? I hoped they would not crush the humor out of him. But it will be difficult to wither anyone who can laugh at himself enough to tell you that his ambition in life is "to be an ex-convict."

A country singer came forward with his guitar and the orchestra backed him up as he sang, not inappropriately, "If I Ever Needed You, I Need You Now." His friends commented pointedly and loudly on the fact that he was getting out soon. When he sang "Just Bummin' Around," the Director of Rehabilitation remarked that that was how he probably got in the pen to begin with.

"Sing 'Just a Closer Walk with Thee,' Jim," Mr. Turner said to an angelic-looking tall blond young man. "I love that song." The lad sang the religious song with charm and sincerity. Here was one more of those absolutely Impossible Interviews: the completely unreal, "it can't be happening" situations in which I find myself the greater part of my life. Here stood a spiritual-looking boy, a convicted murderer, the enemy of society, singing in the voice of an angel, gentle, beseeching words which he obviously felt and loved.

Behind prison walls. Five chaplains. Two protestants. Two Catholic priests. A colored Doctor of Divinity. Five chapters of Alcoholics Anonymous.

"Why?" I asked stupidly, thinking there was no temptation here.

"To help them understand their personality problems. The difficult adjustments that they are going to have to make might drive them to excessive drinking when they go back to the Free World," I was told.

Those prisoners mentally and emotionally qualified serve their time and make their time serve them. They study, or learn a trade or craft. But the real incorrigible, according to my reasoning, is incorrigible for the very reason that he cannot pull himself OUT of himself long enough to do anything constructive that requires co-operation. And he never could! That is why he is the real enemy of society.

I have spent a considerable portion of my life around servicemen. When it comes to the emotions of men cooped up in any place, seeing the same people day after day, whether in a barracks or aboard a ship, it is not difficult to tell whom the men really like or whom they hate.

Huntsville Penitentiary would not be a healthy place for a phony. You've got to be straight and you've got to be right with those guys. The position of Director of Rehabilitation is a job that brings the man in direct contact with desperate, struggling convicts who are "talking straight" to him. They look to him for strength and encouragement, an example of what a first-class human being can be.

Toward Mr. Turner the convicts gave off a quiet emanation of mutual trust, lively affection, and dignified respect. It is to the infinite gain of the State Board of Pardons and Paroles that A. C. Turner is now a member of that group. But the personal loss to the prisoners of the Texas State Prison System is inestimable. He would be the first to say he can do more for them where he is. Anyone can pardon them. It takes a real man to love and understand them.

"Well, what do you think, Mary?" Mr. Turner asked.

That one set me back on my heels. But the question was put straight, and I knew I had to give a straight answer. The past two days had made a profound and lasting impression on me, and I thought I understood the basic question.

"Please don't think me flippant, but my sincere feeling is that THEY NEVER HAD IT SO GOOD. If the Free World had done as much for these men as you have done in here, most of them would not be in prison."

Hank Hornsby, a man convicted of forgery, wrote this song and it voices the feelings of lots of men who have learned contempt, instead of respect, for a quick buck:

EASTHAM TALKING BLUES

I'm a country boy from the heart of the hills;
I came to Texas looking for thrills.
A country boy easily beguiled,
I fell in love with a woman's smile.
I had trouble and finally failed
And ended up in the county jail.
The judge and I had quite a session.
His honor decided to teach me a lesson.
He said two years in the Texas pen
Ought to convince me I couldn't win.
So I rode the chain and made the pen,
That lonely world of misguided men.
When I first arrived at Eastham farm,
I looked around with no alarm.

The beds were clean, the chow was good,
But I didn't know about chopping wood.
The closest I'd ever come to an axe
Was a hardware store where they hang in racks.
Didn't know which was the handle and which the blade;
But that distinction was easily made.
Now you grip the handle and sweat and grunt;
The blade's the thing that wrecks the stump.
You, too, boy, swingin, sweatin, and swearin,
Despising that fountain pen.
It was awful cold about six A.M.
When old Moon holloed, "Let's go, men."
I grabbed my hat and hit the deck with a bounce
When old Moon holloed, "Line up for count."
We left the building and made the yard;
There I saw the captain of the guard.
He was saying something, but I was lost
Till he finally holloed, "Nineteen, Boss."
A guy fell out o' line with his hat in his hand
And walked right up to the captain man.
He was about my size, maybe a little taller;
He laid this story on Captain Laller.
He said, "Captain, don't think me bold,
But I'm awful sick, I have a cold.
My liver's bad, my blood is thin,
I wish you'd kindly lay me in."
The captain said, "I don't think you're bold, but that's a good lick;
Furthermore, I don't think you're sick.
Stop any time and have a try,
But before you do, son, learn to lie.
On this man's farm you're sure outclassed;
These Eastham boys are mighty fast.
Now grab your squad and make the line."
He gave him that famous hitchhike sign.
We made the field and there dismounted
And started work after being counted.
The boss man said, "I want to see
A cloud of white that pleases me.

Now bend your backs when I say, 'Go!'
Chop those trees, and chop them low.
Don't look up till — I'm commanding,
There'd better not be one little twig standing."
I noticed the squads from One to Eight;
I asked the boss how they percolate.
He said the bulls were in Number One,
But when a con was too weak to run,
Too old to try, just buzzard bait,
They place him in old Number Eight.
I said, "Boss, I've got news,
I'm not just making a good excuse,
But I'm so old and scrawny and lean,
Haven't you got a squad Sixteen?"
He looked at me and said kind of rough,
"Now, old thing, that'll be enough.
You conned the merchants with a worthless check,
Now you con me and I'll break your neck.
Grab that axe and blister your hands,
When you leave here, you'll be an honest man."
Now, fourteen months and a dozen days
Have come and gone, I've changed my ways.
I'm going back to the Kentucky hills;
I've had my fill of foolish thrills.
I don't believe that law and I
Will clash again before I die.
But if I'm ever in jail again,
It won't be caused by a woman or gin.
Nor will it be by a drunken lurch;
It'll be plowing too deep or singing in church.

Bustin' a bronc, ridin' a Brahma, or blowin' a horn,

> All the hell-ridin' stars
> Are the boys behind the bars.

When I started out to study Texas and write my impressions
of part of what I saw, "little did I think" I would end up in

prison — especially as a researching anthropologist. But if I run short of obituaries, LITTLE DID SHE THINK! would tell the story.

But I had resolved as far back as page 3 to see all I could of the land that had named me, had marked me for what I am. After seventy thousand miles, I quit keeping track of how far I went, but I saw more than most people do who take Texas for granted, as I did before this pilgrimage started. No writer, it is certain, stands any great chance of conveying Texas — in all its humor, its outrageousness, its heroisms and meannesses, the vastness, the tumult and the shouting — exaggerated enough and sufficiently out of true drawing to emerge in the larger than life picture that has come to be expected of anything Texas Size. Since I was making an I-witness report, my own impressions are views more passionate than detached.

Armadillo

It is always reassuring to see our instinctive choices confirmed by experience and mature reasoning. I felt that a kind of seal of approval had been set on my attitude toward my homeland when I found that the elemental in Texas was both basic and beautiful, lasting and valuable. Three bittersweet years had shown me that the French are right in one thing, at least! "The more it changes, the more it is the same." The more a Texan changes, the more he becomes truly himself. Change and adaptability are among his basic inherited patterns of behavior; resourcefulness is characteristic of him. The country itself is suddenly and violently changeable, often in clashing conflict with itself, elementally, spiritually, and physically, all at the same time, like a Texan's conflict between his pioneer past and his urban present. Storm and stress have characterized the personalities of most of the figures who changed the map of Texas. I began to cast about in my mind for a simile that would be effective in summing up what Texas is and what it is becoming. I wanted a symbol that would convey my feeling for and interest in this unique "country."

As I thought over the range of people and country I had explored, Texas, as I see it now, knowing it intimately — I began to see the outline of a figure emerging, a personification of the spirit of a state. It was the form of a young, vigorous person, standing on the threshold of maturity, someone who had not quite "arrived" at the height of fame, but who knows of a certainty, that fame is coming!

11. TEXAS, TAKE IT OR LEAVE IT

TEXAS is all things to all men. Every man can find in her (or imagine he finds) whatever qualities he loves best: beauty, variety, solidity, riches, tranquillity, and fertility. She has many enchantments in her bag of tricks: austere beauty, rugged majesty, serene drowsiness, bucolic gaiety, and earthy humanity. Her temperament reflects the infinite variety of the weather: gently warm, scorchingly hot, or bitingly cold. Gusty and stormy, showery and sunny within the twinkling of an eye. She can whisper or thunder, caress or crush, melt or freeze — without warning.

She is first spendthrift, then miserly. Frivolous, then profound. Kind, then cantankerous. Jealous, then prodigal. Lovable, then exasperating: a bundle of contradictions and conflicts. How else could she be, with her frontier past scarcely a life span behind her? Her urban present is staggering on widespread feet to keep its balance — a child on roller skates for the first time.

At times she has scorned the old, elemental structures and ways, bulldozed them out of sight, like a new-rich woman shoving the old furniture up into the attic. Now she is becoming aware of the value of her past. Those outmoded values have come back into style again. She is bringing out, one by one, her pioneer virtues, just as she brings out with shy pride her mama's old cut-glass dishes.

For some time Texas has been sticking out too far in the wrong places; sprawly, tripping over her long legs. All on account of her size! She is not quite pulled together yet. When she most wants to put her best foot forward, she seems to have two left feet. Her wrists and hands are a problem. Her voice frequently gets out of control. Endearingly adolescent is her painful anxiety to do the right thing. If she cared less, she would not make so many *gaffes*. Because she is shy, she seems bold. To hide the timidity in her heart, she becomes aggressive. Because she is so pitiably unsure of herself, she sounds too positive. Each day she looks at herself in the glass and groans: "Shall I never grow up? Shall I ever achieve poise and polish? Why can't I be tiny, and dainty, and ladylike?"

When the girl is very, very rich, her conflicts are even greater. She is taught to love culture. She also loves money — and because she is inexperienced, she cannot always distinguish between them. Her taste has not quite evolved; she has not yet learned to use the fascinating pots of color on her toilet table with a delicate touch. Her heels are a little too high and her dresses a little too tight for that burgeoning figure that the money-men of the world cannot take their eyes off.

Those who love her understand her. They know she is growing in grace and loveliness with every maturing hour, as a golden fruit ripens and mellows in the sun. When all her far-flung endowments are brought under control, integrated into a strong and harmonious whole, the warring elements in her reconciled, dominated, and harnessed into a confident, wise, and kindly personality, the ages can say: "Time has wrought a miracle. This Texas is no mere Amazon. She is a goddess."

How can she fail, with such distinguished parents? Was her mother not the Old South? And her father the Young West? Blood lines will tell. When she loses her baby fat and fines down a little, her basic beauty and her essential good breeding will be so well blended that she will be able to take them for granted — and forget them.

She will discover that her greatest riches lie in the minds of her people, and not in the mines of her earth. Contact with the world will teach her to treasure and live by her pioneer principles; to nurture that dogged strength and patience that made her own difficult birth possible. She will learn to hold sophistication lightly, remembering that it is concerned with form and manner, totally lacking in content. She will choose substance over shimmer, goodness over glitter, charitableness over chatter, and virtue over veneer.

Her puppy-dog friendliness will quiet down when the sheer animal exuberance of the young expends itself. With her varied pursuits and pleasures she is unlikely to become blasé for a long time. She has always insisted on being herself, not conforming to what goes against her personal grain. She has the courage her parents had: the courage to stand alone for what she believes to be right, regardless of what the rest of the world may think or say. She has an uncle named Sam who has often been heard to remark: "Texas always was independent-like!"

Because want and hard times are several decades behind her, but not far enough away for her to have forgotten what parched corn tastes like three times a day, she is generous to her neighbors and to the stranger within her gates.

In time she will learn that her wealth, her resources are a responsibility: she must show good stewardship of them for the generations to come. She will guard her heritage well and give a good account of her talents, not burying them under sloth and idleness, nor letting them stagnate in mental laziness and mass-thinking.

Young as she is, foreign flattery is not unknown to her. She knows that all too often their hand-kissing is motivated by self-interest. Because she is young and healthy, Texas loves people. She knows that a complete lack of condescension is the noblest human virtue. From babyhood she was taught that "one man was as good as another, and maybe a damn sight better." Wherever she sits *is* the head of the table. She will keep her guests in control and a few megalomaniacs will not be allowed to foist off their spurious, meretricious "Texanism" as the spokesmen for her rational, clear-thinking, decent people. A continual stream of visitors flows around her. Her hospitality is classic, instantaneously proffered — and from the heart, whether it is caviar and breast of pheasant, or blackeyed peas and cornbread.

"Texas is having growing pains." Her mama has a faint wrinkle between her brows as she and Papa rock on the gallery. "She is growing right out of everything she has. I can't replace her outgrown institutions and outworn ideologies fast enough! And as for her educational needs — we can't keep that girl supplied."

The apple of their eye comes into view, surrounded by admiring and covetous young statesmen. Her papa licks the brown paper of the cigarette he is rolling with one hand: "She's sure beautiful!" He scowls at the young men. "None o' that bunch is man enough to handle her. She's got a hard mouth." "Headstrong is the word for Texas," her mama corrects. "Aw, she's nothin' but a kid," her papa drawls. "Listen at that!"

From the kitchen door comes the black-velvet voice of the Old-South Mammy who raised Texas and taught her her manners: "I'se save you some feesh, Miss Texas."

Mammy's kitchen radio is beating out eight to the bar and as Texas' mama and papa peek in, their erstwhile languorously elegant pride and joy has a piece of fried catfish in one hand and Mammy's hand in the other, doing a weird and wonderful jitterbug.

"Do you suppose she'll ever mature?" Mama murmurs.

"Too damn soon!" Papa snorts. "Have to sit up nights with a shotgun to keep the whole damn world from tryin' to make off with her."

It takes many years to explore this fabled personality, this mythical-reality that is Texas. It's quite a project to watch her come of age. The study is a rewarding one — and well worth anybody's time.

She's only a young thing, but she's learning fast. Her willingness to be taught, and her questioning attitude as to her own omniscience and wisdom are refreshing qualities. She values her own down-to-earth philosophy, and is not likely to be a prey to much that is radical. She is fighting hard for her position as an entity: a force to be reckoned with. So long as she fights for her mental and spiritual freedom, decadence and dry-rot are a long way off. Texas, you're a strange land hard to describe.

> This is the Empire; this is the hand flung out
> The large western dream and the tongue staggers
> To speak it for the size or where to take it.*

Where, indeed?

Pick up a loose thread and wind a smooth, orderly skein from the tangled colors of her canyons, her forests, her shores, and her skies.

Come not in condescension, nor with patronizing mien. Having to eat one's own words is worse than quail every day.

Like the true extrovert she is, Texas welcomes attention.

* Quoted by permission of the author from "A Letter from Texas" by Townsend Miller.

She is always glad to see you, even if you stayed away too long — and forgot to write. Take Texas by the hand and let her show you her world. Take in her *spirit:* not the hustle of her new, nervous cities, but the quiet strength of her limitless plains, prairies, and piney woods; the courage of her pounding seas and time-cleft canyons; the placid beauty of her rivers and hills; the rampage of the Rio Grande; the bucolic humor of her country towns on a Saturday; the inspiring steam from the rich brew of her many nationalities simmering to a harmonious blend in her mammoth melting pot; the pungent mother-wit still heard in the talk of her people; the bright, piercing eye of frontier-blue still to be seen under sunbonnets and old straw hats; the passionate patriotism of her people: "Once you're outa Texas, it cain't be fer to where you're goin'!"

Mix her many-flavored spirits in the great, clean blue bowl that is her limitless sky. It's a heady drink. Over-proof. Certainly not for the puny. You can take it or leave it. But if you can take it, the chances are you'll never leave.

Mesquite